Emergency Politics in the Third Wave of Democracy

Emergency Politics in the Third Wave of Democracy

A Study of Regimes of Exception in Bolivia, Ecuador, and Peru

Claire Wright

LEXINGTON BOOKS
Lanham • Boulder • New York • London

Published by Lexington Books
An imprint of The Rowman & Littlefield Publishing Group, Inc.
4501 Forbes Boulevard, Suite 200, Lanham, Maryland 20706
www.rowman.com

Unit A, Whitacre Mews, 26-34 Stannary Street, London SE11 4AB

British Library Cataloguing in Publication Information Available

Library of Congress Control Number: 2015952385
ISBN: 978-1-4985-1527-6 (cloth : alk. paper)
eISBN: 978-1-4985-1528-3

∞™ The paper used in this publication meets the minimum requirements of American National Standard for Information Sciences—Permanence of Paper for Printed Library Materials, ANSI/NISO Z39.48-1992.

Printed in the United States of America

Contents

List of Illustrations vii

Acknowledgments ix

Introduction xiii

1 The Emergency Politics Concept 1

2 Regimes of Exception in Latin America 25

3 Peru: The Repressive Paradigm 51

4 Bolivia: The Disaster Paradigm 85

5 Ecuador: The Administrative Paradigm 121

6 Lessons Learned 157

References 167

Index 181

About the Author 185

List of Illustrations

FIGURES

Figure 1.1	The Relationship between the Norm and the Exception, According to Decisionism	5
Figure 1.2	The Relationship between the Norm and the Exception, According to Republican Exceptionalism	6
Figure 1.3	The Relationship between the Norm and the Exception when the Exception Becomes the Norm	7
Figure 1.4	The Reciprocal Relationship between the Norm and the Exception	7
Figure 1.5	The Exception as Decision within the Norm	8
Figure 1.6	Models of Reaction within Republican Exceptionalism	12

TABLES

Table 1.1	Types of Politics	3
Table 1.2	Paradigms of Emergency Politics	18
Table 2.1	Constitutional and Legislative Models of Emergency Politics in 18 Latin American Constitutions	31
Table 2.2	UN Data on Regimes of Exception in Latin America	41
Table 2.3	Exceptional Situations and Exceptional Measures in Regimes of Exception in Latin American Constitutions	46

Acknowledgments

This volume is the result of reflections, fieldwork, and analyses that have taken place over several years. Many people and institutions have had an important part to play in this and I am indebted to all of them. Any oversights or errors are clearly my responsibility. On a personal level, I hope to have made a small contribution to understandings of emergency politics in practice and the use of regimes of exception in part of Latin America. The issue of emergency politics is one that concerns and challenges me, and I hope that it is clear throughout this text.

The seed of this volume was sown in the summer of 2004 when Ingeborg Schwarz offered me an internship at the Inter Parliamentary Union. As a student of foreign languages and literature, the opportunity to spend a couple of months in an organization dedicated to both democracy and human rights was decisive for me and undoubtedly set me on a new academic path. The study that I carried out during my internship at the IPU on the impact of anti-terrorism measures on press freedom laws introduced me to the fascinating and concerning world of emergency politics, a world that I continue to try to fathom up until the present day. I would like to take this opportunity to thank Ingeborg and the IPU for giving me the chance to discover a real passion.

Publishing as a young scholar on topics that are far from mainstream can prove rather tricky. I would like to thank Lexington Books for accepting this project and working with me with great professionalism throughout the process. Both Justin Race and Joseph Parry have provided great support, insights and enthusiasm and I am extremely grateful to them both for their part in the finished volume.

The content of this book owes a great deal to the research I carried out during my PhD and Master's theses, and I am indebted to Salvador Martí i Puig and Pilar Domingo for all their time, support, advice, and insights.

Furthermore, I would like to acknowledge the academic and institutional support received during my postgraduate studies at the Universidad de Salamanca in Spain, particularly from Manuel Alcántara Sáez. Likewise, I am grateful to the Universidad Autónoma de Nuevo León in Mexico for giving me the chance to continue to do what I love: research and lecture on Latin American Politics.

At different stages of this study, I carried out research visits that were fundamental in moving things forward. I am very grateful to Felipe Burbano at Flacso Ecuador, Detlef Nolte at the German Institute of Global and Area Studies (GIGA), and Matt Flinders at the Crick Centre for the Public Understanding of Politics at the University of Sheffield for offering me the time and space to undertake fieldwork, organize, and analyze the information, and revise this volume. Furthermore, I would like to acknowledge the support received from two research projects financed by the Instituto Internacional Catalán para la Paz[1] and the Fundación Carolina,[2] headed by Anna Ayuso and Salvador Martí i Puig, respectively, which gave me financial support to undertake fieldwork in both Peru and Ecuador. I would also like to thank Ana Soliz Landivar for her help in carrying out fieldwork in Bolivia.

As well as the key support of my two mentors, it is important to acknowledge the time and efforts of several others colleagues who took the time to review earlier progress with this study and offer their feedback. I am indebted particularly to Manuel Alcántara, Alison Brysk, Renato Cristi, Agustín Ferraro, Roberto Gargarella, Rafael Grasa, Claudia Heiss, Mariana Llanos, Andrés Mejía Acosta, Detlef Notle, Timothy Power, Almut Schilling-Vacaflor, and Guillermina Seri. I hope to have moved forward in ways that they suggested and highlighted findings which they believed should be given more emphasis. Any shortcomings are my full responsibility.

Finally, I would like to support my family for their moral and practical support. Special thanks go to my mother, Alyson, for her arduous work on the manuscript and to my father, Graeme, for his sound advice on practical issues. Nick and Bern deserve special mention for keeping me buoyant. I apologize to them and to the rest of my UK and Mexican families for all of those times that I have been distracted or absentminded in my determination to finish and improve this volume. Particular thanks go to my loving husband, Salvador Alvídrez, for revising my manuscript and—most importantly—for consistently supporting me and inspiring me to be the best I can be.

Special mention must be made of the Bolivian, Ecuadorian, and Peruvian experts who offered their time and ideas during personal interviews carried out over the course of several years. While their names have not been included in the volume for the sake of anonymity, their contribution to the study is invaluable. Carrying out fieldwork in Latin America is a truly humbling experience, due to people's kindness and willingness to offer you their side of the story. This volume is dedicated in general to the multitude of people who actively support democracy and human rights in the region and in particular to a dear Bolivian friend who sadly is no longer with us. Narda: *gracias por todo.*

NOTES

1. "Derechos Culturales y Políticos de los Pueblos Indígenas y su Impacto en el Desarrollo," financed by the ICIP (Instituto Catalán Internacional Para La Paz).
2. "Derechos culturales y políticos de los pueblos indígenas y su impacto en la gestión de recursos medioambientales. CEALCI 10/08," financed by the Fundación Carolina.

Introduction

Emergency, exception, urgency, discretion. . . . These evocative concepts give rise to a whole range of questions that together form a very broad research agenda. For instance, what do these abstract concepts mean in and for political life? Moreover, do they sit comfortably with the ideals of democracy? More specifically, in what circumstances do events become a question of emergency, exception, urgency, or discretion, and what measures are taken in their name? And crucially, what have these concepts meant for governments and citizens, at different times and in different places?

One of the key expressions of the exception in politics is the "state of emergency," a blanket term for the declaration of a seemingly abnormal state of affairs which requires special attention or measures. Yet, what does a "state of emergency" really involve in practice? For example, when we read that a "state of emergency" has been declared in Kyrgyzstan after clashes between ethnic groups,[1] what might be going on? If we read in another newspaper that a "state of emergency" has been declared in the Philippines in the face of an attempted coup[2] is it the same situation? Another article in a different newspaper refers to the declaration of a "state of emergency" to deal with heavy rain in Peru[3]; what is going on in this case? And if we find in another newspaper that a "state of emergency" has been declared in Nicaragua's gas supply,[4] what comes to mind now?

These four cases of "states of emergency" are by no means an exception; rather, "states of emergency" and other expressions of emergency politics are declared regularly to deal with situations that are deemed to be extraordinary, in both authoritarian and democratic regimes throughout the world. Sometimes the cases catch the attention of the media and human rights organisms, reflecting their abnormal nature as well as concern over the normative implications of the measures used, particularly when they involve the military or the suspension of certain civil rights.[5] Indeed, in 1985 the United Nations designated a Special Rapporteur to oversee the use of states of emergency throughout the world, finding numerous cases in very different countries and contexts including older democracies (including the United Kingdom), newer democracies (such as Argentina), and authoritarian regimes (Zimbabwe).[6] Nevertheless, the lack of a clear conceptualization of "states of emergency" or "state as exception" as well as a reliance on press sources and governmental reports means that the data are incomplete. Apparently withdrawn from the international agenda, the states of emergency database that had been promised was never fully delivered[7] and as of 2005 no more reports have been produced.[8] Nevertheless, the reports that were produced point to a clear problem: the widespread use of emergency politics and confusion over what it means in practice.

The starting point of this volume is a concern over the fact that concepts such as emergency, exception, urgency, and discretion permeate political discourse and life; yet we know very little about how they work in practice. What we do know about emergency politics, a concept that will be discussed in some depth in the following chapter, has been largely dominated by two bodies of literature: legal, normative, or juridical studies; and specific debates within the post 9/11 context. Consequently, it is important to update and broaden our knowledge on how emergency politics works in practice, moving beyond legal forms and US-dominated debates. An empirical political study from the global periphery would deepen and broaden our knowledge about emergency politics more globally.

Historical studies confirm that emergency politics in general and regimes of exception (an emergency mechanism that will be defined and discussed in Chapter 1) in particular have been an important political instrument in Latin America since Independence, in both authoritarian and democratic regimes. According to the constitutionalist Fix-Zamudio, "states of emergency or exception have been chronic in Latin America. . . ." (Fix-Zamudio 1999: xv). For his part, Colomer Viadel states that in Latin American history "states of emergency" have almost always been used as "the most extreme and arbitrary ways of trying to impose executive power" (1990, 87). Indeed, although emergency politics in general and the use of regimes of exception in particular are by no means a phenomen exclusive to Latin America, it can be said that the use of regimes of exception has become a historical and constitutional feature of the region (Delfino 2000; Despouy 1999; Colomer Viadel 1990).

Recurring to regimes of exception in a democratic context is a phenomenon that is worthy of study, particularly in Latin America, given that these mechanisms continue to be used throughout the third wave of democracy. Importantly, there are few empirical studies on the subject, despite concern at the beginning of the democratic transitions during the 1980s. Consequently, given the lack of previous studies and empirical data, it is important to establish if emergency politics in Latin America—observed through the institutional mechanisms of regimes of exception—is still expressed in terms of "national security" and coercive measures, according to a repressive paradigm that will be more fully established in Chapter 1; or if on the contrary it has shifted to other paradigms, including the administrative or natural disaster type. Given that my concern is decidedly political rather than legal, my interest in this volume is firmly on exceptional situations, exceptional measures, and how the two dimensions relate to one another.

Importantly, over three decades after the beginning of the so-called third wave of democratization (Huntington 1991), political scientists agree that democratic regimes are still facing serious difficulties in the majority of Latin American countries (Alcántara Sáez 2008; Barreda 2011). Some authors consider a fundamental flaw of democracy in the region to be the arbitrary use of power by state authorities (Kruijt and Koonings 2002, 44; O'Donnell 1997, 183). In this context, the conditions may be ripe for the use of regimes of exception or—as Loveman puts it—"these constitutional foundations of tyranny" (1993, 9). Indeed, Aguilar Rivera (1996) notes that within the framework of weak democracies, authoritarian solutions become attractive for different actors.

In this sense, in recent years emergency discourses have appeared in relation to political violence or internal unrest. For instance, in the context of ongoing presence of terrorist cells, paramilitary groups and drug traffickers in countries such as Colombia, Mexico, and Peru, security at any cost is still a key issue; one that politicians eager to attract votes make the most of (Hagopian 2005, 319). Likewise, the issue of citizen security in the face of violent crimes by organized groups has become a serious problem (ibid). In a large part of the subcontinent, homicide rates have grown considerably, something which politicians in distant latitudes have taken advantage of in order to invoke a type of "punitive populism," a term employed by Salvador Martí i Puig in the case of Mexico (2014) and which could be applied to several countries in the region.

Furthermore, there continue to be crises of a socioeconomic nature. Indeed, throughout the twentieth century, there were several social and economic crises of this type, from the effects of the great depression of 1929 to those of the debt crisis of the 1980s (Kruijt and Koonings 2002, 24). In recent times, the emblematic economic crisis of Argentina in 2001 provoked an important cycle of violence, which has been repeated—albeit it to a lesser extent—in recent years (Rozenwurcel and Vázquez 2009). It is important to highlight, furthermore, that economic crises have accentuated the profound social inequalities the region suffers from, which have made the democratic exercise of power even more difficult (Bonometti and Ruiz Seisdedos 2010).

Finally, natural disasters have been another, recurring extraordinary situation in Latin America: the earthquakes, volcanoes, hurricanes, floods, and droughts have affected all of the countries in the region, albeit in different ways, throughout history and up until the present day (García Acosta 1997; Charvériat 2000). In the past decades, noticeable examples are Hurricane Mitch that swept through Central America; the devastating earthquakes of Pisco (Peru), Mexico City, and Concepción (Chile); and the effects of global warming throughout the region, as expressed through droughts and floods. Importantly, these disasters have been studied from the risk management paradigm, rather than from the perspective of emergency politics or regimes of exception, despite constant but vague references to them.

The multifaceted nature of the exception in political life must be taken into account when studying emergency politics in practice. As Daniel Zovatto argues, there are various ways of studying regimes of exception including constitutional, political, economic, and cultural perspectives (1990).[9] Likewise, I fully agree that they represent a problem that can be studied from several angles, and in this study we opt for a clearly and exclusively political perspective. That is to say, I am interested in how these constitutional and legal provisions are used in practice, taking into account different political junctures and contexts. Although I acknowledge that juridical concerns are of key importance to the study of regimes of exception, given the nature of this study they are of interest to the extent that they constitute the institutional framework for their use in practice.[10] As Loveman (1993) observes, it may be possible for constitutions to be the basis of "tyranny" but the decision on when to use them and what measures to use in their name is clearly political. Indeed any constitutional or legal mechanism is necessarily a formality; what is interesting is to see is how it works, in practice and in context.

At this stage it is worth making an observation that will be more fully developed in Chapter 1: specifically, in order to understand the use of regimes of exception in practice, it is insufficient to just look for figures, counting the number of times they have been declared, as if they were always used for the same reason and to the same end.[11] Consequently, in this volume I have emphasized the material elements of extraordinary situations and extraordinary measures, constructing three ideal paradigms: repressive, administrative, and disaster emergency politics.

For this reason, the most important and urgent question to be answered is simple: what does emergency politics involve in practice? Bearing in mind the evidence from Latin America, it is also relevant to ask whether the repressive paradigm is still dominant, three decades into the third wave of democracy. Indeed, as will be highlighted in Chapter 2, the repressive paradigm is the legacy of two centuries of institutional development and political practice in relation to regimes of exception, constituting a key concern at the time of the transitions to democracy (Despouy 1999; García Sayán 1987a; Loveman 1997), but which has slipped off the academic agenda in recent years, beyond a few legalist[12] or case studies.[13] Therefore, we do not know much about how regimes of exception have been used in recent years and, consequently, in what ways they pose a challenge for current democracies. Furthermore, our conceptualization of regimes of exception—I argue—has been rather blinded by the dominance of the repressive emergency politics paradigm, as seen in the United Nations' reports. Indeed, Latin American countries have been faced with economic crises and natural disasters too, but these situations have either not been expressed in regimes of exception or—perhaps—have not been written into the history of regimes of exception in the region. Consequently, it is important to update our knowledge and understanding of these mechanisms of emergency politics in Latin American political systems in the third wave to understand in what ways they relate to the consolidation of democracy.

This main research question—how does emergency politics work in practice?—seeks to understand the use given to a specific mechanism in countries that are currently undergoing processes of democratic consolidation. Consequently, in order to answer the question, it is necessary to take into account different countries that are involved in similar political processes. For this reason, the research may be framed as an exercise in comparative politics or more specifically a comparative analysis of similar institutions or processes that have been chosen previously for analytical reasons (Peters 1998). Indeed, my aim is to analyze the use given to a specific mechanism—regimes of exception—in similar political contexts: Bolivia, Ecuador, and Peru.[14] Given the lack of studies on the issue from this political perspective and the exploratory nature of the study, it is logical to reduce the ambit to a limited number of countries, rather than trying to account for all of the Latin American third-wave democracies. With this type of analysis, it may be possible to offer a meso-level theory (ibid).

In this sense, the study is inspired by two types of institutionalism: empirical institutionalism and historical institutionalism. According to Peters (2003), empirical institutionalism seeks to answer the following question via case studies: do institutions matter? Taking into account the observation made by Loveman (1993) and Valadés (1974) about the gap between the normative framework of regimes of exception and how they are used in practice, this perspective is very important. Linked to empirical institutionalism is historical institutionalism—as expressed in the works of Mahoney (2004), Mahoney (2001), Pierson (2000), Steinmo, Thelen and Longstreth (1992), and Skocpol and Pierson (2002)—and which seeks to understand how the paths followed in politics are continued or broken in the present, explaining results in a comparative and historical framework. While this study does not incorporate the formal methodology of historical institutionalism, it shares a concern over the idea of path dependency and the possibility of changing models or paradigms of emergency, together with the vital aspect of context.

So, why Peru, Bolivia, and Ecuador? Ultimately these three countries were selected in the framework of most-similar cases or "natural grouping" study, to paraphrase Peters (ibid, 74). Each country will be studied in-depth separately, before offering some interpretative clues from a comparative perspective in the concluding chapter. There are several studies in political science and sociology that choose to study these countries together precisely for the fact they have several features in common.[15] In this study the following characteristics are of particular interest.

First, Bolivia, Ecuador, and Peru are third-wave democracies,[16] with their transitions beginning in the late 1970s in each case, and currently find themselves in a phase of democratic consolidation (Hagopian 2005). Second, they share similar social, economic, cultural, historical, and institutional features (Pachano 2010). For instance, they all have a considerable indigenous population (Pajuelo 2007) and important reserves of natural resources (Oriol Prats and Acías-Maymar 2007). Furthermore, their political past has been characterized by the alternation between authoritarian and democratic regimes (Alcántara Sáez 1991, 113). Third, in recent years the three countries have suffered from political instability, reflected in presidential interruptions via pressure from below.[17] Finally, the three countries belong to the same geographical area, the central-Andean region, and possibly suffer from a domino effect in terms of their political and social processes.

Another key justification for the choice of these three countries is because of their long-term developments in relation to regimes of exception (Loveman 1997; García Sayán 1987a). All three countries are worthy of study given that over the past two centuries, they have followed the general trend in Latin America, as identified by Brian Loveman (1993) first, the inclusion of mechanisms to suspend judicial guarantees, enacted in the face of social unrest during the nineteenth century; second, an abuse of these powers by military governments in the twentieth century; and, third, the permanence of "regimes of exception" at the constitutional level even after the transition to democracy (Loveman 1997; García Sayán 1987). Indeed, the three States have established a regime of exception in the constitution or law, a necessary criterion for their inclusion in this study.

Generally speaking, therefore, the study is of most similar cases but there is an important difference in the case of Peru: during the 1980s and 1990s it suffered a bloody internal war against Sendero Luminoso (Comisión de la Verdad y Reconciliación 2003; Paramio 2006) and between 1992 and 2001 a very un-democratic regime under President Alberto Fujimori (Marcus-Delgado and Tanaka 2001). Indeed, academics working on Peru tend to refer to a situation of interruption of democracy during the 1990s (Hagopian 2005). Consequently, the decisionist element has been present in the case of Peru until recent years and makes it a particularly interesting case. For this reason, the empirical study carried out here focuses specifically on the post-2000 period—two decades into the third wave—while reconstructing events and trends prior to that date through other studies. In this way, by limiting the empirical study to this time frame, the volume aims to be as current as the newspapers but much more analytical, again to paraphrase Peters (1998, 175).

It is also necessary to be clear about what material will be used in the study. To fill in the historical "gap," the works by Brian Loveman (1993) and García Sayán (1987a) are a very useful starting point. Next, it is possible to piece together the use of regimes of exception in the three countries studied here between the transition and (more or less) the year 2000, thanks to previous studies. For instance, in the case of Bolivia, Stephanie Alenda (2003) described the regimes of exception between 1980 and 2000, as a secondary item of interest. In the case of Peru, the PhD thesis of Jorge Power Manchego-Muñoz (1989) provides an overview of the regimes of exception declared between 1981 and 1988, and the Comisión de la Verdad y de la Reconciliación offers data on states of emergency during the 1980s and 1990s in its final report (2003). In the case of Ecuador, Dávalos Muirragui (2008) counts the states of exception declared between 1979 and 1997, using information from the press. A couple of interesting articles published in the newspaper *Blanco y Negro* also offer a perspective on third wave emergency politics in Ecuador, prior to the year 2000. As of 2000 and in all three cases, however, secondary literature is insufficient to understand the role of regimes of exception and that is where the intended contribution of the study begins.

Given the legal basis of regimes of exception, the first step in the empirical analysis was to consult the respective constitutions and secondary laws on regimes of exception to discover the underlying institutional forms and most recent changes. The next step was to find information about tendencies and concerns over the use of regimes of exception in the three countries, together with significant case studies. Consequently, references to the use of the relative mechanisms were found in bulletins on social conflicts, human rights reports, and press articles.

After this exploratory stage, fieldwork was carried out in the three countries,[18] in order to look for further information and carry our interviews with key informants, including human rights defenders, constitutional lawyers, social and political actors, and political analysts, according to a snowball technique and in line with the information garnered during the study.[19] Together with the interviews, extensive archival research on the respective official, State bulletins was carried out in order to access the declarations of regimes of exception, between 2000 and 2010. A total of 292 declarations of regimes of exception were found in the three countries between this period, undoubtedly a much higher number than one may have thought, given the lack of academic attention to the issue in the literature. At the same time, sentences by the supreme courts of each country and resolutions by the Human Rights' Ombudsmen were also collected at this stage. Having established tendencies in terms of the dominant paradigm, certain representative case studies were researched in more depth, taking into account information collected in newspaper reports, legal resolutions, interviews, reports, etc. This information was stored and organized with the CAQDAS (Computer-Aided Qualitative Data Analysis) program NVivo10.[20]

This focus on interpretations, tendencies, and case studies, together with a whole wealth of textual information, places the study firmly in the realms of *qualitative research* (Flick 2014). Given the generalized lack of knowledge about the use of regimes of exception in practice, the study is largely inductive and consequently positioned within the perspective of *grounded theory*. According to this approach, the researcher's exposition to and sensibility toward data is of vital importance, as well as a flexible posture, free from conceptual schemas previously consulted in the literature. According to Glaser and Strauss (1967) "grounded theory" is based on a constant to and fro between data, concepts, and findings, in a systematic way. Given the lack of theory on regimes of exception specifically and emergency powers in general—beyond the repressive paradigm—this approach is also an interesting route to take.

Indeed, Chapter 1 goes into the constructed nature of the exception in some detail, given that a government has to identify and name an exceptional situation in order to take measures in its name. Both securitization theory in general and Loveman's observations on Latin America (1997) make this a particularly important aspect when studying emergency politics in practice. Furthermore, in order to obtain a contextual understanding of the use of this mechanism in the three countries studies here, it is also important to take into account the social construction of the phenomenon and the way in which public opinion legitimizes it or not. Consequently, *social constructivism*—as understood by Berger and Luckman (1986)—is another useful approach when interpreting the process through which regimes of exception have been created and understood socially, both by the political protagonists as well as their antagonists and, indeed, society as a whole.

It is also worth making some comments about appropriate analytical frameworks in order to understand emergency politics as expressed via regimes of exception in the three third-wave countries considered here and their possible relationship with processes of democratization.

As has already been highlighted, the previous literature on the subject has been predominantly from the perspective of human rights abuses, given the dominance of repressive emergency politics in the framework of the historic national security doctrine (Despouy 1999). His principles of legality, proclamation, notification, temporality, the exceptional threat, proportionality, non-discrimination, and the compatibility, concordance and complementarity with the different norms of international law have constituted a real framework on the suspension of human rights in emergency contexts.[21] Nevertheless, taking into account the possibility of other emergency politics paradigms orientated toward natural disasters and administrative or economic difficulties and an evident need to dialogue with Latin American Political Science, it may be necessary to consult other, broader types of literature or at least a broader theoretical base, in order to offer a complete and adequate framework.

Above, I referred to grounded theory as one of the key approaches for this study. According to the precepts of this perspective, interpretative clues will emerge during the process of the research, according to the findings themselves. Consequently, the concluding chapter will be better placed to carry out this discussion and identify the bodies of literature that will be useful in studying regimes of exception in the third wave, according to their use in practice. Nevertheless, at this stage it is possible to point to two sufficiently ample bodies of political science literature that have been crucial for Latin America and which may be interested in regimes of exception for what we already know of them in practice. These groups of literature can be divided into two broad groups: the first is related to democratic development in the region, including the quality of democracy (Altman and Pérez-Liñán 2002), and democratic consolidation (Schedler 2001); and the second is related to the roles of the different branches of the State and consequently to issues such as the separation of powers (Negretto 2003), presidentialism (Nohlen 1991), and accountability (O'Donnell 1997).

In relation to the first group, much has been written about the quality of democracy, its consolidation, authoritarian legacies, and areas where the State is incapable of reaching.[22] Without a doubt, the concept of democracy in a broader sense goes beyond the idea of free elections, with various attempts being made at measuring its "quality," via several indicators, including (typically) political and civil rights, the respect for institutions, the respect for plurality, the possibility to participate and (sometimes) socioeconomic results.[23] None of these indicators take into account the use of regimes of exception, which not only threaten political and civil rights but also the respect for institutions, plurality, and participation. For its part, the idea of democratic consolidation is particularly useful when considering post-authoritarian regimes. According to Manuel Alcántara (2006) and Andreas Schedler (2001) consolidation occurs when there is a lesser possibility of the regime returning to authoritarianism, even in the face of crisis and the classic difficulties of socioeconomic problems and citizens' frustrated expectations (Alcántara 2006; Martí i Puig 2009). Regimes of exception used in the long term represent a degree of democratic abnormality and run contrary to this idea of consolidation.

On the other hand, in relation to the separation of power, it is important to note that regimes of exception are, generally, competence of the executive power and in the case of Latin America of the president (Delfino 2000). Furthermore, in Latin America they have given power to the armed forces. In this sense, three groups of literature related to the separation of powers could offer an important dialogue on regimes of exception: studies on the fall of presidents in Latin America[24]; studies on executive decree authority[25]; and finally, studies on civilian control of the military.[26]

For its part, the literature on the fall of Presidents refers to factors such as minorities in the congress, weak presidents, popular mobilization, scandals, repressive leadership styles, economic crises, and frustrated expectations as important independent variables or, essentially, interpretative clues. Likewise, the literature on executive decrees refers to the importance of institutional design and the issue of majorities and minorities in the congress.[27] It is worth taking into account these variables when considering why presidents may resort to these mechanisms. In this sense too it is helpful to recall the "strong man" myth of Latin American political history and the concentration of executive power in this particular context offering a reminder of past authoritarian regimes (Pereira, Power, and Rennó 2008).[28] Finally, an important aspect of separation of powers in democratic regimes is civilian control over the military in relation to internal order (Magide and Wright 2014), something that the military regimes of the twentieth century in Latin America turned upside down and achieved by a series of constitutional and legal privileges, including regimes of exception (Loveman and Davies 1997).

A way of summing up the concerns of the two bodies of literature and offering a broad framework for the preliminary evaluation of regimes of exception as they are is the approach of democratic governability, with its two main dimensions: *legitimacy* and *efficiency* (Filmus 2005; Alcántara Sáez 2004). Given that one of the greatest dangers for new democracies, including the majority of political regimes in Latin America, are socioeconomic problems and the frustrated expectations of citizens (Alcántara Sáez 2006; Martí i Puig 2009), the *efficiency* dimension is vital. Nevertheless, in contrast to the general concept of governability, democratic governability is that which offers effective government via democratic resources and therefore the *legitimacy* dimension is equally important (Rojas Aravena and Fuentes Saavedra 2004).

In the context of regimes of exception specifically, the *efficiency* dimension may be evaluated through tangible results of the application of this mechanism, essentially the solution of the problem in question and a return to normality. If a regime of exception does not solve the problem and/or is declared repeatedly, then it cannot be considered efficient.

Conversely, in order to evaluate the *legitimacy* dimension, it is necessary to return to the two bodies of literature outlined above: democratic developments and the separation of powers. Furthermore, the regime of exception-specific concerns, such as international laws on human rights protection (Despouy 1999) and control by the legislative and/or constitutional court, is particularly important (Delfino 2000). In the same dimension, it is also worth taking into account the constructed element of emergencies and the role of public opinion in legitimizing the measures. Indeed, as Loveman notes (1997) the notion of "protecting the patria" has been a key justification for the use of regimes of exception, in the following sense: "The moral, historical, constitutional, legal and strictly military rationales for saving the patria always exist. They become operational only if a crisis occurs" (1997, 402). This is a nod to securitization theory—which is described more fully in Chapter 1—when "audiences" give governments the moral authority to wield exceptional power (Roe 2008).

Ultimately, I expect that regimes of exception will tip the balance away from *legitimacy* for the sake of *efficiency*[29] and, for that reason, are at odds with the concept of democratic governability. Nevertheless, it is also possible—as mentioned above—that they are not even *efficient* in achieving the purposes to which they are put. These possibilities will serve as a broad analytical framework in the analysis of the three empirical cases studied in Chapters 3, 4, and 5.

The volume is organized as follows. Chapter 1 offers a thorough review of existing literature on emergency politics, providing conceptual clarification, identifying three types or paradigms of emergency politics (repressive, administrative, and disaster), and pointing to regimes of exception as a useful route in. Next, Chapter 2 offers an overview of emergency politics in Latin America throughout history, pointing to the predominance of regimes of exception and the repression paradigm. In Chapter 3, I describe the continuance of the repression paradigm in Peruvian emergency politics, to deal with both social protest and the apparent threat of organized crime and terrorism. Chapter 4 shows how Bolivia has moved from a repressive to a disaster paradigm, in the face of pressure to adapt to climate change and to democratize regimes of exception. Last of all, in Chapter 5, I analyze the predominance of an administrative paradigm in Ecuadorian emergency politics, as a response to weak institutions and difficulties in implementing policy. The final chapter summarizes the key findings of the study and their implications for our understandings of emergency politics in practice. To close the volume, some "best practices" or ways to democratize regimes of exception are offered.

NOTES

1. Hulkar Isamova "State of emergency in South Krygyzstan after ethnic clash," article published in Reuters on 19th May 2010, available at www.reuters.com.

2. Efe "El Gobierno de Filipinas decreta el estado de emergencia tras frustrar una intentona golpista," article published in El País on 24th February 2006, available at www.elpais.com.

3. Agencia Andina "Declaran el estado de emergencia en Cajamarca por desastres naturales," article published in El Comercio on 10th April 2008, available at www.elcomercio.com.pe.

4. Dpa "El gobierno de Nicaragua intervino la empresa de gas licuado Tropigás," article published in la Jornada on 26th September 2008, available at www.jornada.unam.mx.

5. An example of a human rights report would be "Bahrain set for renewed protests as state of emergency ends," published by Amnesty International on 5th March 2011, available at www.amnesty.org.

6. United Nations: "Annual reports and lists of States which, since 1st January 1985 have proclaimed, extended or terminated a State of Emergency, submitted by Mr. Leandro Despouy, Special Rapporteur appointed pursuant to Economic and Social Council Resolution 1985/37 1993–2005" available online www.un.org.

7. Despouy (1999, 14). On the website of Queen's University, Belfast www.qub.ac.uk there is a reference to data about the use of emergency powers in East Timor, China, El Salvador, India, Malaysia, Northern Ireland, South Africa, Sri Lanka, and Turkey. From the text of the website it is clear that rather than work in progress it is designed to be a historical reference point.

8. United Nations: "Annual reports and lists of States which, since 1st January 1985 have proclaimed, extended or terminated a State of Emergency, submitted by Mr. Leandro Despouy, Special Rapporteur appointed pursuant to Economic and Social Council Resolution 1985/37 1993–2005" online www.un.org. The reports ceased to be produced when the UN Human Rights Council was created in 2006, given that the issue of states of emergency was not included within its remit. See the Council's report: A/HRC/Sub.1/58/36, September 2006.

9. This last approach has been superbly applied in the cases of Colombia (Ochoa Gautier 2004) and the US (Feldman 2007; Wall 2011).

10. As Espin Templado argues, political science should be interested in the law as a further piece of data on social and political reality (1994). For his part, Carl Friedrich (1950) reminds us that continuities in legal and constitutional form often mask changes in practice.

11. In this sense, we adopt a different posture from Power and Rennó (2008), who look for data on how many legislative decrees were proclaimed by Brazilian presidents and a similar perspective to that of Ferreira Rubio and Goretti (1998), who also look to understand the *content* of the decrees. Clearly, it is worth stressing that the two aforementioned studies are related to legislative decrees and not to regimes of exception.

12. Studies from the perspective of law or constitutional law include Delfino (2000), Ríos Álvarez (2009), and Carbonell (2008).

13. For studies that approach (either directly or indirectly) the issue of states of exception published in the last decade see on Colombia, Iturralde (2003); on Ecuador, Dávalos Muirragui (2008); on Argentina, Rosatti (2004); and on Bolivia, Alenda (2003).

14. Again, it is worth remembering that the analysis carried out here is not on emergency politics in general but rather on one institution that has been used as an instrument of emergency politics, specifically regimes of exception.

15. For example, Pérez Murillo (2007), Zúñiga García-Falces (2005), Tamayo Herrera (1998), Del Álamo Pons, (2007), González Pérez y de la Torre Gómez (2004), Oriol Prats and Macías-Aymar (2008), Irurozqui Victoriano (2005), Pachano (2010), and Pajuelo (2007).

16. The third-wave concept was formulated by Samuel Huntington (1991) and has been widely adopted by Political Scientists, historians and Latin Americanists.

17. For example, Sánchez de Lozada in Bolivia in 2003, Fujimori in Peru in 2000, and Lucio Gutiérrez in Ecuador in 2005. On the case of Bolivia, see Buitrago (2010), on the case of Ecuador Mejía Acosta and Polga Hecimovich (2010), and on Peru Berntzen and Skinlo (2010). With regard to the crises in the three countries' political systems, see Alcántara Sáez (2004).

18. In Bolivia and Peru in 2007, in Peru in 2009, in Ecuador in 2010, and in Bolivia (with the help of Ana Solíz Landivar) in 2012.

19. The in-depth, semi-structured interviews were carried out taking into account the methodological concerns of Miguel S. Valles (2009). More information is given on the different interviewees in the following chapters but it is important to note here that their names are not given but rather their profile, given that this information is more relevant rather than personal identity.

20. On the use and operation of this program see Wright and Hinojosa (2015).

21. As previously highlighted, in this volume—while acknowledging its vital importance—the juridical debate on regimes of exception is not entered into beyond these key precepts of Despouy (1999). For further important works and discussions from Latin America see Delfino (2000), Fix-Zamudio (2004), Carbonell (2008), Ríos Álvarez (2009), and Zovatto (1990).

22. See, for example, Hagopian and Mainwaring (2005), O'Donnell (1997), Schedler (2001), and Alcántara (2003).

23. See, for example, Alcántara (2008), Altman and Pérez-Liñán (2002), and Kekic (2007).

24. See Pérez-Liñán (2007) and Llanos and Marsteintredet (2010).

25. See Carey and Shugart (1998).

26. See Lösing (1996).

27. According to Pereira, Power and Rennó (2005), some studies point to considerable opposition to using these decrees while other studies refer to considerable support in congress for the use of these decrees.

28. See Pérez-Liñán (2007, 213).

29. This trade-off is presented as a more general alternative to the liberty versus security debates in the current literature on emergency politics.

Chapter 1

The Emergency Politics Concept

Carl Friedrich once asked, "How are we to get effective, vigorous governmental action, and yet limit the power of governmental bodies so as to forestall the rise of despotic power?" (1950, 596). This question, the question of emergency politics[1] and its intrinsic relationship with authoritarian rule, has been a source of great debate for political theorists for centuries, in different latitudes and different contexts. Indeed, much of what we know and think about emergency institutions in Western politics starts off in Ancient Rome with the figures of the dictatorship, *iustitium* and the decemvirate (Agamben 2005; Wright 2012). Later, thinkers such as Machiavelli (1987), Hobbes (1996), Rousseau (1990), Constant (1989), and Schmitt (1985) grappled with the tenets of emergency government in very different historical and political contexts, ranging from city states to absolute monarchies, Republics, Liberal Republics, and democracies that found themselves slipping into authoritarian regimes. After the Second World War, Rossiter (2002) and Friedrich (1950) revised key models of emergency government and sought to find checks and balances that would safeguard democracy from tyranny.

More recently, as a result of the tragic events of 9/11 and the global reaction to the threat of radical Islamist terrorism, there has been a renewed interest in emergency politics, particularly among North American academics. From the disciplines of political and legal theory, scholars including Bruce Ackerman (2004; 2006), Andrew Arato (2006), and David Cole (2004) have established an intense and fruitful debate on how a government could design emergency powers to prepare itself in the face of other possible attacks permanently without undermining individual rights. This debate—which has been on-going for over ten years—equates the concept of emergency with terrorism and asks about the problematic trade-off between security and liberty in a globalized world (Issacharoff and Pildes 2004).

Without a doubt, this debate among US scholars has been relevant and important when thinking about an adequate framework to approach the problem of terrorism. However, these discussions have dominated recent academic literature on emergency politics[2] and limited our understanding of the concept, for two main reasons. First, it has reduced the idea of emergency politics to one type of threat and a specific context: a military or security response to radical Islamic terrorism. Second, it is based on a legal or formal rather than political approach. The importance of the "war on terror" at a global level cannot be underestimated and should certainly not be overlooked. Indeed, its study certainly requires "all the wisdom man can muster," to quote Friedrich (1950, 596). Nevertheless, it is important to go beyond this specific issue in order to understand the diversity of ideas, problems, implications, and variables involved in emergency politics in practice, in different contexts. This study seeks to (re)open the debate on what is a vital issue for all political regimes, whatever their nature: extraordinary times and the extraordinary responses that are deployed as a result.

It is important to note that emergency politics is a particularly ambiguous and multifaceted concept, that does not fit into neat categories (Loveman 1993; Neocleous 2006) but precisely for that reason it is important to start with some conceptual clarity and then find real-life evidence from different contexts in order to improve our understanding of this aspect of political life. The aim of this volume is to offer a contribution to our understanding of the emergency "black-box" from the geo-political periphery, via an analysis of emergency politics in recent years in Bolivia, Ecuador, and Peru. Importantly, these three countries share similar historical and political backgrounds (including recent transitions to democracy) but—as I demonstrate—the role of emergency politics in recent years has shown clear differences.

Consequently, the main aim of this chapter is to offer a conceptual framework of emergency politics, defining the idea and systemizing the existing approaches in the literature, which are undoubtedly more formal or legal in nature.[3] I argue that it is necessary to consider the material or political elements of emergency politics in order to understand its role in political life. The conclusion reached in this chapter is that the availability of a specific institution in certain context—the "regime of exception"—offers a helpful route to analyzing emergency politics from a decidedly political and markedly empirical perspective. Furthermore, given the prevalence of this mechanism in Latin America both in the past and in the present day, the three countries in question offer fertile ground for its study.

EMERGENCY POLITICS

At this stage, it is important to ask a simple but vital question: what does emergency politics really mean? The answer to this question in practice will vary in time and place, depending on the legal definitions, external threats, political circumstances, and governmental capacities. Indeed, one of the main aims of this volume is to offer solid answers to this question in different contexts. However, it is necessary to start from a more abstract level in order to offer a broad but distinct category that can be dealt with separately from other types of politics.

Perhaps the simplest way of defining emergency politics is to consider its two component parts: the classification of a situation as extraordinary and the use of extraordinary measures as a response to this situation. This definition is similar to, but broader than, a conceptualization offered by the author elsewhere, which defines emergency politics as an alteration in any of the three powers of government (executive, legislative, or judicial) when it is perceived that there is a necessity to do so (Wright 2012). Emergency politics, consequently, is different from ordinary politics, which is characterized by an ordinary state of affairs and ordinary measures.

Another simple but important question follows: if only one of the aforementioned elements is present, are we still talking about emergency politics? That is to say, if there is a situation that is classified as extraordinary but extraordinary measures are not employed; or conversely if extraordinary measures are employed but there is no situation classified as extraordinary. In both cases, the answer would be no. In the first case, it would be a case of resistance politics, given that ordinary measures are used to confront what is considered to be an extraordinary situation. In the second case, it is a question rather of discretionary politics, given that extraordinary measures are taken without any particular justification.

As a result of this reflection, it is possible to create a typology of the four different types of politics, isolating emergency politics in this way and offering much-needed conceptual clarification, as is clear in Table 1.1.

Table 1.1 Types of Politics

		Situation	
		Extraordinary	*Ordinary*
Measures	Extraordinary	Emergency politics	Discretionary politics
	Ordinary	Resistance politics	Ordinary politics

Source: Table created by author

Consequently, emergency politics can be understood as a considerable departure from ordinary political life, in which there is both an "exceptional" state of affairs and an exceptional response. In this sense, to understand the true nature of emergency politics, it is necessary to identify the nature of extraordinary situations and extraordinary measures and how they fit together. That is to say, how does the response correspond to the situation that is classified as an exception? The task of finding real-life examples to improve our understanding of the emergency politics concept in practice is of great importance, particularly when considering that it constitutes a departure from the ordinary ways of doing things and has the potential, therefore, to give rise to more despotic or discretional forms of power.

Part of the difficulty in this sense is the fact that the existing literature on emergency politics, which—while referring broadly to the two dimensions established above—has focused on formal rather than material elements of the concept. Simply put, the literature asks: how does the norm relate to the exception? Rather than, what situations are classified as exceptional in real-life politics? Likewise, it asks, what are the possible governmental reactions, from a procedural point of view? Rather than, what exceptional measures are used in real-life politics? Consequently, in the sections that follow I first review the formal literature on the topic and then offer a more political perspective. Finally, I point to regimes of exception as an ideal route in to the study of emergency politics, moving from a formal to a political approach, in line with the suggestion made by Gross and Ní Aoláin (2006).

Formal Approaches to Emergency Politics

Revising the ample but rather diverse literature on emergency politics, it is logical to start by offering considerable attention to formal approaches as they have undoubtedly dominated the debate. This is not surprising, given that legal and political theorists have busied themselves with its study. Consequently, the sections that follow aim to systemize the vast literature on emergency politics from this formal or procedural perspective: first, the debates on the norm versus the exception (the first dimension of the emergency politics concept) are analyzed; next, the debates on the models of reaction to the exception (the second dimension of the emergency politics concept) are revised; and finally, a more holistic analysis of the emergency politics concept from a formal perspective is offered, taking into account the two different dimensions and how they relate to one another.

The Norm/ Exception Dichotomy

From a formal point of view, the first dimension of the emergency politics concept revolves around a fundamental distinction between what is normal and what is exceptional. Logically, in order to refer to an "abnormal" situation there must be agreement on what is considered to be a normal and regular situation, but this is a political issue that has not been comprehensively approached by the literature. Instead, the dichotomy of the norm versus the exception has structured how exceptionalism is thought of, as Nomi Claire Lazar (2006) argues. However, this section highlights how the division between the norm and the exception in formal terms is highly complex.

Throughout the history of Western political thought, two main currents have dominated our thinking of the norm and the exception: *decisionism* on the one hand and *Republican exceptionalism* on the other (Lazar 2006). For its part, *decisionism* refers to a totally pessimistic conception of political life in which the search for the common good will be in vain, given that human nature and the world are inherently chaotic. The exception is in fact the rule. This vision finds its roots in the thought of Hobbes (1996 edition) and is developed in the twentieth century by Carl Schmitt (1985 edition; 2009 edition). More recently, this idea has been applied to the understanding of political history in Mexico (Williams 2011). The central idea of the exception being the normal state of affairs is represented graphically in Figure 1.1.

Figure 1.1 The Relationship between the Norm and the Exception, According to Decisionism. *Source*: Figure created by author.

For its part, *Republican exceptionalism* starts from the idea that a well-formed and stable State needs protectors to save it in times of crisis that are properly identified as such. The exception is precisely that: the exception. For Machiavelli (1987) and Rousseau (1990), the Republic is the only place where justice and virtue are possible and, consequently, it may be necessary to protect it with a special figure in situations that depart from the norm, until the ordinary state of affairs returns. According to this perspective, the norm and the exception are totally different and separate situations that do not affect each other. Figure 1.2 reflects this separate life of the norm and the exception, as well as the predominance of the former state of affairs in political life.

As already mentioned, the two currents of political thought identified by Lazar have to a great extent dominated the way in which we conceptualize the exception in politics. Nevertheless, it is worth noting that—according to the

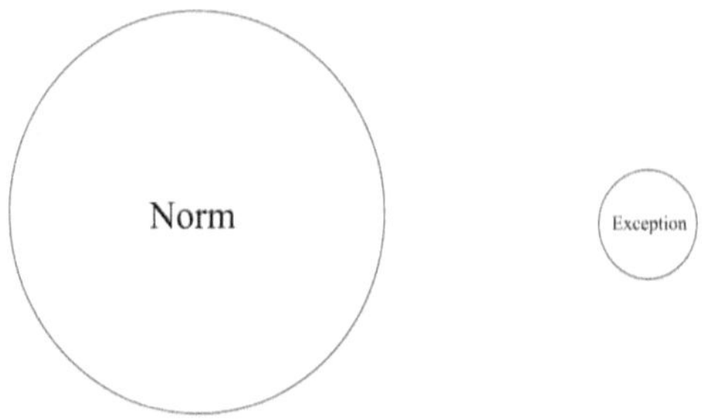

Figure 1.2 The Relationship between the Norm and the Exception, According to Republican Exceptionalism. *Source*: Figure created by author.

conceptualization of emergency politics in this study—*decisionism* is closer to the idea of discretionary politics rather than emergency politics given that if an emergency is permanent it can no longer be thought of as an extraordinary situation as such, notwithstanding any exceptional measures that may be employed. In this sense, the *Republican exceptionalism* perspective is more in keeping with our definition of emergency politics, given that it foresees the possibility of both extraordinary and ordinary situations. However, the literature has also pointed to three additional variations to the norm/exception dichotomy in practice, making it rather more complex.

First, it seems that the exception can easily become the norm, however clear the initial division between the norm and the exception is (Friedrich 1950). In other words, in practice, *Republican exceptionalism* gives way to *decisionism*. For example, as noted previously, after the terrorist attacks of 9/11, there has been a proliferation of studies on the concept of the exception in politics, particularly—but not exclusively—among US academics.[4] According to many of these jurists and political theorists, the situation presented by radical Islamist terrorism has become a completely new, long-term exception that defies the norm-exception dichotomy.[5] From a normative point of view, the same academics appear to be divided over whether this type of exception can be justified or not, nevertheless their way of thinking challenges both *decisionism* and *Republican exceptionalism*. Figure 1.3 depicts this variation in the relationship between the norm and the exception that occurs when there is initially a differentiation between the two but then the exception becomes a new norm in the long term.

The second variation is related to the observation that the understanding of what is normal change and what is exceptional change every time an exceptional situation occurs (Gross and Ní Aoláin 2006). In other words, the framework of what is "normal" and what is "exceptional" is in a constant state of evolution due to the normalization of circumstances that were once considered extraordinary. In this perspective, extraordinary circumstances that occur

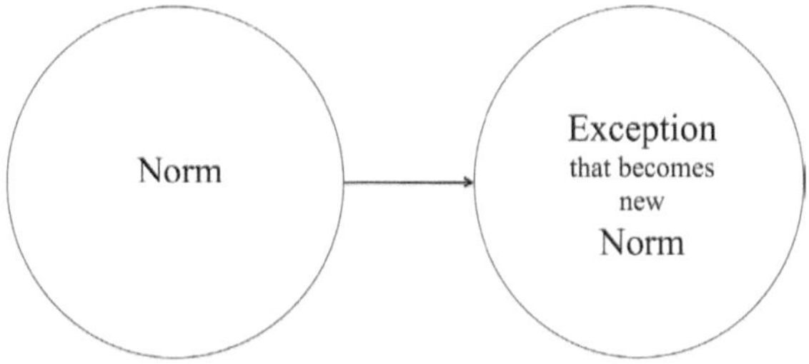

Figure 1.3 The Relationship between the Norm and the Exception when the Exception becomes the Norm. *Source*: Figure created by author.

(or are declared) with certain frequency eventually form part of the norm rather than the exception, because they do not—or should not—come as a surprise. In this way, the norm and the exception are in a constant state of change and dialogue, although the norm is still the predominant state of affairs, as understood by *Republican exceptionalism.* Figure 1.4 displays this reciprocal or dynamical relationship graphically:

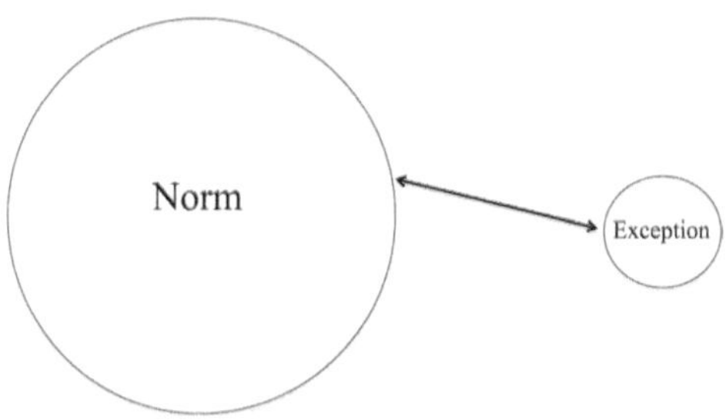

Figure 1.4 The Reciprocal Relationship between the Norm and the Exception. *Source*: Figure created by author.

The last variation is a sort of half-way house between *decisionism* and *Republican exceptionalism*, in the sense that the exception is rather a part of everyday politics, although the norm still predominates. The idea is developed by Honig (2009) who argues that decision is an important part of everyday politics and is contemplated within the framework of a generally ordinary state of affairs. For his part, Neocleous (2006) argues that emergency has been a characteristic of twentieth-century politics and, in that sense, the exception in the framework of the War on Terror is rather nothing new or permanent. In another paper, I argued that the exception is something that permeates ordinary politics, occurring every time there is an alteration within any of the three powers of government—legislative, executive, or judicial—in the name of a special circumstance (Wright 2012). Given that this vision does not rule

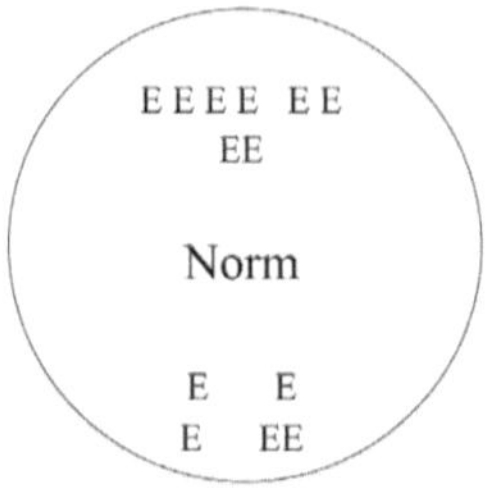

Figure 1.5 The Exception as Decision within the Norm. *Source*: Figure created by author.

out the existence of ordinary politics, it is compatible with *Republican exceptionalism*, and yet given that it permeates political life it once again points toward political *decisionism*. Figure 1.5 reflects the possibility of everyday exceptions within the norm.

Having briefly presented the possible relationships between the norm and the exception, it is evident that the idea of the "exception" is rather blurred. In this study, the division established by the *Republican exceptionalism* current is followed, due to its conceptual clarity and defense of the idea of the "extraordinary," an idea that is reflected in our definition of the emergency politics concept. However, it is also important to acknowledge the historical weight of *decisionism*, despite the fact that it has more to do with discretionary politics rather than emergency politics. Furthermore, the three variants of *Republican exceptionalism* highlighted above (the transformation of an initial exception into a long-term norm, the changing nature of what is exceptional and what is normal, and the occurrence of everyday exceptions within the norm) are particularly interesting as they challenge the norm-exception dichotomy. Consequently, while starting from a generally clear-cut approach within the framework of *Republican exceptionalism*, it is also important to pay particular attention to those occasions when it seems that the norm-exception division is not quite so clear-cut in practice.

Models of Reaction

Having discussed the relationship between the norm and the exception, it is necessary to explore the second dimension of the emergency politics concept from a formal point of view, that is to say the extraordinary procedures that are resorted to in the name of the exception. In this sense, the discussion in the previous section is vital when considering what measures a government will use. For instance, according to the *decisionist* vision, which sees the exception as the normal state of things, the whole apparatus of power must focus on trying to put this chaos into order, which is considered to be a permanent fact of political life. In this sense it is more akin to discretionary politics.

This is the vision that underpins the political systems of absolute monarchs and authoritarian regimes (Hobbes 1996 edition; Lazar 2000 edition; Schmitt 1985 edition) and, as argued before, in essence is more akin to discretionary rather than emergency politics.

On the other hand, following the Republican vision of political life, in which the norm (in theory) prevails over the exception, there are several ways of reacting in the face of a situation that is classified as extraordinary. It has already been noted there is considerable literature on emergency politics from a legal or formal point of view and this is particularly true in relation to the idea of emergency powers or measures.[6] In this sense, Gross and Ní Aoláin (2006) offer a particularly parsimonious approach, with three models of response to situations that are classified as exceptional. In this way, they offer a solid starting point for revising the key contributions to the existing theory on emergency powers. Importantly, the models are formed from a procedural point of view and are based on the idea that, faced with exceptional circumstances, governments have three main options: i) to carry on as normal; ii) to resort to preexisting mechanisms; or iii) to take whatever measures are deemed necessary.

The first model is termed "business as usual" (Gross and Ní Aoláin 2006), and is based on a conviction that nothing can justify a departure from the normal way in which things are done, for fear that it could lead to a permanent and negative change in the political system that has been constructed over time. According to this model, it is better to simply follow normal procedures, on the premise that governments should count on institutions that are strong and designed to resist all possible attacks. Classic liberalism is the great defender of this model and its exemplary thinker is Benjamin Constant, who underlined the tendency for emergency powers to become permanent and despotic. As he saw it, the arbitrariness presented at the start as an extreme resource in very exceptional circumstances becomes the solution to all problems and a daily practice (Constant 1989). It is important to note that, according to my conceptual scheme, this model would not constitute an example of emergency politics, given that no extraordinary measures are employed. Consequently, it would be akin to resistance politics.

The second model proposed by Gross and Ní Aoláin is the model of accommodation (2006), which consists of establishing exceptional procedures to be followed in case of an exceptional situation in the future. There are two main rationales behind the model of accommodation: on one hand, to offer a minimal institutional framework and therefore legitimacy in a crisis situation; and on the other, to offer a rapid response in case of necessity, given that the rules do not have to be made up from scratch (Delfino 2000). In turn, Gross and Ní Aoláin (2006) identify three sub-categories of the model of accommodation, whose principal characteristics are described below.

The constitutional type: Gross and Ní Aoláin note that many constitutional democracies based on civil law traditions (including France, Germany, and the Latin American Republics) count on a preprepared institution to deal with a crisis, in order to act quickly and efficiently (2006). These mechanisms can be established in the constitution or ordinary legislation[7] and are more frequently called "regimes of exception," offering a special normative framework in the face of an "exceptional threat" (Friedrich 1950). The classic model of a regime of exception is the Roman dictatorship, which was divided into two types: i) *dictadura rei gerundae causa* (dictatorship in order to get things done) and ii) *dictadura seditionis sedandae* (dictatorship in order to repress insurrections) (Rossiter 2002). The institution has been praised by various thinkers over the centuries, including Machiavelli (1987), Rousseau (1990), Friedrich (1950) and Rossiter (2002), for simultaneously facilitating and restraining executive power in emergencies thanks to a sophisticated institutional design of checks and balances.[8] The two main characteristics of the regime of exception as it is known today—via the Middle Ages, the Renaissance, the Absolutist states of Europe, the French Revolution, with the mechanism of the "state of siege," and finally in the Weimar Constitution, with its Article 48 (Wright 2012)—are the concentration of power (normally in the executive branch but also in the Armed Forces) and the suspension or restriction of rights or guarantees (in itself an institutional innovation, given that it did not form part of the Roman dictatorship) within a preestablished time limit (Cruz Villalón 1984; de Wilde 2010). It is important to note that in recent years, despite certain institutional checks and balances, regimes of exception have been criticized as an excessively repressive measure (Despouy 1999).

The legislative type: According to Gross and Ní Aoláin (2006), this type of reaction to an exceptional situation involves designing procedures with regard to *what* laws can be made during an emergency and *how* they can be made. Again, the basis of this type of emergency power can be found in Rome, with the figure of the *decemvirate* that is the special law-making body called upon in times of emergency (Wright 2012). The rationale behind this type is that it is not always possible to know what will be necessary in a crisis situation but it may be possible to formulate adequate rules in order to make the changes that are considered necessary in exceptional circumstances (Gross and Ní Aoláin 2006). At the same time there are two categories within the legislative sub-type: i) modifying ordinary laws or ii) drawing-up emergency legislation. The legislative type of accommodation has been of particular interest to the philosopher Giorgio Agamben (2005) who points to a breakdown in the separation of powers as a result, with power generally being concentrated into the executive branch, an argument taken up and applied to the United States recently by DePlato (2014). For her part, Naomi Klein argues that emergency legislation has changed political regimes that were constructed via pacts over time and in circumstances that were considered to be normal, and therefore it has proved to be particularly harmful to democratic forms of government (Klein 2007).

The interpretive type: Again, according to Gross and Ní Aoláin (2006), another preprepared response to extraordinary situations passes through an interpretive filter. In this case, the extraordinary procedure involves interpreting existing laws in a way that takes into account the exceptional situation that has occurred. In other words, it is not the formal law that changes but rather the way in which it is applied, on the basis of the prevalence of certain principles over others. Consequently, in an emergency situation, it is probable that a justification on the grounds of order will take precedence over an interpretation on the grounds of liberty.

The third and final model contemplated by Gross and Ní Aoláin (2006) is the extralegal model, which tends to be found in States with common law traditions (such as the United States and the United Kingdom). In this case, the rationale is that it is impossible to make provisions for the exception given that, due to its very nature, it is impossible to predict the best way to respond to it. Hence, the famous Roman maxim "necessity knows no law." In this model, civil servants must take all the measures considered necessary as and when they are required in order to face different and unexpected aspects of the "exceptional" situation. Gross and Ní Aoláin (2006) insist that the model is not extra-constitutional since it responds to principles such as the hierarchy of power and force against force, it demands accountability over decisions taken in benefit of the common good, and respects the difference between the norm and the exception. Likewise, the extralegal model would not be equivalent to Schmitt's sovereign dictator, given that in this case the only underlying principle is the search for order in the face of what seems to be a never-ending chaos (Schmitt 2009 edition). In this sense, it is more akin to the Roman figure of *iustitium* in which all citizens were called up to take whatever measures necessary in the face of an emergency (Agamben 2005; Wright 2012). It is this model of reaction that corresponds to the long-term situation of exception in the post 9/11 context and which has been a source of heated debate among US authors such as Ackerman (2004) and Cole (2004).

It is clear that Gross and Ní Aoláin (2006) account for an extensive, varied and complex body of procedural or legal literature on emergency politics with their different models of reaction. In order to offer further clarity, Figure 1.6 presents a conceptual map of these models, all of which essentially follow the norm versus exception dichotomy as understood by *Republican exceptionalism*.

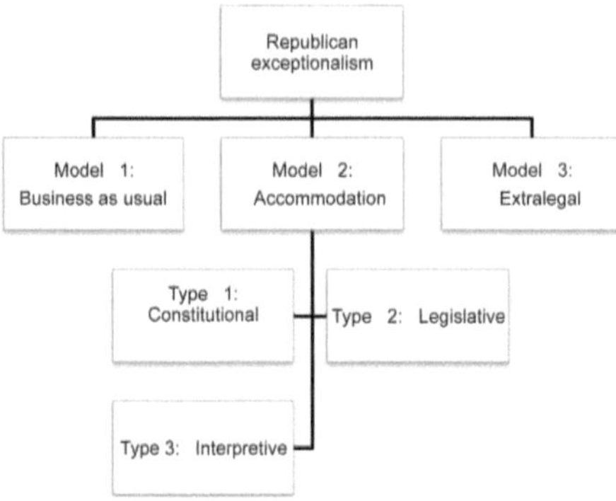

Figure 1.6 Models of Reaction within Republican Exceptionalism. *Source*: Figure adapted from Gross and Ní Aoláin (2006).

Again, it is important to establish two important caveats regarding this scheme, in the same way that three variations on the norm/exception dichotomy were also established.

First of all, it is important to acknowledge that a government may react with different models at the same time or at different points in time. For example, the United Kingdom—despite its historical inclination toward the extralegal model—opted for a legislative type of accommodation model during the First World War (Agamben 2005; Rossiter 2002). Second, it would be a mistake to think that these categories are mutually exclusive which do not change over time. For example, the "state of siege" in fact began as an extralegal mechanism in the French revolution rather than a constitutional-type accommodation model (Rossiter 2002), but it has changed over time, acquiring more institutional limitations and a constitutional format. As Loveman reminds us (1993), emergency politics changes according to the circumstances and over time and therefore does not always respect ideal types or fit into categories. The slippery nature of the emergency politics concept has formed part of its intellectual appeal for scholars over the centuries. Nevertheless, it is important to try to make some sense of this complexity, and Gross and Ní Aoláin's models (2006) offer a very useful approach in that sense.

Emergency Politics from a Formal Perspective

As established at the start of this chapter, the emergency politics concept consists of two main dimensions: extraordinary situations and extraordinary measures. Consequently, having discussed the different approaches in the formal or procedural literature in relation to both dimensions, it is now possible to make some observations about how the two dimensions fit together. It is also worth bearing in mind that some of the categories or ideas in the literature on emergency politics do not fit in neatly with the conceptualization of emergency politics that forms the basis of this study, as will be highlighted below.

In terms of the debate on the first dimension, that is to say the norm versus the exception, the *decisionist* perspective confuses the norm and the exception, referring to a state of permanent chaos. Consequently, it cannot fall into our conceptualization of emergency politics, but instead should be understood as discretionary politics. Rather, the perspective of *Republican exceptionalism* is more useful, given that it establishes a clear difference between the norm and the exception, contemplating the possibility of an ordinary state of affairs. Nevertheless, the caveats about the exception becoming a new norm, the reciprocal relationship between the exception and the norm, and the exception as decision within the norm constitute discordant notes to the simple norm versus exception dichotomy that should not be overlooked when studying emergency politics empirically.

Next, in terms of the debate on the second dimension, that is to say procedural responses to the exceptional situation, the models suggested by Gross and Ní Aoláin (2006) offer a parsimonious summary of the extensive literature on the subject from a procedural point of view. Nevertheless, the "business as usual" model would be excluded from the emergency politics concept, given that it does not represent an extraordinary measure as such. Consequently, the accommodation model (with its legislative, constitutional, or interpretive sub-types) as well as the extralegal model fits more comfortably with the emergency politics concept offered here. Again, it is important to understand that a government may resort to all of the different models at different times and that the categories may change according to the legal framework and historical experiences.

Consequently, from a procedural or formal point of view, the conclusion reached here is that emergency politics can best be understood when there is a clear differentiation between the norm and the exception (as established in the perspective of *Republican exceptionalism*) and a clear use of extraordinary measures, such as is the case of the different types of accommodation model or the extralegal model, proposed by Gross and Ní Aoláin (2006). It has been, repeatedly, stressed that these categories are largely ideal, as in practice there may well be significant variations and blurring of lines, yet they offer a necessary starting point to structure the complex emergency politics concept, based on the important contributions of political theorists and legal scholars of both past and present.

Political Approaches to Emergency Politics

Building on the significant contributions from a formal or procedural perspective, the aim of this study is to approach emergency politics from a decidedly political and empirical perspective. By political I understand a more contextualized approach that has to do with concerns such as agency, capacity, conflict, and governability rather than legal and philosophical concerns. By empirical I refer to how emergency politics works in practice. The literature on emergency politics from a decidedly political perspective is scarce, given that it has not been a classic object of study for political scientists. Consequently, this section is relatively brief. Nevertheless, it includes a revision of the existing literature on emergency politics from a political perspective in the two key dimensions: extraordinary situations and extraordinary measures. Finally, a research agenda on emergency politics in practice is established, together with three main ideal types or paradigms, according to real-life situations and measures.

Extraordinary Situations

Having considered the possible relationships between the norm and the exception in formal terms, an important question remains to be answered: what type of circumstances or situations constitutes an exception? It is a question that has barely been touched upon by the existing literature and which nevertheless is vital when opening up the conceptual black-box of emergency politics and understanding its role in political life.

For its part, the nearest that constitutional law has come to defining a political concept of the exception is the doctrine of the "exceptional threat" and, yet, there is a great divergence of opinion over what this actually means. For example, Delfino (2000) notes that there are many different exceptional situations but what they share is a capacity to impede the State's normal way of functioning, as well as its institutions and ordinary legal framework. In other words, the exception is a relative concept given that is a question of governmental *capacity*. For Despouy (1999), the exceptional threat refers to a situation that is of such gravity that it puts in danger the *life* of a community. Clearly the two definitions are different: one speaks of a lack of capacity to respond and the other of an unexpected and sizeable threat.

It is also important to note that after 9/11 a new, more political, approach to the exception in politics has been developed: securitization theory. According to this perspective, the exception is rather a process through which issues are framed by political elites in order to convince citizens that they are problems of security (Neal 2006). Huysmans (2006) shares this vision, arguing that what makes a situation exceptional is not the degree of violence it involves but rather its politicization as such. Securitization theory foresees the possibility of the political elite constructing certain circumstances as exceptional in order to disorientate the population, gain support from "audiences" and impose measures that are favorable to their own interests (Roe 2008).

Naomi Klein (2007) develops this idea further, arguing that over the past forty years the neoliberal economic model has been imposed by manipulating different crises and applying exceptional measures when the population finds itself in a state of disorientation, or, to use her metaphor, "shock."

In any case, it is clear that it is up to each government to decide which situation is exceptional, far from an objective standard, and in line with the rather vague concept of the exceptional threat. For example, although Amnesty International publishes opinions and recommendations over human rights violations in emergency situations, it does not question the decision to declare the emergency[9] and consequently appears to respect each State's sovereignty in this matter. In any case, in the literature there is some basic agreement over what types of situations can be considered extraordinary: armed conflict, socioeconomic crises, and natural catastrophes or disasters (Klein 2007; Loveman 1993; Zovatto 1990). Nevertheless, it is worth asking if these categories are mutually exclusive, if they hold up in practice, and if there are other situations that should be taken into account, such as the threat by organized crime identified recently as an emergency situation by Frankenberg (2014). Likewise, it is also important to consider the political origins and implications of these different exceptional situations. Offering a reply is an important and pending task for research on emergency politics, from a decidedly political and empirical perspective.

Taking into account these observations, moving from an abstract analysis of the relationship between the norm and the exception to an empirical analysis of the specific situations that have been classified as extraordinary in recent times would constitute a considerable contribution to this important discussion, which—despite some noticeable regional and case studies[10]—has yet been more theoretical in nature. Again, although there is currently an important and fruitful debate in the literature on the norm and the exception but, it focuses almost exclusively on the paradigm of radical Islamist terrorism from the perspective of the United States (Ackerman 2004; Cole 2004; Ferejohn and Pasquino 2004; Ralph 2013),[11] and thus dominates the way we think of and conceive of emergency politics.[12] This volume seeks to offer a contextual understanding of circumstances and situations that are classified as exceptional, in a very different geopolitical context, specifically Latin America.

Extraordinary Measures

It is also clear that existing approaches to emergency politics have focused mainly on procedural or formal elements in reply to extraordinary situations, with options ranging from doing nothing, resorting to a previously established model (a regime of exception, an exceptional law-making capacity, or a different interpretation of existing laws) or using any measures possible. Although this literature is certainly extensive and useful, helping to classify different models of emergency procedures, in essence it tells us little of what emergency politics has involved in practice, in political terms. Indeed it is necessary to understand what measures are employed in practice, beyond their formal or procedural nature, and what they mean in political terms.

Nevertheless, it is possible to tease out certain groups of measures from the literature on the topic, including the suspension of certain civil liberties, special economic or administrative measures, and technical or scientific measures. Below I analyze what the literature has to say about these different types of exceptional measures.

The extraordinary measures that have most successfully captured the imagination and concern of scholars are those that are repressive in nature. The suspension of certain civil liberties and the use of military courts to try civilians are particularly concerning from the perspective of democratic governability and has been dealt with extensively both in the academic literature and by international organizations such as the United Nations (Despouy 1999). Indeed, between 1985 and 2005, the United Nations dedicated a Special Rapporteur to the issue of "states of emergency" understood as cases in which repressive measures were used in the face of an exceptional situation (Wright 2012). While the use of extraordinary, repressive methods has slipped off the UN's agenda (since 2005 it no longer produces its annual lists of states which have declared "states of emergency"), in the context of the war on terror there have been numerous treatise and recommendations on the issue, mainly in the United States (Cole 2004), but more recently in other regions including Asia (Ramraj and Thiruvengadam 2010),[13] and Europe (Brysk and Shafir 2007).

Another group of extraordinary measures found to be used in emergency situations are those that are administrative in nature, changing the way things are done, how policy is implemented, or even who is in charge. In many ways, this group of measures runs parallel to the legislative type model of accommodation discussed above, as extraordinary policies are often implemented via fast-track laws (Agamben 2005). Likewise, Naomi Klein's study of 2007 highlights how episodes such as Hurricane Katrina were used to change the structure of social programs in New Orleans via fast-track administrative measures or the "shock therapy" of structural adjustment measures with the pretext of restarting troubled economies. For her part, Jacqueline Best (2007) refers to exceptionalism and states of emergency ruling economic governance at the global level. Nevertheless, it is also important to contemplate other possibilities that are more executive or administrative than legislative in nature within this group of measures. As Carey and Shugart (1998, 13) argue, the great majority of executive decrees, rather than new laws or policy per se are generally "executive decisions taken in the course of implementing existing laws or exercising what are typically inherent executive prerogatives, such as establishing interagency task forces, commuting sentences of convicted felons, or pinning medals on veterans." These prerogatives become exceptional in nature when they are prioritized over other plans or laws, via fast-track implementation or the use of special funds or economic measures, as established in the "shock doctrine" (Klein 2007).

The final group of measures that can be identified in the literature is either scientific or technical in nature and are related to exceptional situations that need a response based on specific knowledge. Although the literature on the exception has not concentrated on this sort of response, first the disaster (McEntire et al. 2002) and later the "risk management" (Smith 2013) paradigms have busied itself with the study of the different types of technical (and sometimes economic) mechanisms that can be employed to deal with exceptional situations. More recently, the volume by Alemanno (2011) has dealt with contingency plans, communication strategies, technical knowledge, and exercises of futurology in the face of extraordinary and unexpected events as a paradigm of emergency politics.

It is important to identify to what extent these different measures are used in real-life emergency politics and to find out if others exist. It is also worth noting that the three broad groups of exceptional measures that have been found in the literature are not necessarily exclusive. Indeed, the so-called war on terror appears to blend exceptional repressive, administrative, and technical measures together in a semipermanent exception from the norm.

Emergency Politics from a Political Perspective

Having established the broad groups of extraordinary situations and extraordinary measures in practice, it is necessary to understand how they fit together in order to identify different types or paradigms of emergency politics. It is also important to reiterate that the different categories are not mutually exclusive, as different types and combinations of extraordinary situations and extraordinary measures must certainly exist. Ultimately, there may be further groups of situations and measures in practice, which have not yet been caught by the literature on the subject. Again, we are reminded that despite our best efforts, emergency politics does not fit into neat categories.

Nevertheless, it is possible to point to three dominant types or paradigms of emergency politics that can be teased out from the literature on the topic, according to the type of extraordinary situations and extraordinary measures. First, there is "repressive emergency politics" in which, faced with situations of political violence, governments employ exceptional coercive measures. Such is the case of the War on Terror, dealt with by authors such as Ackerman (2006) and Cole (2004). Next, there would be "administrative emergency politics," in which, faced with (real or constructed) situations of extraordinary administrative difficulties and socioeconomic crisis, governments respond with extraordinary administrative measures. This is the case of the shock doctrine, established by Naomi Klein (2007). Finally, there is "disaster emergency politics," in which extraordinary technical or scientific measures are employed when governments are faced with a natural disaster (Alemanno 2011). Table 1.2 offers a simple taxonomy to represent these "ideal" types or paradigms.

Again, it is likely that the lines between these ideal types may become blurred in practice. Indeed, the war on terror has also involved important administrative and technical measures, including complex surveillance systems (Paye 2006); the shock doctrine (Klein 2007) often supports itself with violence and on occasions has been justified by the presence of natural disasters[14]; and the disaster paradigm does not rule out the potential for conflict, administrative/economic measures, or physical coercion. Nonetheless, the three paradigms offer a useful starting point when moving from a more formal or procedural perspective to a more political one and undoubtedly reflect different over-arching or dominant models or logics behind emergency politics.

For its part, the repressive emergency politics paradigm has undoubtedly dominated debates on the issue, which have revolved around the playoff between security and liberty (Ackerman 2006). In an interesting turn, recent debates have moved onto the idea of security versus economy, in the context of classic disaster emergency politics (Alemanno 2011). However, these debates are fresh, generally orientated toward the crisis or risk management paradigm rather than the emergency one, and lack vast empirical evidence. In this sense, it is important to identify and understand the implications of different paradigms of emergency politics, particularly for democratic regimes, which—in line with the *Republican exceptionalism* perspective—should strive to operate in ordinary situations and ordinary measures.

Finally, it is worth remembering the important "constructed" element of emergencies,[15] in line with securitization theory and the different interpretations of the "exceptional threat." The need to find legitimacy for the

Table 1.2 Paradigms of Emergency Politics

Situations	Political Violence	Administrative Crisis	Natural Disaster
Measures	Coercive Measures	Administrative Measures	Humanitarian Measures
Paradigm	Repressive Emergency Politics	Administrative Emergency Politics	Disaster Emergency Politics

implementation of certain measures and the strategies with which they are communicated are of vital importance from a political perspective. Hence, in our quest for understanding emergency politics, it is important to remember that rather than extraordinary situations being the source of extraordinary measures—as Gross and Ní Aoláin suspect (2006)—the relationship between the two different dimensions may in fact be the other way around. Indeed, it may be that extraordinary situations may be just a way of justifying extraordinary measures, in line with securitization theory and the "shock doctrine," described so vividly by Naomi Klein (2007).

REGIMES OF EXCEPTION AS A ROUTE IN

The aim of this chapter has been to formulate a useful and consistent concept of emergency politics and to review the extensive literature on the issue. Many observations have been made but there are three that are vital for our understanding of emergency politics. First, the concept is highly complex and should be subject to further research and clarification. Second, the current debate revolves largely around the US-led war on terror, obviating other regions and types of emergency politics. Finally, the concept has—up until now—been dominated by procedural, normative, or formal approaches in the literature, and consequently we know very little about emergency politics in practice, particularly from a political perspective.

The rather chaotic knowledge we have of emergency politics is reflected in the biggest attempt to date to chart emergency powers empirically. Indeed, despite excellent intentions to safeguard citizens from human rights violations, the global reports produced by the United Nations between 1985 and 2005 suffered from several shortcomings.[16] First, there was a lack of a clear definition of "states of emergency," beginning with an idea that included human rights abuses in the framework of the repressive paradigm and ending up with a broader idea including what is understood here as the disaster model. Second, different types of emergency powers from a procedural point of view were included in the annual reports, including legally declared and de facto exception; hence the metaphor was mixed even further. Finally, the use of newspaper articles and governmental reports to the UN (rather than national level declarations) meant, inevitably, that the information was incomplete. Consequently, this global attempt at identifying all of the instances of emergency politics producing, in the first instance, human rights violations was fundamentally flawed. Indeed, the full database that had been promised was never delivered (except for some limited data on specific countries)[17] and the UN's systematic monitoring of states of emergency came to an end in 2005, although its support in emergency situations has continued.

Undoubtedly, the study of emergency politics in a systematic and empirical way is a considerable and complicated undertaking. Consequently, in order to be consistent and comprehensive, it is necessary to define and reduce the scope of the emergency politics concept from the outset. The first place to start would be from the perspective of *Republican exceptionalism* in which—in theory at least—the norm and the exception lead separate lives. Next, it is worth bearing in mind the importance of procedural literature as a way of isolating different emergency mechanisms and tracking their use empirically. For example, the possibility of analyzing an extralegal model or interpretive type accommodation model is very difficult to do in practice given that by their nature they avoid simple definition or identification. On the other hand, the constitutional and legislative models of accommodation lend themselves to empirical analysis, as they tend to be officially declared by the government (Despouy 1999). In this study, the scope is reduced further by focusing on the constitutional accommodation model (otherwise known as regimes of exception).

There are three main reasons to reduce the scope of the study to regimes of exception: first, because regimes of exception (in essence) respect the norm versus exception dichotomy established by *Republican exceptionalism,* as by their very nature they should be *transitory*; second, because they are officially declared by the executive and so they can be tracked more easily; and finally—unlike the legislative model of accommodation[18]—regimes of exception explicitly articulate the type of extraordinary situations as well as the type of extraordinary measures when they are declared and therefore offer us an important perspective on the two dimensions of emergency politics established in this study, as well as how they fit together.[19] They involve a narrative in which an exceptional situation is outlined and exceptional measures are declared in response.

In this sense, the study takes on board a suggestion of Gross and Ní Aoláin (2006) who argue that—particularly in the case of the constitutional accommodation model (regimes of exception)—it is both necessary and possible to establish a typology or scale of emergency powers, given that different situations must sure call for different measures. As of yet, the literature has left this task unfulfilled. Regimes of exception are known principally for their functioning as a mechanism of repressive emergency politics and yet we have to consider other paradigms under which they might work, such as the administrative or disaster paradigms, established above.

In the first instance it is vital to understand how regimes of exception are used in practice—taking into account their legal form but allowing for an ample degree of improvisation—in order to understand their place in politics. My starting point is from clear-cut categories in which the norm and the exception are different states of affairs and in which extraordinary measures are used to deal with extraordinary situations. On the ground, however,

I expect to find many challenges to these ideas as a result of real-life political practice. In this sense, the study is embedded in the traditional of empirical institutionalism (Peters 2003). As a result of this more in-depth understanding of how they are used in practice, in the second instance it will be possible to understand the ways in which they may protect or indeed damage democratic regimes. Indeed, the different paradigms—repressive, administrative, and disaster—are likely to create very different challenges, as will become clear in the empirical analysis.

Thus far, the debate on regimes of exception has focused on the issue of human rights in the framework of repressive emergency politics and a great deal of effort has been dedicated by the international legal system and legal theorists to limit abuses of power in this sense (Fitzpatrick 1994; Svensson McCarthy 1998; Despouy 1999). For example, the principles formulated by Despouy have offered restrictions on the suspension of human during emergency situations: legality,[20] proclamation,[21] notification,[22] temporality,[23] the exceptional threat,[24] proportionality,[25] non-discrimination,[26] and the compatibility, concordance and complementarity with the different norms of international law.[27] Two of the Syracuse principles are also very relevant when considering regimes of exception from a political point of view: the need for congress to revise the necessity of the measures and the need for courts to retain their ordinary functions.[28]

Crucially, there is a division of opinion in the literature over whether departing from human rights norms for the sake of exception can *ever* be justified (Gross and Ní Aolaín 2006). Some authors reject the compatibility of emergency powers in general and regimes of exception with democracy from the outset. For instance, Jon Elster is skeptical about the possible combination of democracy and the "exception," given that the temporary suspension of human rights can easily lead to a permanent dictatorship (1988, 9), something that troubled Benjamin Constant over two centuries ago (1989 edition). On the other hand, other authors, including José Antonio Aguilar Rivera (1996), Leandro Despouy (1999), Clinton Rossiter (2002), and Ferejohn and Pasquino (2004), emphasize the need for a government to protect citizens in the face of unforeseen situations by using regimes of exception, in the framework of strict controls and the exigencies of the situation. One of the strictest controls mentioned by authors, and the basis of "constitutional dictatorship," is the idea of the "exceptional threat" (Friedrich 1950; Delfino 2000), which amounts to a water-tight justification. While this is difficult to establish in practice, it is important to consider in the name of what "exceptional threats" regimes of exception are declared in order to gauge whether such measures can be considered legitimate.

Given this focus on repressive emergency politics, it may well be necessary to consult other bodies of literature in order to evaluate other uses given to regimes of exception. Indeed, it is important to bear in mind the possibility that these mechanisms may also correspond to the disaster and/or administrative paradigms. If so, it would be necessary to go beyond the (enormously important) issue of human rights. Consequently, potentially useful theoretical approaches from political science will be referred to throughout the empirical study, and summarized in the final analysis, in the framework of grounded theory (Glaser and Strauss 1967). Nevertheless, it should be remembered that concerns over the use of regimes of exception in practice (including and beyond the repressive paradigm) are likely to include old concerns over the separation of powers (Manin 1995) and newer ones over the quality of democracy (Altman and Pérez-Liñán 2002), democratic consolidation (Schedler 2001), democratic governability (Rojas Aravena and Fuentes Saavedra 2004), democratic accountability (O'Donnell 1997), and transparency (Dahl 1971).

Finally, in order to reduce the scope of the study even further, it is necessary to identify a specific context in which regimes of exception are contemplated in legal frameworks and employed in practice, in order to approach their use empirically. As already mentioned, Latin America offers fertile ground for their study, due to the historic use of these measures (Loveman 1993) and their continuing presence in constitutional and legal frameworks (Delfino 2000). Furthermore, the relatively recent wave of transitions to democracy in the region (Hagopian and Mainwaring 2005) and the authoritarian undercurrents of the emergency politics concept make its study all the more urgent. Consequently, the following chapter locates the emergency politics discussion in the Latin American context, revising legal provisions and historical precedents and establishing the continuing dominance of regimes of exception throughout the region.

NOTES

1. In this volume the term "emergency politics" is used, in line with the concept formulated by Bonnie Honig (2009). In the following section, a definition of the concept is offered, presenting it as a broad category that incorporates the similar ideas of emergency powers, emergency government, emergency rule, states of exception, states of emergency, martial law, and so forth.

2. There are a few noteworthy exceptions that will be pointed out during this chapter.

3. Some of the ideas that are developed here were expressed in a preliminary form in a publication in Spanish, see Wright 2014c.

4. See for example the following studies: Ackerman (2004); Agamben (2005), Arato (2006), Ben-Asher (2010), Cole (2004), Ferejohn and Pasquino (2004), Issacharoff and Pildes (2004), Tribe and Gudridge (2004), and Vladeck (2004).

5. Some scholars, including Chappell (2006) and Neocleous (2006), reject this idea, however, arguing that the exception has been a feature of Western politics for a considerable time.

6. See for example, Ackerman (2006); Ferejohn and Pasquino (2004), Friedrich (1950), Rossiter (2002), and Schmitt (1985).

7. In, fact Ferejohn and Pasquino (2004) claim that the use of ordinary legislation to enact emergency powers rather than constitutional mechanisms (often due to a rejection of these mechanisms because of previous abuses) has become increasingly common and cite India as an example.

8. First of all, a respected and well-known person (but not an active politician) was chosen to steward the dictatorship, in order to avoid the concentration of power in the hands of the Consuls; second, a time limit of six months was imposed, in order to avoid long-term emergency powers; third, the Senate classified the situation as an emergency while it was the Consuls who chose the dictator; fourth, no profound changes could be made to the Republic during the reign of a dictatorship; and, fifth, this means of ruling could only be proclaimed once per year (Rossiter 2002, 18–22).

9. See for instance "Nigeria. State of emergency must not lead to more human rights abuses." Available at www.amnesty.org.

10. Alemanno (2011); Ramraj and Thiruvengadam (2010); and Williams (2011).

11. See also the special edition of *Theory, Culture and Society* edited by John Armitage (2002).

12. Several, very recent studies have looked at emergency powers more broadly in the history of the United States, see for instance DePlato (2014) and Edelson (2013).

13. It is important to acknowledge the excellent study on states of emergency in India, prior to the War on Terror, by Tummala (1996).

14. The case of the economic reforms deployed after the Lisbon earthquake in 1755 would be a similar example (Cardoso 2006).

15. In this sense, constructivism could be a useful frame to analyze emergency politics, in line with Berger and Luckmann (1986).

16. United Nations: "Annual reports and lists of States which, since 1st January 1985 have proclaimed, extended or terminated a State of Emergency, submitted by Mr. Leandro Despouy, Special Rapporteur appointed pursuant to Economic and Social Council Resolution 1985/37 1993–2005" available online www.un.org.

17. Despouy (1999, 14). On the website of Queen's University, Belfast www.qub.ac.uk there is a reference to data about the use of emergency powers in East Timor, China, El Salvador, India, Malaysia, Northern Ireland, South Africa, Sri Lanka, and Turkey. From the text of the website it is clear that rather than work in progress it is designed to be a historical reference point.

18. On the important question of whether the legislative model of accommodation constitutes an emergency power per se see the excellent volume by Carey and Shugart (1998).

19. In some cases, these aspects are also established at constitutional level, although the mechanisms themselves tend to be vague. Chapter 2 goes into this issue in more detail.

20. That is to say that the state of emergency is regulated by a series of norms, as well as internal controls. In order to avoid circumstantial reforms in the mechanism, Despouy (1999) argues that it must be established at the constitutional level or in a norm that has constitutional status, something also suggested by Colomer Viadel (1990).

21. In this case, the regime of exception must be declared by the competent authority so that the population affected can understand the nature of the exception. Furthermore, the declaration must be ratified by the national legislative power or another competent authority, as a counterweight mechanism to prevent abuses.

22. The next principle defended by Despouy is notification to the international community, in order to inform that the government in question will not be able to fulfill some of its responsibilities under international human rights law. It also alerts the international community as an important counterweight to abuses of power.

23. The fourth principle suggested by Despouy is temporality, that is to say the duration of the declaration must be strictly necessary, taking into account the nature of the situation. Furthermore, once the declaration has come to an end, it is not possible to continue applying the norms that are used. Despouy suggests a limit of three months and extensions subject to careful revisions.

24. The fifth principle formulated is the concept of the exceptional threat, developed by the constitutional doctrine. This refers to the circumstances (internal commotion, external attack, public danger, natural or man-made disasters) that constitute situations of exception. He underlines that the threat must be real or imminent and that general concepts (including those used by authoritarian regimes in Latin America throughout the twentieth century) such as national security or subversion do not automatically constitute situations of exceptional threat. Second, in order to classify a situation as exceptional, it must be of such a nature as to threaten the organized life of a community in a given territory, endangering citizens' rights and security or that of State institutions.

25. The next principle is proportionality, in the sense that the measures adopted should be those necessary to deal with the crisis. Any excess in this sense would be an abuse of power.

26. The penultimate principle regarding regimes of exception is that of non-discrimination, so that the measures do not affect one social group (e.g. according to age, gender, ethnicity etc.) over another.

27. Despouy's final principle is related to the protection of civil rights and the obligations of States under international law. It implies the preeminence of laws favorable to the protection of human rights, which include the International Pact of Civil and Political Rights of 1966 and which establishes that certain rights can never be subject to derogations, even in exceptional circumstances: the right to life, to physical integrity, freedom from slavery, from forced labor, from illegal detention, freedom of religion, though, conscience and the right to a juridical personality (Article 4). Furthermore, the jurisprudence of the Inter-American Court of Human Rights has underlined that it is not possible to suspend guarantees but rather restrict the enjoyment of certain rights during a regime of exception (García-Sayán 1989).

28. These measures are referred to in García-Sayan, 1989.

Chapter 2

Regimes of Exception in Latin America

The main question posed in this book is the following: what does emergency politics involve in practice? Given the ambiguous nature of the emergency politics concept, its apparent refusal to avoid definition and shirk empirical study, it is necessary to reduce the scope of the task at hand. In this volume I do so by studying a specific emergency mechanism,[1] from a political perspective, in similar sociopolitical contexts. Indeed, this volume seeks to identify the predominant emergency paradigms in Bolivia, Ecuador, and Peru, as expressed in the use of regimes of exception, three decades into the third wave of democratization. The rationale behind this study is simple: if we know more about how emergency politics in general and regimes of exception specifically work in practice—beyond the legal debates and the context of the US war on terror that has dominated academic literature since 2001—we will also be able to establish the specific ways in which they may protect or indeed be harmful to democratic regimes.

Regimes of exception are known principally for two key measures—the concentration of power in the executive branch and the suspension of the enjoyment of certain human rights—in the face of political violence. I termed this use of regimes of exception as corresponding to a political paradigm or model of repressive emergency politics. Consequently, in the first instance it is important to establish not only to what extent regimes of exception have been used in practice, but also to what degree this use has corresponded to a repressive paradigm. Likewise, it is also important to identify other uses these mechanisms may have, remembering the origins of modern-day regimes of exception in the multifaceted Roman Dictatorship which could be either repressive or administrative in nature (Rossiter 2002). Indeed, the previous chapter formulated a further two paradigms under which regimes of exception may also operate: administrative emergency politics (where extraordinary administrative measures are employed to deal with administrative difficulties) and disaster emergency politics (in which extraordinary technical measures are employed to deal with extraordinary situations created by the forces of nature).[2]

Once I have identified how regimes of exception are used in practice and under which paradigms they operate it will be possible to establish how their use relates to democratic concerns. Thus far, the debate in the literature has focused on the crucial issue of human rights in the face of repressive emergency politics and a great deal of academic effort has been dedicated to limiting abuses of power in this sense (Despouy 1999). However, whenever regimes of exception are also employed within the administrative or disaster paradigms, it may be necessary to broaden the frameworks with which they are evaluated, particularly in relation to ideas and evaluations of democratic regimes, including and beyond the human rights issue.

As pointed out in the Introduction and Chapter 1, Latin America offers fertile ground to update our knowledge on emergency politics through the filter of regimes of exception. This chapter will highlight the reasons why this is the case and offer an overview of the current state of our knowledge regarding the use of these mechanisms in the region.[3] To guide the analysis, I will continue to refer to the two key dimensions of emergency politics—extraordinary situations and extraordinary measures—and the three emergency politics paradigms—repressive, disaster, and administrative—in order to approach the concept from a markedly political perspective.

Consequently, this chapter is structured as follows: the first section highlights the prevalence of regimes of exception as the classic emergency model of accommodation[4] in Latin America, with reference to history as well as modern-day constitutions; the second section underscores the use of regimes of exception within the repressive emergency politics paradigm, from the newly independent States of the nineteenth century, through the military regimes of the twentieth century, and until the critical juncture of the third wave of democracy which started to ripple through Latin America in the late 1970s; and finally, in the third section of the chapter, the use of regimes of exception in Latin America in this third wave of democracy is approached, referring to their constitutional features and highlighting the lack of systematic information and scarcity of academic studies on the subject.

The main conclusion reached in this chapter is that—in line with classic conceptualizations of this mechanism—the historical use and constitutional form of regimes of exception in Latin America undoubtedly correspond to the repressive emergency politics paradigm. The lack of systematic studies on the issue makes it all the more urgent to determine whether this is still the case, in practice.

REGIMES OF EXCEPTION AS THE CLASSIC MODEL OF ACCOMMODATION IN LATIN AMERICA

To start with—and following the argument of Chapter 1—it is logical to establish whether there has been a tendency in Latin America in relation to the use of emergency politics from a procedural point of view, before considering under what paradigms it has operated. In this way it is possible to reduce the scope of the study and offer a more systematic empirical analysis.

In this sense, it is important to highlight how the relationship between the norm and the exception has evolved in the Latin American States since Independence. In general terms, it is possible to speak of a *decisionist* vision during various decades of the nineteenth century, when the nascent States found themselves in situations of crisis that were considered to be permanent (Loveman 1993). In the same way, throughout a large part of the twentieth century, the Latin American States were in the hands of military, authoritarian, or sultanistic governments, with the justification of trying to confront different types of chaos (ibid). Finally, the third wave of transitions to democracy as of 1978 defended a more Republican idea of the difference between the norm and the exception, thanks to the predominance—at the symbolic level at least—of the Rule of Law (Hagopian 2005). In this sense, the decisionist legacy of the past is still an important obstacle to the consolidation of Latin American democracies, as is clear in studies such as those carried out by Kruijt and Koonings (2002, 24) and Williams (2011).

Notwithstanding these oscillations between *decisionism* and *Republican exceptionalism* in Latin American history, it is important to consider the procedural replies to the exception, in line with Gross and Ní Aoláin's models of reaction (2006), described in the previous chapter. In this sense, several key studies on emergency politics from both procedural and historical perspectives have given rise to some heated debates and contrasting perspectives on what is the most prominent model of reaction in Latin America. Indeed, some authors point to a legislative model of accommodation and others point to a constitutional model, and in many cases the two models seem to become mixed. The terms of the debate are highlighted below, followed by evidence from Latin American history, and from 18, present-day constitutional frameworks. Our conclusion is that the constitutional accommodation model—or regime of exception—is undoubtedly the classic emergency power from a procedural point of view, notwithstanding the considerable role of the legislative model.

Within this procedural perspective, there has been a tendency to identify executive powers to legislate as *the emergency power* in Latin America. Indeed, Cheibub, Elkins, and Ginsburg (2011; 1721) argue that a typical characteristic of Latin American presidents is their capacity to employ emergency powers and that these are legislative in nature. According to this perspective, faced with an emergency situation, the powers typically given to presidents would be to legislate, in the context of or beyond a regime of exception. Importantly—in line with Ferejohn and Pasquino's (2004) argument—the aforementioned authors (Cheibub, Elkins, and Ginsburg 2011) state that in many cases ordinary legislation can facilitate emergency powers and therefore in practice the constitutional level may not be the most adequate when considering or looking for emergency powers. However, their measure of emergency provisions in Latin American constitutions mixes elements of the two different models of accommodation, given that they include: "(1) the participation of the legislature in the emergency process; (2) the reference to internal security reasons as a justification for emergency powers; (3) the explicit provision for the suspension or restriction of rights during emergency; and (4) the prohibition of constitutional amendments during emergency rule" (ibid, 1722).

On the other hand, Carey and Shugart (1998, 14) argue that executive emergency powers in Latin America are normally mechanisms to suspend civil liberties and to take control of public administrations, particularly in moments of internal disorder. For them, the authority to change a policy via a legislative decree is conceptually different and—given that in many Latin American constitutions it is a faculty that the Congress can delegate to the President—is not an extraordinary measure as such.[5] For these authors, there may be cases when governments make the most of emergency situations in order to define new policies, instead of restricting their powers to the suspension of certain human rights. In these cases, they speak of a "paraconstitutional" initiative, given that it is not always contemplated in the constitution.

In both cases there appears to be a blurring of conceptual lines: in the first case, the legislative model does not deny the possibility of regimes of exception, and in the second case, the constitutional model does not rule out the possibility of legislative powers. However, it is clear that the first perspective is strongly orientated toward law-making capacity and the second to the suspension of civil liberties in the face of internal disorder. Consequently, in order to evaluate which of the two perspectives has stronger foundations, I shall first consider the historical argument (what is the predominant model of reaction according to historians?) and then the procedural argument (what is the dominant model in present-day constitutions?)

The Historical Argument

From a historical perspective, the hypothesis of Carey and Shugart finds ample evidence in Latin America. For their part, Negretto and Aguilar Rivera (2000) underline the predominance of regimes of exception in Latin America, after an initial attempt to employ a "business as usual" model faced with exceptional situations of a political nature during the nineteenth century, which in practice ultimately lead to an extralegal model (Aguilar Rivera 1996, 327). The consequence was that, by the end of the nineteenth century, practically all of the Latin American constitutions included a clause of exception (Aguilar Rivera 1996, 244; Safford 1987, 62; Loveman 1993, 64). In the twentieth century, the use of regimes of exception was linked to the political rise of the Armed Forces in Latin America after the global economic depression of 1929 (Rouquié and Suffern 1997, 289). Later, in the transitions to democracy, regimes of exception survived, despite numerous legal and constitutional changes, as the great legacy of authoritarian regimes (Loveman and Davies 1997). Without going into specific details about the specific uses of regimes of exception throughout Latin American political history (this will be dealt with in a separate section), there seems to be general agreement that they have characterized emergency politics in the region.

On the other hand, Vázquez Carrizosa (1979) emphasizes the importance of executive decree powers throughout Latin American history and the concentration of legislative power in the executive branch, within and beyond the specific figure of regimes of exception, and—with reference to the case of Colombia—particularly to deal with economic crises. For his part, Brian Loveman includes a whole series of emergency powers within his conceptualization of a regime of exception (including the suspension of guarantees and martial law), something which—as Negretto and Aguilar Rivera (2000) point out—go beyond traditional conceptualizations of regimes of exception, such as that used in this study. Nevertheless, he acknowledges the possibility of creating new legislation within the framework of a regime of exception but does not identify it as the main feature of the mechanism. For his part Aguilar Rivera (1996) notes that, in the case of Mexico, suspension of guarantees ultimately became a way to transfer power from the legislative to the executive.

Consequently, from a historical perspective, the predominance of regimes of exception as the classic model of reaction to emergency situations finds plenty of evidence. Nevertheless, as Loveman (1993) and Aguilar Rivera (1996) point out, there may be the possibility of executive decree authority within the declaration of a regime of exception. These ideas are taken up and put to the test in the following sub-section, by considering evidence from present-day constitutions.

The Constitutional Argument

As well as confirming that regimes of exception—rather than the legislative model—have been the paradigmatic emergency power throughout Latin American history, it is also helpful to offer a constitutional basis for the argument. Consequently, I checked 18 present-day (as of 2015)[6] Latin American constitutions, in order to ascertain the relative weight of the two procedural models that have been the source of debate for scholars. Bearing in mind the reflections made as a result of the historical argument, it is necessary to establish in the case of each constitution whether i) a regime of exception is included; ii) the regime of exception explicitly contemplates giving the President extraordinary legislative faculties; and iii) the constitution explicitly contemplates extraordinary legislative faculties for the president faced with situations of emergency, exception, crisis, or urgency.[7] In this way, the relative weight of the constitutional accommodation and the legislative accommodation models of emergency politics can be ascertained, at least at the constitutional level.[8]

In all cases, a regime of exception[9] or clause permitting the suspension of rights[10] in the face of crisis or emergency situations is firmly established. Consequently, as Brian Loveman argued in 1993, it seems that there appears to be an "acceptance of regimes of exception as an essential ingredient of Spanish American constitutionalism" (1993, 392). In only three cases[11] does the mechanism *explicitly* contemplate the use of extraordinary legislative powers, confirming that to a large extent and at the constitutional level, the constitutional model of accommodation does not merge with the legislative model of accommodation, rather they are conceptually distinct, in line with the argument made by Carey and Shugart (1998). Finally, with regard to legislative power that is delegated to the executive—beyond the framework of regimes of exception—such powers are *explicitly* contemplated in eleven present-day constitutions in the region.[12] However, in only five cases[13] are they presented as an emergency power as such, apparently confirming the observation made by Carey and Shugart (1998), in the sense that most often executive decree power is a delegated, discretional faculty rather than an emergency power *per se*. The results of this analysis are displayed in Table 2.1.

In summary, it is clear that regimes of exception are a particularly relevant object of study in the Latin American context. They have been shown to be the primary model of accommodation in emergency contexts from both historical and constitutional point of views and conceptually different from the legislative model, although on certain occasions—as Loveman (1993) points out and is clear from our analysis of 18 Latin American constitutions—they may converge. Given the lack of studies and empirical information on the subject, what is not clear is which model of accommodation has been used more frequently in Latin American politics in recent years. Nevertheless, proving the current predominance of regimes of exception in the region in empirical terms is not the purpose of the study. Rather, the starting point is that regimes of exception are the paradigmatic emergency power in the

Table 2.1 Constitutional and Legislative Models of Emergency Politics in 18 Latin American Constitutions

Country/Constitution	*Regime of Exception*	*RoE Contemplates Extraordinary Legislative Powers*	*Presidential Legislative Powers Beyond RoE*
Argentina 1994	Yes. Art 23	No.	Yes. Art 76
Bolivia 2009	Yes. Arts 137–140	No.	No.
Brazil 1988	Yes. Art 137–141	No.	Yes. Art 68[a]
Chile 1980	Yes. Arts 40–45	No.	Yes. Art 64[b]
Colombia 1991	Yes. Arts 212–215	Yes.	Yes. Art 150[c]
Costa Rica 1949	Yes. Art 121[d]	No.	No.
Dominican Republic 2010	Yes. Art 262–266	No.	No.
Ecuador 2008	Yes. Arts 164–166	No.	Yes. Art 148[e]
El Salvador 1983	Yes. Arts 29–31	No.	No.
Guatemala 1985	Yes. Arts 138–139	No.	No.
Honduras 1982	Yes. Arts 187–188	No.	Yes. Art 245
Mexico 1917	Yes. Art 29	Yes.	Yes. Art 131[f]
Nicaragua 1987	Yes. Art 185	Yes.	Yes. Art 138[g]
Panama 1972	Yes. Art 55	No.	Yes. Art 159
Paraguay 1992	Yes. Art 288	No.	No.
Peru 1993	Yes. Art 137	No.	Yes. Art 118
Uruguay 1967	Yes. Art 168	No.	No.
Venezuela 1999	Yes. Arts 337–339	No.	Yes. Art 236[h]

[a] Importantly, this special executive legislative faculty is not framed as an emergency power as such in the Brazilian constitution.

[b] Again, this special executive legislative faculty is not framed as an emergency power as such in the Chilean constitution.

[c] While this special executive legislative faculty is framed as an extraordinary power but no mention is made of the idea of exceptional circumstances in the relevant article.

[d] In this case no specific name is given to the emergency power, rather the legislative—and in its absence the executive—has the power to suspend certain rights.

[e] In this case, the President is given the power to dissolve the Congress and (with the Constitutional Court's approval) to issue decree-laws of economic urgency until the new Congress is elected. This power can be granted once in the first three years of the mandate and in case of political crisis or internal commotion, or if Congress "takes on attributes that are not stipulated in the constitution". (Article 148)

[f] These powers to legislate are exclusively in economic and trade matters, although no mention of emergency or exception is made in this case.

[g] These powers are not considered exceptional per se but rather as a measure for when Congress is in recess.

[h] Importantly, this special executive legislative faculty is not framed as an emergency power as such in the Venezuelan constitution.

region (from a historical and constitutional perspective) and consequently are a worthwhile route in to studying the rather messy concept of emergency politics from an empirical perspective. Furthermore, given that executive decree power has received a great deal of attention in Latin America political science literature—particularly in the cases of Argentina[14] and Brazil[15]—whereas regimes of exception have not, there is all the more reason to update the knowledge we have of them.

Now, what needs to be clarified is what it has meant to declare regimes of exception in Latin American history, or in other words under what paradigm they have operated. Below, I describe how, over the past two centuries, emergency politics in Latin America—as expressed via the use of regimes of exception—has been characterized by the repressive paradigm, as a result of military intervention in civilian affairs and the suspension of certain human rights.

THE REPRESSIVE EMERGENCY POLITICS LEGACY

Beyond the formal distinction between the norm and the exception and the different models of reaction, it is important to identify the material or political elements of emergency politics. That is to say, to understand how regimes of exception have been used, in practice, in the history of Latin America. As seen in Chapter 1, existing literature on emergency politics has not offered much clarity over both exceptional circumstances and exceptional measures, although in general terms three types or paradigms were established: repressive emergency politics, administrative emergency politics, and disaster emergency politics. In this section I show how over the centuries and up until the period studied here (the third wave of democracy) regimes of exception in Latin America have been associated mainly with a repressive emergency politics paradigm, that is to say as a means of repression during episodes of (mainly internal) political unrest.

Not only has the repressive paradigm dominant, but authors also agree that it is synonymous with authoritarian styles of power, that infringe human rights and show a disregard for the separation of powers. As Colomer Viadel (1990, 87) states: "Generally [states of exception] have been applied with an aim that goes against their constitutional form. . . . In the political history of Latin America they have nearly always been instruments with which the most extreme and arbitrary forms of the predominance of executive power have been tried to be imposed. . . ." For his part, Brian Loveman notes that: "Incorporating provisions into the legal and political culture of Spanish America made them invisible but yet hegemonic premises of political life" (1993, 7).

The analysis carried out in this section—which is undoubtedly an overview and owes a lot to Loveman's seminal work of 1993—reads the history of emergency politics in Latin America through the use of regimes of exception in different political systems. Indeed—in line with our reflections on *decisionism* and *Republican Exceptionalism*—it is not the same thing to use regimes of exception in authoritarianism as it is in democracy. Reflecting these systemic-level differences in general terms, this section is divided into three sub-sections: first from Independence until the end of the nineteenth century; next between 1900 and 1978, representing the rise of the Armed Forces in the region; and finally in the transitions to democracy, which is the start of the period of particular interest in this study.

Regimes of Exception after Independence

Since the wars of Independence, with the power struggles to construct new States, and until the War of the Pacific, the Latin American Nation States were born and constructed over bloody battles (Colomer Viadel 1990, 31; Loveman and Davies 1997, 3; Safford 1987, 80–84). These conflicts that characterized nineteenth-century Latin American politics gave rise to a relationship between the norm and the exception that essentially came closer to *decisionism* than to *Republican Exceptionalism* (Loveman 1993).

What could be regarded as the great "achievement" of Independence in Latin America in fact gave rise to a very serious problem: a vacuum of power, where previously there was the authority of the King of Spain. Those who fought to fill this vacuum, the founders of the Latin American Republics, were the soldiers who had been victorious in the anticolonial wars (Loveman and Davies 1997, 3; Colomer Viadel 1990, 31; Safford 1987, 80–84). As Loveman notes, the notion of the soldier came much before the notion of the citizen in the region (1997). Furthermore, over the first few decades after 1812 (when Venezuelans declared independence from Spain) a series of social and economic problems created political upheaval and civil strife (Loveman 1993, 53). Consequently, therefore, it is important to take into account that the Latin American States were founded via a violent redistribution of political power that was carried out via armed conflict and that endured throughout the nineteenth century.

In this context, the nascent states faced the following dilemma: whether they should follow Iberian, authoritarian traditions or instead introduce the liberal constitutionalism that was being championed in France, Great Britain, and the United States at the time (Safford 1987, 57). As Roberto Gargarella explains, although conservatives and radicals had an important impact on the constitutionalism of this period, it was the political activism of liberals that led to the adoption of predominantly liberal constitutions in the region (2005, 219). The main tenets of liberal constitutionalism were: to protect individual rights, to limit state power, to restrict the president's powers, and to establish a system of checks and balances (ibid, 197). In this sense these efforts marked a desire to end the "tyranny" of Spanish Rule (Loveman 1993, 3). For this reason, the first Latin American constitutions did not include emergency powers, instead following the "model of resistance"[16] that had been proposed by thinkers such as Benjamin Constant in the aftermath of the *terreur* of the French Revolution (Aguilar Rivera 1996, 232).

Nevertheless, without constitutional responses to the crisis situations faced by these nascent states having been crafted (Loveman 1993, 62), on several occasions only two options were left at their disposal: i) the removal of presidents via *golpes de estado* [coup d'états] or ii) the violation of the constitution and of liberal principles, in order to cling on to power (Aguilar Rivera 1996, 28). Consequently, various political historians argue that these liberal-oriented states were undermined by this deficiency in their institutional make-up. As Gargarella explains, Latin American liberals thus often had to resort to more conservative principles—including the concentration of power and the use of violence in order to achieve stability (2005, 247). The consequence of this was that, despite an initial reluctance to do so, by the end of the nineteenth century, practically all Latin American constitutions had come to include a framework for a Regime of Exception, understood as a mechanism to concentrate power in the executive to essentially do anything it wanted, suspend rights and liberties, and offer more power to the military (Aguilar Rivera 1996, 244; Loveman 1993, 64; Safford 1987, 62). As a blanket justification, the vague notion of "conmoción interna" (internal commotion) was also introduced (Loveman 1993, 6) to justify these repressive measures.

It appears that there was a clash between liberal ideals and the political, economic, and social upheaval of postindependence in Latin America. On the one hand, the constitutional model did not offer instruments that could be used to confront the crises that invariably emerged during the foundation of a new State, meaning that extralegal or paraconstitutional faculties were employed. On the other hand, the culture of "antipolitics"[17] on the part of the *caudillos*, nascent military sectors, and liberals themselves undermined the values established by these fragile young republics. The systematic reply to this situation was the use of regimes of exception as a mechanism of repression disguised beneath a minimal framework of legality (Loveman 1993, 203).

1900–1978 The Military Legacy

During a large part of the twentieth century, the Latin American States were in the hands of military, authoritarian or sultanistic governments, with the justification of confronting different political, economic, and social chaos (ibid). Although the military had an important role at the time of independence and toward the end of the nineteenth century, with the founding of the first national armies at that time, the armed forces in Latin America gained true political prominence after the Great Depression of 1929 (Rouquié and Suffern 1997, 289). Between February and December of 1930, the governments of Argentina, Bolivia, Brazil, the Dominican Republic, Guatemala, and Peru were all ousted by military coup d'états. This became a common occurrence in Latin America during the twentieth century, in many cases up until the end of the 1980s, even despite the brief period of "democratic euphoria" that came after the end of the Second World War (ibid.).

Later on in the twentieth century—particularly in the 1960s, 1970s, and 1980s—the political violence that had become a characteristic of the Independence era continued, although its features and dimensions were substantially different. In this period, the violence occurred specifically within the frontiers of these States in the framework of the Cold War. This so-called "national security doctrine" to a great extent constituted a discursive excurse in order to justify repressive measures, in line with the perspective of "securitization theory" discussed in Chapter 1. In this context, the military again gained increasing importance after the Cuban Revolution of 1959, given the Cold War circumstances and support from the United States in their fight against communism. Between 1962 and 1972 there were a series of *golpes de estado*, which were followed by the brutal repression of the opponents of these military regimes. As Rouquié and Suffern explain (ibid, 291), any aspiration to social change or support for left-wing parties was considered to be "revolutionary." It was in this context that the national security doctrine was developed, with public order therein becoming the key priority for governments and justification for a whole battery of repressive measures, including regimes of exception (Zovatto 1990).

Although the political persuasions of the military have shown some degree of variation—from the historical authoritarian-bureaucratic model in the Southern Cone to a more progressive one in the Andean region (Rouquié and Suffern 1997)—the regimes established in Latin America during the twentieth century were ultimately characterized by their common rejection of democracy (Loveman and Davies 1997). Their solution to the range of problems they faced was to concentrate power, and in many cases to limit civil rights in general, whether the objective was the repression of left-wing opponents or national economic development. In order to achieve a concentration of power in the Executive the military resorted to the use of decrees, which they aimed to legitimize by using the regime of exception clauses that had been incorporated in national constitutions during the nineteenth century (Loveman 1997). Indeed, by the end of the 1970s two-thirds of Latin American countries lived under "states of exception" (Despouy 1999, 16).

In real terms, the use and abuse of Regimes of Exception was more common among the dictatorships of the Southern Cone. As Leandro Despouy (1999) explains, regime of exception clauses were regularly enacted in this region, leading to the perpetual abuse of human rights. For example, in Chile 200,000 citizens were detained between 1973 and 1980 under special measures during the declaration of "states of siege." In Uruguay, between 1971 and 1983, a third of the population was detained or interrogated in the framework of similar measures (ibid). Likewise, a state of exception was in place in Paraguay between 1954 and 1987.[18] As Despouy also explains, regimes of exception are the most critical situations for the protection of human rights particularly when, as was the case of the authoritarian regimes of the Southern Cone, emergency becomes routine (ibid).

Indeed, it was under the authoritarian governments of the twentieth century that the repressive nature of regimes of exception was consolidated, propped up by two main pillars: the intervention of the military in politics and the use of force to repress social disturbances.[19] As García-Sayán notes (1989), these situations rarely constituted a threat to a constitutional order and were rather localized protests that resulted from social and economic injustices. The real problem with the use of the mechanism during this period is that they became permanent (Despouy 1999) and consequently did not respect the difference between the norm and the exception within Republican Exceptionalism, again becoming instruments of a decisionist, discretionary politics, as they had been during the nineteenth century.

The Transition Period

Finally, the third wave of democratization that rippled through Latin America as of 1978[20] ushered in a more Republican idea of the difference between the norm and the exception, thanks to the predominance—at the symbolic level at least—of the Rule of Law. Undoubtedly, there have been a number of authoritarian interruptions such as Fujimori's dissolving of Congress in Peru in 1993 or the *golpe de estado* in Honduras in 2009. Nevertheless, the *decisionist* legacy of the past is still an important challenge in the consolidation of Latin American democracies, as is clear in studies such as those carried out by Kruijt and Koonings (2002, 24) and Williams (2011). In any case, the general rule is that democracy (whatever its current limitations and states of consolidation) is the "only rule of the game" in the region.

The so-called "third wave of democratization" in Latin America began at the end of the 1970s—with the Dominican Republic the first to turn, in 1978—and ended with the return of democracy to Chile in 1990 (Rouquié and Suffern 1997, 330).[21] The new democracies faced two main challenges: on the one hand, the legacy of institutionalized violence and, on the other, widespread social inequality amid the economic crisis of the 1980s (Kruijt and Kroonings 2002, 24). With regard to the first challenge, as Terry Lynn Karl explains (1996), the military carried out a series of foundational pacts with the new democratic actors in order to maintain its power and influence in certain areas. Consequently, the new governments opted for a pragmatic approach, one that may have led to foundational weaknesses such as impunity and the weak rule of law (Loveman and Davies 1997).

In the majority of Latin American countries, the withdrawal of the military from government coincided with new electoral legislation and new constitutional arrangements (ibid, 1997). However, Bolivia, Chile, and Uruguay chose to retain preexisting constitutions that had either been drawn up by or used to support military regimes. Foundational pacts were vital for the emerging democracies to survive and succeed, with the influence of the military being reflected in these nascent entities coming to represent "protected" democracies, including such elements as criminal codes that included special clauses for political crimes or that gave autonomy to members of the Armed Forces (Loveman and Davies 1997). Another mechanism that was very important in maintaining the influence of the military was precisely the regime of exception itself, by then synonymous with repressive emergency politics. In fact, every new constitution adopted between 1978 and 1993—with the exception of the one in Paraguay—reaffirmed and broadened the measures that could be employed in emergency situations (ibid, 376). Table 2.1—with the analysis of 18, contemporary Latin American constitutions—reflects the degree to which these constitutional arrangements that survived the transition period are still present in the region.

At the time of the transitions there was considerable academic concern over the use of regimes of exception to repress protests and their possible impact on human rights. For instance, in 1986 the Comisión Andina de Juristas and the Instituto Interamericano de Derechos Humanos organized the seminar: "Los Estados de Excepción en la Región Andina" (Figallo 1987) which led to a collective volume of case studies on the Andean Region (García-Sayán 1987a). At the end of the seminar, a declaration was made pointing to the abuses carried out under states of exception in the region in the past, including the vagueness of constitutional mechanisms, the important issue of undefined emergency situations, the use of military force, a tendency to use in the face of protest, and the lack of explicit time limits or "institutionalised use of states of exception as a means to violate human rights" (ibid, 273). It is important to note that particularly Colombia and also Venezuela have not been exempt from the use of regimes of exception, despite having democratic regimes before the transition period in Latin America (Loveman 1997).

In the same way, Zovatto offered an overview of human rights and states of exception in 1990. Furthermore, in the case of Peru there was considerable academic output at the time, given the repeated use of the mechanism in the struggle against *Sendero Luminoso*.[22] At the regional level, it was in 1993 that Loveman published his seminal and exhaustive work on regimes of exception in Latin America from a historical point of view: *The Constitution of Tyranny*. Consequently, at the start of the transitions there appeared to be an acute awareness of the dangers involved in the use of regimes of exception—which by then had been firmly established within a repressive emergency politics paradigm—but little constitutional development to avoid their use and abuse.

To summarize this section on the use of regimes of exception since Latin American Independence, it is abundantly clear that they have become synonymous with repressive emergency politics. This reading of emergency politics in the region is undoubtedly due to the scope of this study, restricted to one specific mechanism. In that sense, two observations—and perhaps caveats—need to be made. First of all, the norm/exception dichotomy has, undoubtedly, been put to the test on repeated occasions in the region, particularly in the form of authoritarian regimes. Second, the history of regimes of exception in the region has been written firmly within the repressive emergency politics framework. While the existence of other types of exceptions situations in the region, including natural disasters[23] and economic crises,[24] is unquestionable, what is not clear is whether they have been dealt with through the application of regimes of exception. In any case, it remains to be seen whether regimes of exception are still used according to the repressive paradigm as understood by the literature and/or if they have been used under different paradigms (i.e. administrative emergency politics or disaster emergency politics) in the third wave of democracy. Finding an answer to that question is one of the main objectives of the present volume.

EMERGENCY POLITICS IN THE THIRD WAVE

As highlighted in the previous section, repressive regimes of exception have been an important legacy of previous constitutional arrangements and political practices throughout Latin America, surviving the transitions to democracy pretty much unscathed. However it is important to ask if these mechanisms of emergency politics have been used in practice in the third wave of democracy and if so according to what paradigm. These are important questions which nevertheless have not received a consistent or systematic answer in the literature. In this section I focus on our (limited) existing knowledge of regimes of exception in the third wave, as a starting point for the case studies that are the empirical core of this volume. This knowledge comes from monitoring by the United Nations, a handful of academic studies, and a more in-depth examination of present-day Latin American constitutions.

Monitoring of States of Emergency by the United Nations

As noted in the Introduction and Chapter 1, throughout the 1980s the issue of states of emergency was considered a priority at the United Nations, who designated a Special Rapporteur to monitor the application of regimes of exception throughout the world and sought to create a database to monitor derogations from international human rights norms in situations of emergency. Indeed, the conceptualization of the United Nations of "states of emergency" at the start was rather a juridical instrument used in a situation of conflict to concentrate power in the executive—and particularly—restrict the enjoyment of certain civil rights. In that sense, the UN's conceptualization is essentially in line with the repressive emergency politics paradigm.[25] As well as efforts in terms of establishing international normative standards, the United Nations Rapporteur was in charge of monitoring the use of regimes of exception throughout the world, which it did between 1985 and 2005. While the information gathered is highly interesting, two reservations must be made.

First, the information is likely to be incomplete and indeed underestimate the use and scope of regimes of exception. Initially, the "states of emergency" were identified via press articles and later on via reports that the States handed in to the Rapporteur's office. In terms of press articles, it is important to point out the possibility of censorship or at least restricted information during a regime of exception. Likewise, as García Sayán (1989) notes, few countries in Latin America actually handed in reports to the United Nations. Both methods are clearly insufficient and the lack of consistency in the methodology means that the results cannot be compared easily over time.

The second—and crucial—reason is given that the UN's conceptualization of a regime of exception is not clear and appears to change over the years. As mentioned above, in line with the report by Questiaux, at the start the United Nations referred uniquely to a juridical instrument that is in line with the repressive emergency politics paradigm and firmly based on existing norms (Fitzpatrick 1994). However, in the annual lists of states of emergency produced by the UN Special Rapporteur, both formally declared "states of emergency" based on constitutional regimes of exception and informal (para legal) "states of emergency" are included[26] Later, as of 1998,[27] no further references are made to these para legal states of emergencies and only "states of emergency" with an explicit legal base are included. In the same way, at the start only those cases related to internal conflict or disturbances and the suspension of human rights were included. Later on, several cases relating to natural disasters and socioeconomic problems were included.[28] Furthermore, having used the term "state of emergency" as a generic term since 1985, as of 2003 the term "state of exception" is used as a generic term for measures ranging from "states of war" to "states of disaster" and "state of siege."

Rather than a criticism as such, these observations show how difficult the conceptualization and identification of regimes of exception can be in practice. Nevertheless, the data—which as has been highlighted are likely to *underestimate* the extent of the problem—are revealing. Indeed, the United Nations' reports between 1985 and 2005[29] confirm that over this period of twenty years, multiple declarations of "states of emergency" have occurred in Latin America, with either the restriction of human rights or the deployment of military forces. Indeed, the vast majority of Latin American democracies gave rise to at least one declaration of a state of exception between 1985 (or after the transition, if it was later) and 2005.[30] Furthermore, according to the same data, the governments of the Andean countries have resorted to the use of regimes of exception much more frequently than their neighbors. For instance, in Ecuador there were over thirteen declarations of states of emergency between 1985 and 2005. The case of Peru reveals a concerning, semipermanent use of regimes of exception whilet in Bolivia and Venezuela there have been declarations on several occasions. The situation in the Andean region contrasts with cases such as Chile, El Salvador, and Panama, countries with recent authoritarian pasts and yet in which no regimes of exception have been declared since the return to democracy, at least according to the—rather conservative—UN data.

This information is presented in Table 2.2, separated according to country and whether the state of exception/emergency was a one-off or a long-term event. For the reasons above, the figures are by no means conclusive but at least they offer an orientation and confirm that regimes of exception are very much "alive and kicking" in the region. Unless otherwise stated, the declarations appear to be within the repressive emergency politics paradigm; however cases that appear to fit in more with the administrative or disaster paradigms are duly noted. It is important to take into account that the data are from 1985 onwards except in those States which transited to democracy after this date. In those cases, the data are taken since the year of their return to democracy.

Unfortunately, and despite the shortcomings in the data, the issue seemed to slip off the UN agenda somehow and since 2005 no further monitoring reports have been published on the issue of regimes of exception.[31] Indeed, by that year the data itself was noticeably very limited, with just a handful of countries mentioned. Furthermore, the UN Special Rapporteur on the issue no longer exists and the database that was promised has not appeared.[32] Despite giving priority to the issue for a period of twenty years, the United Nations has turned its attention to other issues rather than emergency politics, perhaps as a result of the events of 2001.[33] In any case and despite the shortcomings mentioned, its contribution to the monitoring of the use of regimes of exception in the past cannot be underestimated and offers vital lessons for future studies and reports on the issue—including the current volume—particularly in relation to the need for conceptual clarity and going beyond the juridical or rights-orientated approach to regimes of exception that has undoubtedly dominated the literature. Furthermore, the data available, which if anything *underestimate* the problem in numerical terms, confirm the concerns of

Table 2.2 UN Data on Regimes of Exception in Latin America

Country	*One-off States of Emergency*	*Long-term States of Emergency*
Argentina	4 (1985, 1999, 2001, 2001)	
Bolivia	5 (1985, 1986, 1990, 1995, 2000)	
Brazil	—	—
Chile	—	—
Colombia	2 (1992, 1994)	4 (1984–1991, 1992–1993, 1995–1996, 2002–2003)
Costa Rica	—	—
Dominican Republic	—	—
Ecuador	12 (1986, 1988, 1988, 1989, 1999, 1999[a], 1999, 2000[b], 2001[c], 2002[d], 2002[e], 2002)	1 (1999–2000[f])
El Salvador	—	—
Guatemala	3 (1993, 1998[g], 2001)	
Honduras	1 (1988)	
Mexico	—	—
Nicaragua	2 (1988, 1993)	1 (1982–1988)
Panama	—	—
Paraguay	1 (2000)	
Peru	3 (2000[h], 2002, 2003)	3 (1981–1990, 1988–1990[i], 2003–2005)
Uruguay	—	—
Venezuela	4 (1989, 1992, 1993, 1993)	2 (1994–1995[j], 1995–1999)

Source: Table adapted by author from United Nations annual state of emergency reports
[a] The situation referred to here is in relation to the transport system.
[b] The situation referred to here is economic crisis.
[c] The situation referred to here is economic crisis
[d] The situation referred to here is a storm.
[e] The situation referred to here is in relation to the transport system.
[f] The situation referred to here is a crime wave.
[g] The situation in this case was Hurricane Mitch.
[h] There is also reference to an extension of a state of emergency in the same year, but it is not clear which one hence it is not counted here.
[i] During this period, 13 separate declarations of regimes of exception appear to have been made.
[j] The situation here was a financial crisis.

scholars such as Zovatto (1990) and García-Sayán (1987a) at the start of the transitions, in that regimes of exception have been used as mechanisms of repressive emergency politics throughout Latin America in the third wave of democracy.

Academic Concern over Regimes of Exception in the Latin American Third-Wave

Despite a widespread concern over the use of these mechanisms at the time of the transitions (García-Sayán 1987a) and Brian Loveman's seminal, historical study (1993), there have been very few academic studies on regimes of exception in recent years. Indeed, since the transition period, academic interest in regimes of exception as a political mechanism seems to have diminished in the region, following the tendency established at the UN level. Importantly, since the 1980s—when most of the key literature on regimes of exception was published and several important conferences were held—there have been no further conferences on the topic in Latin America.

Nevertheless, there have been a handful of interesting studies on emergency politics during this period, albeit of limited scope, without touching upon elements of conceptualization or going beyond the issue of human rights within the repressive emergency politics paradigm. In relation to regimes of exception specifically,[34] it is worth highlighting the following studies, which fall into three groups. The first is those that offer case studies on one country such as those carried out by Dávalos Muirragui (2008) on Ecuador, Vázquez Carrizosa (1992) and Iturralde (2003) on Colombia,[35] and Rosatti on Argentina (2004).[36] The second group offers brief analysis of declarations of regimes of exception as an item of secondary interest in studies related to broader political processes, such as Alenda on Bolivia (2003), and Jaskoski on Peru (2012). The final—most extensive group—are those studies that approach regimes of exception in Latin America in the third wave from a mainly juridical or constitutionalist point of view (Delfino 2000; Fix-Zamudio 2004; Carbonell 2008; Ríos Álvarez 2009).

Latin American Political Science, for its part, has largely overlooked regimes of exception as an object of study in their own right, focusing instead on executive powers to legislate, particularly in the cases of Argentina and Brazil.[37] Curiously, despite a concern for the quality of democracy, democratic consolidation, and authoritarian legacies, as pointed out in an earlier article (Wright 2012), political studies in the third wave have not busied themselves with the systematic study of regimes of exception. Nevertheless, as Loveman (1993, 9) argues, they constitute a troubling foundational legacy of third wave democracies that undermine their consolidation. In his own words: "No elections, no delicately orchestrated set of musical chairs, and no transitions from authoritarian to elected governments will succeed in consolidating constitutional democracy without drastic reform of these constitutional foundations of tyranny bequeathed by liberals and conservatives in the nineteenth century and reaffirmed by social democrats, and revolutions in the twentieth."

I would add that, in accordance with our existing knowledge of them, regimes of exception present (at least) three fundamental incompatibilities with the concept of polyarchy as understood by authors such as Dahl (1971) and O'Donnell (2004): i) when they restrict the enjoyment of human rights; ii) when they concentrate power in the executive branch or the army; and iii) because they may offer few opportunities for accountability. Furthermore, if regimes of exception stay in place over time or are repeatedly declared they represent a profound challenge for a political regime's status as a democracy. I expect to adjust this list according to the findings of the study.

As well as an apparent literature gap, it is important to note that there have been fertile conditions for the use of regimes of exception in the region. Indeed, in Latin America the three main emergency situations identified in Chapter 1 have persisted in the third wave of democracy: political violence, economic crisis, and natural disasters. What remains to be seen is how these "external threats" relate to emergency politics in practice, as it is expressed via regimes of exception. Given the lack of systematic studies on these material or political elements of emergency politics, it is necessary to revise real-life practice and offer interpretations, as is the intention of the present volume. As a result, it will be possible to establish if the repressive paradigm of emergency politics—which has dominated the literature on regimes of exception[38]—has continued in the region, or rather if the two other models, administrative or disaster emergency politics, have co-existed with, or even, replaced it. This is important because the way in which regimes of exception are used in practice will likely have different impacts and relationships with processes of democratic consolidation.

Features of Regimes of Exception in Present—Day Latin American Constitutionalism

Throughout this volume it has been stressed that the legal aspects of regimes of exception are secondary to the political or material aspects of these mechanisms of emergency politics. Our thinking is in line with Friedrich's observation in that constitutional or legal continuity can often hide changes in practice (1950). Essentially, the legal nature of regimes of exception is a route in to exploring emergency politics in practice as it makes them easier to identify. In any case, in order to add support to the empirical study—and supplement the rather sketchy knowledge we have of regimes of exception in the third wave—my prior analysis of Latin American Constitutions (up until 2015) is broadened in this section. At this stage, the aim is to establish whether the repressive emergency politics paradigm is still dominant at the constitutional level, at least, beyond what national jurisprudence, legislation, regulations, and juridical interpretations may have to say on the matter. Despite important observations that could be made over checks and balances by the congress and/or the constitutional court, these concerns are not included here given that the focus is on extraordinary situations and extraordinary powers, and how they fit together.

In terms of extraordinary situations, in almost all cases there are references to situations of political violence, external warfare, or the disturbance of public order.[39] In several cases, reference is made to the idea of "conmoción interior" or "internal commotion" which is a highly ambiguous expression,[40] seemingly related to the idea of an exceptional threat and which—according to Loveman (1993)—was first introduced in Latin American constitutionalism in nineteenth century. Next, it is important to note that around half of the regimes of exception refer to situations of natural disaster (as well as pollution and epidemics)[41] and a handful to the economic and social order.[42] In one case there is no reference to a specific situation as such but rather simply to exceptional situations in general terms which—notwithstanding posterior legal interpretations—represents a great deal of ambiguity at the constitutional level.[43] Consequently, it is clear that while situations of political violence are still predominant at the constitutional level, natural disasters and socioeconomic crises are also contemplated.

Then, with regard to extraordinary situations, the suspension of rights or even of guarantees is the most frequently referred-to measure. In some cases the specific rights that can be suspended are listed and in others there are rather references to rights that may not be subject to derogation. In any case, the possibility of restricting liberties relating to freedom of movement, assembly, and lawful detention is frequently referred to. Furthermore, there are reiterated references to extraordinary powers of coercion and in the case of Ecuador and Peru it is explicitly established that control of internal order may be handed the Armed Forces. As has already been established (see Table 2.1), in three cases extraordinary legislative powers are offered to the executive within the regime of exception[44] and in the case of Chile and Ecuador several administrative powers are offered, relating to collecting taxes and public administrations. Curiously, no explicit mention is made of technical measures as such, at this constitutional level. Consequently, it is clear that regimes of exception are intricately related to the use of coercion, following on from the historical paradigm in the region. However, references to administrative type measures—although there are clearly few of them—remind us of the more administrative type of regime of exception contemplated in the Roman dictatorship.

It is important to recall that the conceptual pillar of this study is that emergency powers consist of two main dimensions: extraordinary situations and extraordinary measures. Consequently, it is necessary to offer some comments on how the two dimensions fit together in the regimes of exception established in contemporary Latin American constitutions.

In the majority of cases, the classic schema of external war/internal disturbances plus the use of coercion is established. However, in some cases there is a rather surprising combination of the two dimensions. For instance, Article 148 "state of exception" of the Bolivian constitution of 2009 contemplates a restriction of civil rights in the face of various circumstances, including natural disaster. It is worth asking if this is the most logical—or justifiable—response in this type of situation, rather than technical or humanitarian aid. In the same way, in Article 265 of the Dominican Republic's 2010 constitution, faced with situations of natural disaster or socioeconomic crisis, there is also a suspension of rights in the framework of a "state of emergency." On the other hand, the Constitutions of Chile, Colombia, Guatemala, and Venezuela are interesting given that they establish different regimes of exception according to the type of emergency. Nevertheless, although the situations vary, the measures do not go much beyond the suspension of rights and/or legislative measures, in the case of Chile and Colombia. The idea of clear-cut paradigms or types with extraordinary measures relating to extraordinary situations is particularly interesting for the concerns of this study but is largely absent from Latin American constitutionalism which—as stated before—suffers from a degree of vagueness and ambivalence at the constitutional level, something that was already highlighted as a key concern by jurists at the start of the third wave (García Sayán 1987a).

A summary of the results of the analysis can be found in Table 2.3.

As a result of the analysis carried out in this section, it is clear that the classic formula of political violence together with coercion predominates in regimes of exception as they are contemplated in current constitutions, reflecting historical models described in the first section of this chapter. However, in the same constitutions some differences can be observed in both extraordinary situations and extraordinary measures, leaning toward the administrative and/or disaster paradigms. Furthermore, in several constitutions, the two dimensions of emergency politics simply do not concord with the classic taxonomy. Taking into account that regimes of exception in Latin America have been characterized by discretion and improvisation by presidents (Loveman 1993)—often departing from their constitutional form and purpose (Colomer Viadel 1990)—it becomes even more necessary to carry out an analysis of how these dispositions have been used in practice, beyond constitutions, history and a few, scarce NGO reports or press analyses.

As stated before, in this section I have refrained from looking at possible oversight mechanisms or limitations on power in the framework of regimes of exception in order to highlight the more material aspects of their constitutional form, something that in turn has been largely overlooked by previous studies. Indeed, before considering the possible effects of regimes of exception on fragile democracies it is necessary to ask: what does their use correspond to? Once we understand better how these mechanisms have been used in the three countries studied here, it will be necessary to understand how they may affect democracy and at that stage, return to important issues of oversight. In any case, our current, sketchy knowledge on regimes of exception in

Table 2.3 Exceptional Situations and Exceptional Measures in Regimes of Exception in Latin American Constitutions

Constitution	*Regime of exception*	*Situations*	*Measures*
Argentina 1994	"state of siege" Art 23	Internal commotion or external attack.	Suspension of guarantees, special powers of detention.
Bolivia 2009	"state of exception" Arts 137–140	Danger for state security, external threat, international commotion, or natural disaster.	Suspension of certain rights.
Brazil 1998	"state of siege" Arts 137–141	Grave commotion or declaration of war.	Suspension of certain rights.
Chile 1980	"state of assembly" Art 40	External warfare.	Suspension of certain rights.
	"state of siege" Art 40	Internal warfare/grave internal commotion.	Suspension of certain rights.
	"state of catastrophe" Art 45	Public calamity.	Suspension of certain rights. Chief of National Defense in charge of measures.
	"state of emergency" Art 42	Grave alteration of public order of danger for the security of the Nation.	Suspension of certain rights Chief of National Defense in charge of measures.
Colombia 1991	"state of external warfare" Art 212	External warfare.	Legislative decrees can suspend incompatible laws. Use of force.
	"state of internal commotion" Art 213	Disturbance of public order that goes beyond the police's capacity.	Legislative decrees can suspend incompatible laws. Use of force.
	"state of emergency" Art 215	Grave and imminent threat to the country's economic, social and ecological order, or public calamity.	Legislative decrees to face the crisis. Raising taxes.
Costa Rica 1949	suspension of individual rights and guarantees Art 121	"Evident public necessity."	Suspension of certain rights and guarantees.
Dominican Republic 2010	"state of defense" Art 263	In case national sovereignty or territorial integrity are in grave and imminent danger due to external armed aggression."	Suspension of certain rights.
	"state of internal commotion" Art 264	In case of a grave disturbance of public order which imminently attacks institutional stability, the security of the State, or citizen coexistence and which cannot be resolved via the authorities' ordinary faculties.	Suspension of certain rights.
	"state of emergency" Art 265	When other events than those included in Articles 263 and 264 that disturb or threat in an imminent way the economic, social or environmental order of the country, or constitute a public calamity.	Suspension of certain rights.

Guatemala 1985[a]	States of exception Arts 138–139	Invasion, grave disturbance of the peace, activities against the security of the State, or public calamity.	Suspension of certain rights and others in law.
Honduras 1982	Restriction or suspension of rights Art 187–188	Invasion, grave disturbance of the peace, epidemic, or any other general calamity.	Suspension of certain rights and guarantees.
Mexico 1917	Suspension of individual guarantees Art 29	Invasion, grave disturbance of the peace, or any other cases that put society in serious danger or conflict.	Suspension of guarantees and powers to legislate available to executive.
Nicaragua 1987	"state of emergency" Art 185	War, cases where the security of the nation, the economic conditions or natural catastrophes demand it.	Suspension of certain rights and guarantees and powers to legislate available to executive.
Panama 1972	"state of urgency" Art 55	In case of external warfare or internal disturbance that threatens the peace and public order.	Suspension of certain rights.
Paraguay 1992	"state of exception" Art 288	In case of international armed conflict or grave internal commotion that puts in imminent danger the constitution or the regular functioning of the organs created by it.	Suspension of certain rights.
Peru 1993	"state of emergency" Art 137	In case of a disturbance of the peace or internal order, a catastrophe or grave circumstances that affect the life of the nation.	Suspension of certain rights. Armed Forces can take control of internal order.
	"state of siege" Art 137	In case of invasion, external warfare, civil warfare, or imminent danger that it will occur.	Suspension of certain rights. Armed Forces take control of internal order.
Uruguay 1967	Security measures Art 168	In grave and unpredicted cases of external attack or internal commotion.	Suspension of certain rights.
Venezuela 1999	"state of alarm" Art 338	Catastrophes, public calamities, or other similar events that seriously endanger the security of the Nation or of its citizens.	Suspension of certain rights.
	"state of economic emergency" Art 338	Extraordinary economic circumstances that seriously affect the economic life of the Nation.	Suspension of certain rights.
	"state of internal or external emergency" Art 338	Internal or external conflict that seriously endangers the security of the Nation, its citizens, or its institutions.	Suspension of certain rights.

[a] Clause 139 of the constitution establishes five regimes of exception—state of prevention, state of alarm, state of calamity, state of siege, and state of war without giving further details about situations or measures. (They are to be regulated in the Ley de Orden Público y Estados de Excepción).

the third wave places them firmly within the repressive paradigm, with a few discordant notes among the UN data and relevant constitutional clauses that point toward the disaster and administrative paradigms.

The three case studies that follow aim to offer a contribution to this debate.

NOTES

1. Regimes of exception lend themselves to empirical, political analysis given that they are officially declared by the competent authority and by their very nature are structured around specific situations and specific measures (Gross and Ní Aoláin 2006).

2. The last chapter stressed that these ideal models are unlikely to be so clear-cut in practice (Loveman 1993).

3. Some of the ideas that are developed here were expressed in a preliminary form in a publication in Spanish, see Wright, 2014c.

4. According to the schema of Gross and Ni Aoláin, 2006.

5. It is important to note that their study is on executive decree powers rather than emergency powers as such, which nevertheless makes the distinction even more interesting. In that sense, executive decree authority appears to be a discretionary power, if it is not made in the name of the exception or emergency. Colomer Viadel (1990) also agrees that states of emergency in Latin America have not really been orientated toward legislative powers but rather the suspension of guarantees and the use of temporary statutes.

6. Argentina 1994; Bolivia 2009; Brazil 1998; Chile 1980; Colombia 1991; Costa Rica 1949; Dominican Republic 2010; Ecuador 2008; El Salvador 1983 ; Guatemala 1985; Honduras 1982; Mexico 1917; Nicaragua 1987; Panama 1972 ; Paraguay 1992; Peru 1993; Uruguay 1967; Venezuela 1999.

7. We do not consider the possibility of sending legal bills to the Congress as a matter of urgency as an extraordinary legislative faculty given that it simply implies that the Congress will have to study the project more quickly and there is no breakdown of the separation of powers.

8. It is important to remember that regimes of exception and legislative type emergency powers may also be established in ordinary legislation. Indeed, Ferejohn and Pasquino (2004) suggest that the shift from constitutional to legal level increasingly common.

9. Argentina, Bolivia, Brazil, Chile, Colombia, Costa Rica, Ecuador, Guatemala, Nicaragua, Panama, Paraguay, República Dominicana, Venezuela.

10. Costa, Rica Honduras, Mexico, Uruguay.

11. Colombia, Mexico, Nicaragua.

12. Argentina, Brazil, Chile, Colombia, Ecuador, Honduras, Mexico, Nicaragua, Panama, Peru, and Venezuela

13. Argentina, Ecuador, Honduras, Panama, and Peru.

14. Several authors have offered interesting analyses on the legislative emergency model in Argentina (particularly Leiras 2012; Bercholc 2009; Quiroga 2005; Serrafero 2005).

15. On the extensive use of these powers in the case of Brazil see Cheibub Figueiredo (2010); Pereira, Power and Rennó (2008); and Pereira, Power and Rennó (2005).

16. Gross and Ni Aoláin (2006).

17. Loveman and Davies (1997).

18. Data from UN annual reports and lists of states, United Nations: "Annual reports and lists of States which, since 1st January 1985 have proclaimed, extended or terminated a State of Emergency, submitted by Mr. Leandro Despouy, Special Rapporteur appointed pursuant to Economic and Social Council Resolution 1985/37 1993–2005" online www.un.org.

19. It is worth pointing out that there is no clear record in the literature on Latin America of more administrative-oriented regimes of exception, even though we suspect that the model of *dictatura rei gerundae* may have been present in the past.

20. On this process, see the volume edited by Hagopian and Mainwaring (2005).

21. It is important to point out that El Salvador and Guatemala both underwent a transition to democracy in the 1990s and Mexico its "alternancia" in 2000. It is equally important to note that Colombia, Costa Rica and Venezuela did not form part of this third wave as they were already (formally) democratic regimes.

22. García-Sayán (1987b); García-Sayán (1989); Eguiguren Praeli (1989); Power Manchego-Muñoz (1989).

23. Natural disasters have been another, recurring extraordinary situation in Latin America: earthquakes, volcanoes, hurricanes, floods, and/or droughts have affected all of the countries in the region, albeit in different ways, until today. Brian Loveman refers to them on several occasions as a situation that has provoked the use of regimes of exception (1993; 1997) but does not offer examples on how they have worked in practice, rather absorbing them within the repressive emergency politics paradigm. There is nothing apparently new in this situation: during the nineteenth century, Peru's rulers dealt with different types of natural disaster which were affecting both the people and agricultural production. (Carcelén Reluz 2011).

24. It is important to consider the economic crises that have struck the region, from the effects of the great depression of 1929 to the effects of the debt crisis of the 1980s (Kruijt and Koonings 2002, 24), Leslie Bethell (1997).

25. See Despouy, 1999.

26. De facto states of emergency are those which are not based on a specific juridical norm.

27. See for example UN report E/CN.4/1998/41/Add.1

28. For instance, the report of 1999 refers to a declaration of "state of public disaster" in Guatemala, in the face of the effects of Hurricane Mitch. E/CN.4/Sub.2/1999/31; and the report of 2003 refers to problems with public transport in Ecuador E/CN.4/Sub.2/2003/39.

29. United Nations: "Annual reports and lists of States which, since 1st January 1985 have proclaimed, extended or terminated a State of Emergency, submitted by Mr. Leandro Despouy, Special Rapporteur appointed pursuant to Economic and Social Council Resolution 1985/37 1993–2005" online www.un.org.

30. Namely, Argentina, Bolivia, Colombia, Ecuador, Guatemala, Honduras, Nicaragua, Paraguay, Peru, and Venezuela.

31. United Nations: "Annual reports and lists of States which, since 1st January 1985 have proclaimed, extended or terminated a State of Emergency, submitted by Mr. Leandro Despouy, Special Rapporteur appointed pursuant to Economic and Social Council Resolution 1985/37 1993–2005" online www.un.org. The reports ceased to be produced when the UN Human Rights Council was created in 2006, given that the issue of states of emergency was not included within its remit. See the Council's report: A/HRC/Sub.1/58/36, September 2006.

32. (Despouy 1999, 14). On the website of Queen's University, Belfast www.qub.ac.uk. The database is limited to the countries of China, East Timor, El Salvador, India, Malaysia, South Africa, Sri Lanka and Turkey and is designed to be a historical reference point.

33. It is important to note, however, that the UN has several mechanisms to offer assistance during humanitarian crises or emergencies, although it no longer offers data or monitoring on emergency situations.

34. On recent approaches to emergency politics in Latin America beyond the formal regime of exception framework, several authors have offered interesting analysis on the legislative emergency model in Argentina (particularly Leiras 2012; Bercholc 2009; Quiroga 2005; Serrafero 2005) and on an extra legal or mixed model in Mexico (Williams, 2011) and Argentina, Brazil, Venezuela and Peru (Leiras 2010).

35. Although Colombia is not a third-wave democracy, it is important to mention here due to considerable academic concern over human rights violations in the context of semipermanent states of siege during the 1980s, particularly, and also in the 1990s.

36. In the cases of Iturralde (2003) the conceptualization of states of exception or emergency is much broader than that employed in this study, more in line with Loveman's conceptualization (1993). Interestingly, Rosatti's study (2004) focuses on executive intervention in the context of economic crisis.

37. As already mentioned, several authors have offered interesting analysis on the legislative emergency model in Argentina (particularly Leiras, 2012 and Bercholc, 2009, Quiroga, 2005, Serrafero, 2005). On the extensive use of these powers in the case of Brazil see Cheibub Figueiredo (2010); Pereira, Power and Rennó (2008); and Pereira, Power and Rennó (2005).

38. It is important to note that the fact that the other two paradigms of emergency have not been singled out in the literature does not necessarily mean that these mechanisms were not used for that purpose in the past. It may just be that the type of literature (more concerned about human rights abuses) has meant that they have been exempt from analysis.

39. Argentina, Bolivia, Chile, Colombia, Dominican Republic, Ecuador, El Salvador, Guatemala, Honduras, Nicaragua, Panama, Paraguay, Peru, Uruguay and Venezuela.

40. On this issue see Valadés, 1974. This term is used in the following cases: Argentina, Bolivia, Chile, Ecuador, Paraguay and Uruguay.

41. Bolivia, Chile, Colombia, Dominican Republic, Ecuador, El Salvador, Honduras, Nicaragua, Peru, and Venezuela.

42. Colombia, Dominican Republic, and Venezuela.

43. For instance, in Costa Rica, there is a situation of "evident public necessity" (Article 121).

44. Colombia, Mexico and Nicaragua.

Chapter 3

Peru

The Repressive Paradigm

"Declaring a state of emergency makes more sense in places where the law is always applied. There are many areas in Peru where the law doesn't apply. People take the law into their own hands, the State is almost non-existent and therefore we are already living in a natural state of emergency where everyone can do what they want."[1] With those words my first in-depth interview in Peru (and for that matter in Latin America) came to an end. A rather cutting comment that nevertheless sheds light on the context in which states of emergency should be understood in Peru: a democratic regime that is far from fully consolidated and with clear systemic fault-lines or fractures.

Nevertheless, this does not mean to say that regimes of exception have not had an important role to play in recent Peruvian history. On the contrary, in this chapter I show how historical trends have continued well into the twenty-first century, almost three decades into Peru's transition to democracy, with the proliferation of both transitory and semipermanent regimes of exception proving a profound challenge for democratic governability. My findings are based on fieldwork that was carried out during a visit to Peru first in 2007 and then again in 2009. During these visits, I learned of and gained access to diverse and relevant sources, including declarations of regimes of exception published in the official state bulletin *El Peruano*,[2] secondary laws,[3] in-depth interviews with key informants,[4] reports by NGOs,[5] and newspaper articles.[6]

The chapter is structured as follows: first of all, a starting point is established, in which historical tendencies and relevant normative frameworks prior to 2000 are identified; next, an in-depth analysis is offered of regimes of exception as they have been used in practice in Peru between 2000 and 2010; and third, an ending point is established, offering an overview regarding developments in regimes of exception in practice and changes or continuities at the formal level, three decades into the third wave of democracy.

Furthermore, some reflections are offered regarding the relationship between regimes of exception and democracy in Peru, taking into account possible trade-offs between legitimacy and efficiency.

THE STARTING POINT: HISTORICAL USE AND LEGAL FRAMEWORKS PRIOR TO 2000

As stated in the Introduction of this volume, the focus of the empirical study is on the period between 2000 and 2010, given that our knowledge after the first date is rather sketchy and in order to offer a degree of distance and greater analytical capacity, the latter date is a useful place to stop. Nevertheless, taking into account the possibility of "path dependency" in the use of regimes of exception, it is important to highlight how their constitutional form and use developed prior to the twenty-first century. Consequently, this section explores the historical use and principal legal developments regarding regimes of exception prior to 2000, bearing in mind the two key dimensions in the study—extraordinary situations and extraordinary measures—and the three possible emergency paradigms: repressive, administrative, and disaster. First of all, more distant historical precedents and legal figures are briefly analyzed, before summarizing developments in the first twenty years after Peru's transition to democracy. As a result, it will be possible to establish a "starting point" to contextualize the in-depth empirical study that constitutes the core contribution of this chapter.

As established in Chapter 2, the processes of independence from colonial rule in Latin America were fraught with violence, conflict and antipolitics led by soldiers and caudillos (Loveman 1993). While debates at the constitutional level raged on between liberals and conservatives throughout the nineteenth century, the emerging State's political reality bore more resemblance to discretional rather than ordinary or even emergency politics. Indeed, as Loveman (ibid) points out, no effective civilian governments were established in Peru until the end of the century and constitutions were drawn up and discarded in quick succession. In this context, the possibility of suspending citizen guarantees was included in every constitution in place during this period, that is to say the Constitutions of 1823, 1826, 1828, 1834, 1839, 1856, 1860, and 1867 (Gargarella 2005, 132). In this section (which draws heavily on Brian Loveman's seminal work of 1993) I shall outline the context in which these provisions were included, their main features, and their use in practice.

It is important to highlight that when San Martín claimed Peru's Independence in 1821, he did so within a regime of exception. In 1822 a document outlining guidelines for a future constitution was drawn up, in which the liberal idea of rights was coupled with the conservative idea of reserving a central role for the armed forces. The independent Peruvian State's first, liberal-orientated constitution was adopted in November 1823, but after just two months was immediately suspended by the Congress which gave full powers to Bolívar (Loveman 1993, 213). It is worth noting that this constitution included a clause to suspend guarantees, limited to offering the executive the power to detain people and set them before a judge within 24 hours. In 1826, a new constitution under Bolívar was drawn up and approved, establishing a healthy dose of liberal rights as well as further regimes of exception.

After Bolívar was ousted, a new constitution was drawn up in 1828, giving the president extraordinary powers for specified periods when national security demanded it. At that time—in a wave of nationalism and under General Pablo Pedro Bermúdez—foreign liberals were deported, the sessions of the congress were interrupted, and a series of military coups took place. In a context of serious political instability with the continuous application of regimes of exception, another constitution was drawn up in 1834, including further regimes of exception and more extraordinary powers for the President. Nevertheless, the regimes of exception contemplated at the constitutional level were still more restrictive than in many parts of Latin America at that time. As Loveman notes (ibid, 218): "Executives had no constitutional authority to suspend the constitution, to declare a regime of exception unilaterally, or to suspend operation of the legislature." Hence while real-life politics was dominated by *caudillos* and conflict, the constitution emphasized legislative control.

The new constitution of 1839—promulgated after the end of the rather unsuccessful Bolivia-Peru Confederation—focused on order and pacification and gave the executive ample powers over congress. Curiously, a special council including military officers and churchmen was drawn up that could declare the *patria* (fatherland) in danger and grant special powers to the president. These broad, vague powers were essential to suspend constitutional guarantees and could even be passed on to prefects. Indeed, the political regime at that time was undoubtedly much more authoritarian and centralized than before, something that was reflected at the constitutional level.

After another period of political turmoil, in1856 a much more liberal constitution was drawn up which established that Congress would be in charge of the measures to be employed under a regime of exception, although the President retained extraordinary powers to save the *patria*. This extremely liberal Constitution was at odds with the rather chaotic political reality. Indeed, a Conservative revolt ensued and the President (Ramón Castilla) asked for extraordinary powers in October 1857, with the following justification: "The state of war is, by its nature, extraordinary and abnormal. It requires, therefore corresponding extraordinary measures, beyond routine procedures"

(Quoted in Loveman 1993, 225). Once the conservatives had been defeated, the military closed congress. During this period of crisis, the congress itself declared a regime of exception, a manoeuver that is at odds with the executive-orientated understanding of emergency politics in Latin America.

Given this situation of turmoil, in 1860 a new constitution was drawn up that, with brief interruptions (1867–1868 and 1879–1881), would be in force until 1920. Not only was it the most "successful" of the nascent State's constitutions in terms of longevity, it also set the standard regarding current-day regimes of exception in Peru (Gargarella 2005). While the legislative was given a degree of control, regimes of exception were once again established when the *patria* was in danger, this time including the suspension of specific guarantees relating to the freedom of assembly and association and restrictions on arrest without a warrant. For his part, President Castilla left office in 1862 after creating a watershed in Peruvian politics and setting a key precedent in terms of the constitutional form of regimes of exception. The twenty years after Castilla's rule were marked by a series of coups and military governments, as well as the War of the Pacific (1879–1883).

Consequently, the political legacy of the nineteenth century was a constant struggle for power and a series of failed civilian governments. In relation to regimes of exception specifically, it is clear that by this time, the suspension of guarantees and restrictions of the freedoms of assembly and expression, all in the name of the *patria*, were not just a question of constitutional law but rather of political reality, to paraphrase Loveman (1993, 230).

The situation of instability and coups that had characterized Peruvian politics in the nineteenth century continued well into the twentieth. Indeed there were several military coups during the century, in 1914 (Benavides), 1919 (Leguía), 1930 (Ponce), 1930 (Sanchez Cerro), 1932 (Jiménez), 1948 (Odría), 1962 (Godoy), 1968 (Velasco Alvarado), and 1975 (Morales Bermúdez) (Gorman, 1997). What is important, however, is that during this period several civilian governments became consolidated, in contrast to the situation in the nineteenth century, when military *caudillos* consistently ruled the roost. In any case, as Eguiguren Praeli notes (1989, 252), throughout this period, states of exception were used to repress popular mobilizations, strikes, and the political opposition. According to García Sayán (1987b, 96), between civilian and military governments in power between 1960 and 1980, more than 50 repressive states of exception were decreed.

After reaching power via a coup, Leguía promulgated a new constitution in 1920 dealing with workers' rights, limiting executive power, and prohibiting the suspension of rights and liberties, effectively excluding regimes of exception from the constitutional framework. Nevertheless, in practice he nullified the constitution and ruled as a dictator, imprisoning political dissidents, students, and indigenous people. Indeed, his term in office represented the rise of the military as an organized group in Peruvian politics, given that they propped up his regime for eleven years (Villanueva 1997, 83). Following the economic crisis at the end of the decade, and Sánchez Cerro's coup of 1930, the Emergency Law of 1932 was promulgated to deal with unrest and in place until 1945.

In this context, a new constitution was drawn up in 1933, which—while of little relevance during the dictatorship—is key to our understanding of the development of regimes of exception in the twentieth century. Indeed, in its Article 70 it restored presidential authority to suspend individual rights and liberties during emergencies. This "suspension of constitutional guarantees" is the basis for the later regimes of exception discussed in the following section, although nothing is said of the armed forces in such situations (Eguiguren Praeli 1989). Importantly, this constitution was of considerable longevity, constituting the supreme norm—albeit with clear interruptions—until July 1980.

As already mentioned, however, the constitutional regime of exception was of little relevance in the context of the discretionary, authoritarian regime of the period between 1932 and 1945. During this time, further emergency laws were decreed, including one that foresaw the possibility of military courts judging civilians and the reestablishment of the death penalty (García Sayán 1987b, 97). At the same time, there were massive summary trials, and members of the APRA opposition who had revolted in Trujillo were shot by firing squad (ibid). As Villanueva notes (1997), during this autocratic period democracy was seen as an obstacle and dictatorship more benevolently. Indeed, when democratically elected President Bustamente y Rivera reached power in 1945 and the constitution of 1933 was reinstated, the democratic honeymoon lasted for just three years.

Indeed, after yet another *golpe*, this time in 1948, the dictatorship of General Odría was installed and would remain in place until 1956. During this time the Decree Law 11049 Security Law of the Republic (Ley de Seguridad de la República) was promulgated to deal with acts of a political social nature. The penalties included arbitrary detentions and deportations of foreigners, on the basis of the slightest signs of opposition to the regime. As García Sayán (1987b, 99) notes, in this context and with the security law, there was no real need to declare a regime of exception.

In 1956, the political wind changed back to democracy and the security law was revoked. Nevertheless, this did not mark the end of emergency politics in Peru. Indeed, during this period, rather than emergency laws, the suspension of guarantees clause of the newly reinstated 1933 constitution was used to repress mass protest. In order to facilitate military intervention in these cases, Article 213 of the Constitution of 1933 was invoked, given that Article 70 (in which the suspension of guarantees was established) made no mention of their deployment. Likewise—after yet again another *golpe* in 1962 and the mass detention of left-wing politicians (ibid)—Belaúnde Terry came to power as a democratically elected President. During his (first mandate), Belaúnde Terry was faced with several mobilizations by peasants, decreeing Law 15590 to typify violent attempts to change the constitution as a crime against the *patria* and declaring suspension of guarantees with particular force in those areas of the country affected by the mobilizations (ibid).

After this oscillation between military and civilian governments, in 1968 a new type of military regime would transform Peru (Gorman 1997). Via a decree-law called the *Estatuto del Gobierno Revolucionario* (Statute of the Revolutionary Government), the constitution was only observed when it met the government's aims (García Sayán 1987b). Interestingly, rather than issuing an emergency decree law,[7] there was a systematic use of suspension of guarantees to restrict labor rights and freedom of expression in the face of mobilizations. Importantly, in 1972, the suspension of guarantees used to deal with a student movement in Puno was called a "state of emergency," a figure that did not exist in the Constitution of 1933 (ibid). Indeed, it was increasingly used to refer to regimes of exception between 1968 and 1980, when they were used to repress popular protest (Eguiguren Praeli 1989). In an interesting innovation, during this time the newly "invented" states of emergency were used to "reorganize" sectors and dismiss workers, in an interventionist approach (García Sayán 1987b).

In summary, regimes of exception were used throughout the twentieth century by both civil and military governments. During this period they were mainly used to deal with social unrest and became more relevant when emergency laws were not in force. Mainly facilitating the suspension of liberties and freedoms, they also gave power to the military, vie ample interpretations of the 1933 constitution. While Article 70 of the same constitution—"suspension of guarantees"—was the basis for these declarations, in the 1970s they were informally referred to as "states of emergency," an innovation that would later become institutionalized during the transition to democracy.

In the face of a weakened military regime and following the handover from General Velasco Alvarado to General Morales Bermúdez, Peru began its transition to democracy in 1978 (Hagopian and Mainwaring 2005). Likewise, by this stage there was a clear, historic tendency toward the usage of emergency powers in general and regimes of exception specifically, notably within the repressive paradigm. In fact, during the central transition years of 1978 and 1979, states of emergency were issued on 6 occasions,[8] to put an end to various union strikes. Indeed, the suspension of individual guarantees under a state of emergency could be considered an incongruent aspect of the transfer of power to civilians (Comisión de la Verdad y de la Reconciliación 2003, 24).

In 1978 and 1979, a Constituent Assembly was drawn up in preparation for a process of political change, to great expectations. However, the military publicly stated on 22nd July 1978 that the Constituent Assembly would have to follow its guidelines, causing a wave of protests in Lima. Ultimately, the military's influence was maintained, as the constituent Javier Alva Orlandini declared, later on in the same year, that the constitution was "the military government's lady-in-waiting." (ibid, 21) Indeed, once the new constitution had been signed, the military government rejected part of the text, claiming that the constituent assembly had exceeded some of its functions (Rubio Correa 1989, 223)

In this political context, two regimes of exception were incorporated in the 1979 Constitution, in its Article 231: the state of emergency ("estado de emergencia") and the state of siege ("estado de sitio"). In the same constitution it was also established that the President could apply extraordinary measures in economic matters or for national security (Colomer Viadel 1990, 123).[9] As García Sayán explains: "It would seem that the military regime must have had some bearing on the wording that was applied to measures referring to situations of exception," given their vagueness (García Sayán 1987c, 281).[10] Indeed, in relation to the state of emergency, the military successfully changed the time limit to sixty days rather than the thirty that had been approved by the Constituent Assembly with reference to the mechanism of the 1933 constitution (García Sayán 1987b, 110). Again, this seems to be in line with the transitional experience of many countries in Latin America (Loveman 1993, 375). In any case, it is important to highlight at this stage what exceptional situations and measures were contemplated in the two regimes of exception of the Constitution of 1979, given that they are the basis of the regimes of exception that continue to be available in Peruvian constitutionalism.

In the case of the state of emergency, the following circumstances were established as constituting an exceptional situation: "a breach of the peace or internal order, a catastrophe or serious circumstances that affect the life of the Nation." With regard to the exceptional measures that could be employed, the restriction of guarantees related to four liberties[11] (personal freedom and security, the inviolability of the home, and the freedom of assembly and movement within the country) was established and the (previously paraconstitutional) possibility of handing over control of internal order to the Armed Forces was included.[12] Beyond these measures, the Constitution was typically vague. Consequently—in line with the interpretation of Eguiguren Praeli (1989)—the "state of emergency" established at the constitutional level at the start of the transition is firmly placed within the repressive paradigm, except for the idea of a catastrophe, which points, rather ambiguously, to the disaster paradigm. Indeed, as Eguiguren Praeli (ibid) notes, there are no specific measures to deal with natural disasters or economic crises, which can also constitute exceptional threats.

For its part, the "state of siege" could be declared "in case of invasion, external war, civil war, or an imminent danger from which they might arise," and therefore the exceptional situations are strongly linked to external war rather than internal violence or conflict, as in the case of the "state of emergency." In terms of the extraordinary measures, there is an implicit provision for the restriction of human rights given that the clause stipulates that the declaration of the state of siege should include specific "mention of the fundamental rights of which the exercise may not be restricted nor suspended." Beyond this, nothing more is said. Consequently, the "state of siege" contemplated in the constitution of 1979 is an even more vague and ambiguous clause, most likely a consequence of the military influence at the time.

Having outlined the emergence of normative frameworks in relation to regimes of exception at the start of the transition, it is important to understand how these measures were used over the following two decades. Curiously, there were no declarations of states of siege during that period. Rather, there was a systematic and semipermanent use of states of emergency to confront the internal conflict provoked by the actions of *Sendero Luminoso* (Shining Path), financed to a great extent by coca plant production in several departments, including Huánuco, Ucayali and San Martín.[13] As a prominent Peruvian human rights lawyer noted: "Real-life is always much more complicated than we expect, so they (the constitution-makers of 1979) never imagined that the same day that the democratic regime began, Peru would enter into a war, I don't think they could ever have imagined it." (Personal interview with the author, Lima, April 2007)

Indeed, the emergence of *Sendero Luminoso* coincided with and to a large extent overshadowed the return to democracy in Peru under President Beláunde Terry. The burning of the presidential electoral ballot boxes in Chuschi on 17th May 1980 was a symbolically- charged beginning to the subversive group's activities, which would remain intense until the mid-nineties. According to the Institut Internacional de Gobernabilitat de Catalunya, *Sendero Luminoso* "consciously and constantly sought to incite disproportionate responses on the part of the State." (IIGC 2005, 17).

After these initial attacks by *Sendero Luminoso*, there was a heated debate as to whether the state of emergency would be an efficient mechanism for combating terrorism. Indeed, there appeared to be reticence to do so in an attempt to protect a newly restored democracy.[14] For instance, in December 1980, the then Minister of Interior—José María de la Jara y Ureta—publicly stated that there was no need to resort to this constitutional mechanism in order to combat terrorism (Comisión de la Verdad y Reconciliación, 2003). Importantly, the government dealt with the political violence without recourse to states of emergency for fifteen months. However, on 11th October 1981, the police post in the district of Tambo, Ayacucho, was attacked and a state of emergency was decreed in the country for the first time since the transition to democracy. The decision to resort to states of emergency would later be classified by the Comisión Verdad y de la Reconciliación as akin to an abdication of "democratic responsibility."[15]

After this episode, states of emergency were declared increasingly frequently and became a key weapon in the fight against the terror of *Sendero Luminso*. Indeed, between 1981 and 1988, a total of 65 Supreme Decrees were issued which declared or extended states of emergency in the country to deal with this specific threat.[16] During this period, the debate continued over the legitimacy of the repeated use of states of emergency to deal with the terrorist threat. On the one hand, some politicians were of the opinion that a state of siege should be declared—which as has been established was designed to deal with external warfare—, the death penalty should be reintroduced, and the role and autonomy of the Armed Forces should be increased. On the other hand, other politicians and even some army generals argued that handing over power to the military and suspending guarantees was not the best way to combat *Sendero Luminoso* and the MRTA but rather a political, social or economic transformation was necessary (Rubio Correa 1989, 235).[17] For example, Colonel Huamán asserted that the solution:

> "is not military, because if it were military I could solve it in minutes . . . the thing is that we are talking about human beings, of forgotten peoples who have been making demands for a hundred and sixty years and nobody has taken any notice of them. . . ." (Comisión de la Verdad y Reconciliación 2003, 92)

The colonel was swiftly removed from his position as a result but was not the only high-ranking military officer to question the government's use of the armed forces to fight *Sendero Luminoso* (Rubio Correa 1989). Indeed, there was a generalized impression among many sectors that the government was passing the burden of the situation onto the army, shirking its responsibilities (Eguiguren Praeli 1989).

At the time of Alan García's election as President and the subsequent change of government in July 1985, there was severe criticism over the lack of a cohesive strategy to defeat terrorism and the seemingly permanent use of states of emergency. Likewise, there was also hope for greater protection for human rights in the fight against *Sendero Luminoso* (García-Sayán 1987b, 123) under the new government. Nevertheless, President García continued to use this mechanism of emergency politics, especially in Lima and Callao, where a state of emergency was in place from February 1986 until the end of his first mandate in 1990. In fact, in 1986, there was widespread concern that a state of siege would be declared throughout the whole country, a fear which ultimately did not come to fruition.

It is also important to note that, as well as suspending human rights and granting control of internal order to the military, where Political-Military Commands were installed as of 1982, the armed forces coordinated public and private sectors and effectively usurped civil authorities in emergency zones (Degregori and Rivera 1993, 8).[18] Therefore, there was an emerging and highly criticized political-administrative aspect in relation to states of emergency during this period, beyond the repressive measures formally established in the constitution (Eguiguren Praeli 1989; García Sayán 1987b). These Military-Political Commands led to several, very serious human rights abuses, including the disappearance and execution of detainees, torture and inhuman treatment and murders of the civil population (ibid).[19] Indeed, the Military-Political Commands monopolized information coming from emergency zones (in which they revealed how many people had died in their operations and—rather suspiciously—the lack of prisoners taken) and relieved the public ministry of the task of removing corpses in the emergency zones (ibid).

In contrast to the debate and reluctance when it came to using the state of emergency in the decade of the 1980s, the situation was different in the decade of the 1990s. The terrorist threat of *Sendero Luminoso* and the long-term application of repressive states of emergency had coincided to largely neutralize the debate. Consequently, when Alberto Fujimori—an antipolitics politician if ever there was one[20]—came to power he did not hesitate to resort to what had become a well-established mechanism of repressive emergency politics in democracy. Just after coming to power, he declared a state of emergency in several provinces of Cuzco and extended the existing state of emergency in Lima and Callao three times. By December 1991, 47% of national territory found itself under a state of emergency (Jaskoski 2012). The United Nations, in 1992, expressed its concern over the situation of a long-term state of emergency in the country in the following terms: ". . . the Committee observes that . . . the assumption of power by military forces in areas where the state of emergency has been declared has meant that the implementation of rights and freedoms guaranteed in the Pact [International Covenant on Social and Political Rights] is ineffective." (Observaciones finales del Comité de Derechos Humanos, Peru, U.N. Doc. CCPR/C/79/Add.8 [1992]). Furthermore, in July 1992, all power over the control of internal order was handed over to the military, even in areas not declared under state of emergency (Comisión de la Verdad y Reconciliación 2003).

To understand fully the implications of regimes of exception under President Fujimori's rule, it is also important to refer to his *autogolpe* or "self-inflicted coup" of April 1992. During this coup, Fujimori dissolved

Congress and the judiciary and gained full powers to issue decree laws—including emergency laws to deal with terrorism[21]—until the formation of the *Congreso Constituyente Democrático* (Constituent Democratic Congress), which would draft a new Constitution in 1993. As well as including the possibility for Congress to delegate legislative powers to the executive in financial and economic matters (Article 118), the same two regimes of exception established in the 1979 constitution—the state of emergency and state of siege—were maintained in Article 137 of the new constitution. The content of the article is virtually the same and therefore the two mechanisms can be understood within the same vague and ambiguous,[22] but markedly repressive, emergency politics framework established above.

Nevertheless, there is one important difference: in the case of the state of emergency, the 1993 Constitution clarified that the *rights* relating to personal freedom and security, the inviolability of the home, and the freedom of assembly and movement within the country can be suspended. For its part, the constitution of 1979 had contemplated the possibility of suspending the *guarantees relating to these rights*, something that had been pointed out in both national and international debates as contrary to international human rights law.[23] Consequently, this change could be seen as a positive step forward in the protection of human rights under states of emergency although in practice during the 1990s it offered little more than lip service. Indeed, in an apparent attempt to cover tracks and create further opacity surround states of emergency, in 1995 two amnesty laws (26479 and 26492) were passed that guaranteed impunity for acts committed in areas declared to be under a state of emergency.[24]

In practice, it proves very difficult to establish when or how states of emergency were declared and managed during Fujimori's time in government, given that—after the *autogolpe*—democracy in Peru seemed to slowly slide into a more authoritarian regime or democratic breakdown (Tanaka 2005). Indeed, in a personal interview with a prominent human rights lawyer, he asserted: "Certainly the state of emergency ended up by being the defining element of a new political scenario and a de facto political regime."[25] For her part, the leader of an important human rights NGO[26] noted that with the state of emergency ". . . the idea was to resort to a more legal mechanism to install a regime of terror."

On the other hand, the editor of a national newspaper claimed that by this time, the fight against terrorism and Fujimori's style of leadership had become so "extraordinary," that to declare a state of emergency was essentially irrelevant, for the following reason: "I don't think that the state of emergency has anything to do with the fact that at one point the army and democratic governments of the time decided to use extra-constitutional actions such as extrajudicial killings. . . . Those killings were going to happen anyway with or without the state of emergency because they are covert actions that go beyond the constitution" (Personal interview with the author in Lima, April 2007).

Finally, it is important to note that at the start of this period there was considerable academic interest in states of emergency in Peru, due to the suspension of human rights in addition to the extension of these declarations over time.[27] Several works of a judicial nature were published on the subject[28] together with reports by human rights NGOs.[29] Nevertheless, as of the 1990s, academic interest in the mechanism lessened[30] and the main attempts to reconstruct the declaration of states of emergency in the framework of the armed conflict was by the Comisión de la Verdad y Reconciliación in 2003 and later by Jaskoski in 2012. In order to understand the generalized lack of academic interest in regimes of exception after the 1980s, a prominent human rights lawyer offers the following explanation: "I think there is a degradation of the institution of the state of emergency linked to the armed conflict, very much related to military control in emergency zones, very much related to human rights violations. I think that people have chosen to avert their gaze and assume that it is not an issue of academic interest" (Personal interview with the author in Lima, April 2007).

To sum up, it is clear that by the year 2000 and two decades into the third wave of democracy, regimes of exception had become synonymous with the repressive emergency politics paradigm, particularly in the devastating fight against *Sendero Luminoso*[31] and to a lesser extent in the face of social protest and mobilization. Specifically, although two regimes of exception were available during this period—the state of emergency and the state of siege—the former were declared extensively while no states of siege were declared. The main characteristics of this mechanism have been its use in the face of internal conflict, the suspension of human rights, the deployment of the military, and its extension over long periods of time to no particular effect. As a prominent human rights lawyer explained, "It's true that there have been many declarations of states of emergency due to natural phenomena, due to other sorts of situations, but I would say that the overwhelming majority of states of emergency in Peru have been related to armed conflict."[32] These other types of uses, if and when they have occurred, have not been written into the history of emergency politics and regimes of exception in Peru.

It is important to note that at many times throughout Peruvian political history, there has been confusion over the norm and the exception due to the long-term application of regimes of exception. This continued to be the case well into the third wave, particularly with the Political-Military Commands that effectively took over control of local authorities in the fight against *Sendero Luminoso*. Of the many problems identified with the use of regimes of exception during this period, the lack of meaningful congressional oversight, the paralysis of civilian authorities, the restriction of habeas corpus, and the free reign given to the armed forces are considered to be the most concerning for democracy (García Sayán 1989, 15)

EMERGENCY POLITICS IN PERU 2000–2010

As outlined at the start of this chapter, the intensive, original empirical research that forms the real contribution of this study on Peru is the collection of information relating to the declarations of regimes of exception by Presidents in the first decade of the twenty-first century.

The main aim of the study is to understand how regimes of exception have been used in Peru in recent years and chart any changes, continuities, or developments in that sense. A secondary aim is to understand how these uses can be analyzed within the prism of democratic governability, with its two pillars of legitimacy and efficiency. In previous sections, it was noted that throughout history regimes of exception in Peru have been used extensively and according to a repressive paradigm. In this section my findings suggest that this historical use, rather than coming to a halt with the return to democracy, has in fact remained strong. However, there is also ample evidence of use of regimes of exception according to the disaster paradigm in the period, something that had been absent from—or perhaps not written into—Peruvian political history.

Before offering an in-depth analysis of these two dominant uses of regimes of exception in Peru, it is important to highlight that my analysis of presidential declarations issued in *El Peruano* revealed that the extensive use of states of emergency in general terms shows no sign of waning, with a total of 115 declarations during the 11-year period,[33] not counting extensions over time[34] or space[35] which—as will be shown—were also very common. In fact, there seems to be a growing tendency for Presidents to declare states of emergency, from 2 in 2000 up to 15 in 2010.

Nevertheless, rather than simply counting regimes of exception as if they were all the same, it is important to understand how they have been used, starting from three broad conceptual categories: repressive, administrative, and disaster. The sections that follow use this conceptual lens in order to understand how regimes of exception have been used during this period.

Old Habits Die Hard: Repressive Emergency Politics

Chapters 1 and 2 of this volume established that regimes of exception have become synonymous with a repressive paradigm of emergency politics, characterized by the suspension of certain civil liberties and/or the deployment of the military to deal with civil unrest or political violence. Indeed, this emergency paradigm has been dominant in Peru since Independence and—according to the analysis carried out here—remains so in recent years. During the first decade of the twenty-first century, 32 declarations of regimes of exception with these two main features were declared. In some cases, there are also references to administrative difficulties because of the unrest but this is a secondary element in an otherwise exclusively and extensively repressive model.

Importantly, the experts interviewed in Lima in 2007 understood that fewer states of emergency had been declared post-2000, in comparison to the years of the fight against *Sendero Luminoso* and after the post-Fujimori return to democracy in 2000.[36] Indeed, compared to the 65 declarations and/or extensions declared between 1981 and 1988,[37] 32 declarations certainly represents a quantitative decrease. Nevertheless, it is still a significant number and has not passed unnoticed by human rights NGOs.[38] Likewise, taking into account the extensions of many of these initial declarations, the image changes somewhat and actually mirrors the situation in the 1980s, as will be discussed in the following pages.

It is also important to note an increase in the repressive states of emergency in Peru as of 2006, which—importantly—occurred when Alan García came to power. Indeed, during the four and a half years in which he was in office during the period studied, he issued a total of 20 decrees of this type, a much higher number than his predecessor Alejandro Toledo.[39] This finding is particularly interesting as President García had also been in power in the 1980s, when—as has been already pointed out—states of emergency were used as a routine mechanism to deal with the conflict with Sendero Luminoso which, at that time, was at its height (Jaskoski 2012). Several academics[40] have pointed to García's autocratic presidential style, something that his in keeping with this extensive use of repressive states of emergency. Hence, the use of repressive states of emergency in Peru should not only be understood as a case of institutional path dependency, but rather the result of a personal "learning process" that President García carried forward nearly twenty years later.

In order to offer an adequate interpretation of the use of these repressive regimes of exception it is helpful to distinguish two main ways in which they have been used and which, importantly, constitute clear continuities with historical practice. On the one hand, there have been repeated declarations of states of emergency to deal with protest or civil unrest, mirroring developments in pre-transition twentieth century; and on the other, there have been a whole series of declarations and extensions of states of emergency to deal with remainders of *Sendero Luminoso* and the illegal cultivation of the coca crop in two key regions of the country, to a large extent in keeping with the situation in the first two decades of the transition.

In terms of the former, throughout the decade under study, regimes of exception were declared at regular intervals to deal with social unrest.

Cases include protests over the privatization of electricity in Arequipa (DS-052–2002), an attempted coup by Antauro Humala (DS-001–2005), social unrest caused by disputes among authorities in the municipality of Chiclayo (DS-067–2006-PCM), protests over the government of Apurímac (Nº-086–2006-PCM), and the potential for violence in relation to elections in the province of Sarayacu (DS-053–2007). Nevertheless, two cases are particularly significant due to the public debate that they provoked: the nationwide protests that occurred in 2003 and the case of the conflict of Bagua in 2009. These cases will be described in some depth below.

In May 2003, a series of strikes took place throughout Peru, initiated by the Sindicato Único de Trabajadores de la Educación del Perú (Education Trade Union), paralyzing the country's education system.[41] For their part, workers of the judicial system and health service also went on strike. Likewise, groups of farmers joined the protest and put up roadblocks in 64 points around the country. As a result, public transport services were interrupted and there were problems in guaranteeing food supplies. It was a moment of great tension and the breaking point of a year of protests. In this "extraordinary" situation, President Alejandro Toledo declared a state of emergency on 27th May for a period of thirty days by issuing DS-55–2003-PCM. The decree refers to the government's responsibility to guarantee human rights and protect citizens from threats against their security, briefly outlining the circumstances mentioned above and a need to control internal order.

The same decree established the suspension of the four rights contemplated in the state of emergency established in the constitution of 1993, that is to say personal freedom, transit, the inviolability of the home, and personal security. The same day, via Resolución Suprema 181–2003-DE, the Armed Forces took control of internal order in twelve of the country's districts. In this context, and with the help of the national police, the Armed Forces employed two key strategies: massive detentions and the use of force. According to the Defensoría del Pueblo (Peru's Human Rights Ombudsman), a total of 348 people were detained during the state of emergency and various shows of force were used particularly tear gas and water cannons to clear the roadblocks. As a result, 117 people were injured and a university student was killed. Despite these measures, the protests carried on and in fact intensified. Faced with this situation, the Minister of Defense, Aurelio Loret de Mola seemed rather exasperated: "Here the excesses have been produced by a crowd that has not respected the state of emergency" (Coordinadora Nacional de Derechos Humanos 2004, 29).

Indeed, on 3rd June—well after the state of emergency had been declared—protests took place in 32 cities. It seemed evident that the use of force was not working. However, at that time, the Defensoría del Pueblo called on all sectors to wage peaceful protest and fewer detentions were carried out. Little by little the conflict died down until on 12th June there were just three isolated protests around the country. At this time the government decided to change its tactic: establish dialogues and accompany the protests rather than trying to detain social leaders. As a result, the state of emergency was officially lifted on 26th June, via DS-062–2003-PCM.

Although certain sectors—including some political parties—supported the declaration of a state of emergency to deal with the mass protests, there were severe criticisms of the measures employed at both national and international level, representing instances of social accountability. On the one hand, concerns were voiced over the legitimacy of using states of emergency to deal with social protest. For instance, on 28th May the NGO Aprodeh declared "We lament that there has been recourse to a state of exception as a way of resolving social conflicts that express the just demands of the population" (Aprodeh 2003). Likewise, the Defensoría del Pueblo criticized the decision to declare a state of emergency for the following reason: "it is an extreme measure that involved serious risks and enormous responsibility and which can be avoided by using the necessary measures to deal with conflicts that have arisen as a result of the current situation" (Defensoría del Pueblo 2003a).

Crucially, the debate surrounding the repressive state of emergency declared throughout Peru in 2003 was unprecedented in the country's history. Likewise, the role of the Defensoría del Pueblo in overseeing the mechanism during its application was a new and transcendent development. Equally important is the fact that, despite arrests and the use of force, the protests actually intensified as a result of the measure—something that previously would have been unthinkable—forcing the government to establish dialogue. Notwithstanding these developments, there was no review of the use of states of emergency to deal with social unrest in the long term. Indeed, they continued to do so throughout the decade, only catching the public's attention again in 2009 with the tragic and bloody conflict in the indigenous province of Bagua.

To contextualize this case, it is important to note that over the decade studied here, and particularly as of 2008, there was a steep rise in the number of conflicts over natural resources, specifically in territories belonging to indigenous peoples or peasant communities (Arellano 2008; Wright and Martí i Puig 2012). A defender of indigenous peoples' rights interviewed by the author explained the situation in the following way:

"The State thinks that it owns all of our country's resources, so it doesn't matter if a peasant has a mine in his *chacra*,[42] they hunt him down and of course they give him a thousand dollars, or 10,000 dollars—which seems a lot to him—and ultimately he is left without his land, without anything. So we believe that indigenous people's right over the lands should be respected . . . the Covenant 169[43] is not respected." (Personal interview with author, Cusco, February 2009).

In this context, when protests turned violent, repressive measures were used, including regimes of exception. Indeed, in December 2008, faced with indigenous peoples' blocking access to work on a gas duct, President Alan García declared a state of emergency (DS-087–2008-PCM), sending the army in, and suspending the rights relating to personal liberty and safety, the inviolability of the home, and freedom of movement and transit in various districts of the province of Huamanga in the department of Ayacucho.

Six months later, on 8th May 2009, President García declared another state of emergency, this time in the conflict that led to the tragic events of Bagua, wherein at least 30 people—between policemen and indigenous protesters—were killed at the *Curva del Diablo*. Several months into a long conflict over two decree laws that effectively handed over indigenous lands to multinational firms for exploitation, without prior consultation or consent,[44] the so-called "Movilización por los Pueblos Amazónicos" took place, obstructing entry points to hydrocarbon plants in different areas. Via decree DS-027–2009-PCM, a state of emergency was declared in different districts of the Departments of Cusco, Ucayali, Loreto, and Amazonas, based on the need to "ensure the country's energetic security" and stating that the measures used in the protests were "acts against public order and the laws." While on this occasion the military were not initially called upon, the four rights established in the constitution—those relating to personal liberty and safety, the inviolability of the home, and freedom of movement and transit—were duly suspended.

Once the state of emergency had been declared, the protests became increasingly intense. At that time, indigenous leaders criticized the political intent behind the measure. For instance, Roger Rumrrill—via the indigenous media platform Servindi—stated: "The violent and repressive reply from García's regime to the indigenous peoples fair demands was inevitable."[45] For his part, Alberto Pizango, leader of AIDESEP, claimed that: "the state of emergency declared on the 9th of May is an act of provocation by the government" which nevertheless "has mobilized more indigenous people."[46] Finally he defiantly added that the "state of emergency didn't mean anything" and that the protestors would radicalize their measures as a result. Similarly, in a personal interview with the author, an indigenous activist involved in the conflict offered the following evaluation: "We know that there is a state of emergency and that the state of emergency is to kill and when we go to the protest we say goodbye to our families in case we don't go back, of course. . . . It is more violent, they lock you up, they hit you, and nothing happens. We are aware of it but you can still carry on fighting" (Personal interview with the author, Bilbao, May 2011).

During the state of emergency, the government set up round tables in order to establish dialogue and the unconstitutionality of the two laws that had been the cause of the conflict was declared. Nevertheless, the roadblocks and occupation of petrol plants continued. In the face of the increasingly intense and disruptive protests, on 4th June the tragic events occurred at the Curva del Diablo.[47] It was at that point that the state of emergency was applied with its full force. Indeed, it was extended to the whole of the Department of Amazonas (DS-035–2009-PCM) and at that time the armed forces were called in (Resolución Suprema 192–2009-DE/SG). Furthermore, a curfew was imposed in the provinces of Bagua and Utcubamba (Resolución Suprema 193–2009-DE/SG). During this intense phase of the state of emergency, 99 people were arrested[48] and the protests came to a very quick end. The tragedy produced a state of shock in Peruvian society in general and particularly among the indigenous people involved in the protests, with the leader of AIDESEP—Alberto Pizango—swiftly going into exile in Nicaragua.

It is important to highlight the debate in the press regarding the state of emergency of May 2009. Many opinion pieces were written about it, referring to a great unease with regard to the measure, claiming that it was the government's typical, knee-jerk reaction without offering a solution to structural problems.[49] Moreover, public opinion seemed to agree that it had an effect of polarizing the situation and was only being used to protect the multinational gas transportation companies rather than citizens. Seemingly, the declaration of the state of emergency brought the conflict to a zero-sum situation: "For the government, the Amazon natives are enemies (and not adversaries) and therefore they must be defeated politically."[50] It appears that the events of Bagua left their mark on the way in which states of emergency are viewed in Peru. Indeed, in a later case a columnist regrets "After what happened in Bagua, it seems that we haven't learnt the lesson and that the resolution of social problems continues to be a task . . . left unfinished."[51]

The impact of the episode of Bagua on Peruvian politics was massive, leading to a brief but signification investigation (Comisión Especial para Investigar y Analizar los Sucesos de Bagua 2009) and—by reaching out to international allies—the eventual promulgation of a law on the consultation of indigenous peoples (Wright 2014b). However, the underlying problem of social conflict over the use of indigenous resources is by no means over, nor is the use of states of emergency to repress indigenous protest. Indeed, beyond the period studied here, further declarations of repressive type regimes of exception have been made to deal with conflict over natural resources between indigenous peoples and the government and/or international firms.[52] Well before Independence, "protecting internal order" had become synonymous with the suppression of indigenous rebellions in Peru (Loveman 1993). This continues to be the case, three decades after the transition to democracy.

Despite the significant uses of regimes of exception to deal with instances of protest, the dominant trend in the first decade of the twenty-first century has been to apply successive states of emergency to deal with cells of *Sendero Luminoso* and illegal cultivations of coca in two specific areas of the country: several provinces of the Departments of Apurímac, Ayacucho, Huancavelica, Cusco, and Junín[53] and several provinces in the Departments of Huánuco, San Martín, and Ucayali.[54] In the case of the former, via a series of extensions, a state of emergency was, in effect, in place continuously from 2003 until—and apparently beyond—2010, the last year studied here. In the case of the latter, again via extensions, a state of emergency was in place continuously from 2005 until—and again apparently beyond—2010. This situation of a long-term application of repressive regimes of exception entails a high degree of democratic abnormality and seems to confirm the fears of liberal thinkers such as Benjamin Constant.

Importantly, the different declarations and extensions of states of emergency in these regions are highly vague and ambiguous, particularly in terms of the extraordinary situations they refer to. Indeed, the first decree applied to the provinces of the Departments of Apurímac, Ayacucho, Cusco, and Junín—to be extended further to Huancavelica in future decrees—is in fact an extension of the declaration of May 2003 that dealt with social protest. That decree states the following:

> the conditions still exist which determined the declaration of State of Emergency solely in the departments of Junín, Ayacucho and Apurímac, and in the province of La Convención, department of Cusco . . . the State of Emergency in the national territory, declared by the Supreme Decree Nº 055–2003-PCM is terminated, except for the departments of Junín, Ayacucho and Apurímac, and in the province of La Convención, department of Cusco, in whose districts the aforesaid State of Emergency is extended for a period of thirty days. . . .
>
> DS-062–2003-PCM of 25th June 2003

This vagueness over the exceptional situations characterizes all of the pursuant declarations and extensions of states of emergency in the region. What is particularly concerning about DS-062–2003-PCM specifically is that the original situation of protests is then used to deal with an unknown, unspecified "exceptional threat," ushering in a long-term repressive regime of exception through the back door. The first full declaration of a state of emergency in several provinces of the Departments of Apurímac, Ayacucho, Huancavelica, Cusco, and Junín (DS-077–2003-PCM) then refers to "acts contrary to public order" in the areas but does not offer any further clarification. This use of states of emergency is one of the greatest risks involved in emergency powers: that is to say, the possibility that measures designed for and justified by a specific exceptional situation will be transferred to a very different one (Gross and Ní Aoláin 2006, 230). Indeed, despite the vague nature of the extraordinary situation as expressed in the decrees, there is clarity over what measures can be used. Indeed, in all cases the four rights contemplated in the constitution are suspended and in the majority of cases related to the Departments of Apurímac, Ayacucho, Huancavelica, Cusco, and Junín, the Armed Forces are called upon to maintain internal order.

Only in 2010 was the real reason behind the declarations explicitly included in a decree. DS-055–2010-PCM, issuing a new state of emergency in several provinces of Huánuco, San Martín, and Ucayali, for the first time offers some clarity on the exceptional situation, stating that the decree is to "allow a sustained and permanent effort for the counter-terrorist operations and prohibition of the illicit Trafficking of Drugs. . . ." (DS-055–2010-PCM). Consequently, it can be ascertained that the motivation for all of these states of emergency would be to control the country's illegal areas of coca production and the supposed remainders of terrorist activity occurring in the same regions. In the case of those declarations applied to Apurímac, Ayacucho, Huancavelica, Cusco, and Junín, the region is known as the VRAE and consequently had become militarized under decrees of exception for over eight years.[55] In the case of Huánuco, San Martín, and Ucayali, the region is known as the Alto Huallaga Valley, where again further illegal cultivation of coca takes place[56] and *Sendero Luminoso* gangs are located, and which has found itself under national police control by means of states of emergency for over five years.

Importantly, by the time that Fujimori fled the country at the end of 2000, the terrorist threat in the country was much reduced, with some very small areas of low intensity activity, specifically in these two areas: the VRAE and the Alto Huallaga Valley (Jaskoski 2012). Importantly, these regions were at the center of the fight against *Sendero Luminoso* in the 1980s and 1990s. For Cáceres Santa María et al., during the 1990s "The coca-growing basins of the VRAE and the Huallaga became the bloodiest scenarios of the war due to *Sendero Luminoso* attacks, state repression and the presence of drug-trafficking hit men" (2007, 162). Likewise, Dreyfus (1999) talks about the militarization of the Alto Huallaga Valley during the fight against *Sendero Luminoso* between 1980 and 1995, which occurred under states of emergency. Seemingly, despite democratic renewal in 2001, history in Peru has repeated itself. The words of the head of a prominent NGO referring to the 1990s could easily be applied to the post-2000 declarations in the VRAE and the Huallaga Valley: "I cannot understand how the state of emergency can become the natural and permanent state of things. That is what happened, the state of emergency was declared for 30 days, which is what the law allows, but afterwards it is extended indefinitely. That is not democracy. . . ." (Personal interview with author, Lima, April 2007).

Several of those interviewed during fieldwork in Peru,[57] confirmed that drug trafficking and remainders of *Sendero Luminoso*[58] were the reason behind the majority of the states of emergency recently declared in the country, which—as shown here—went on to become permanent. Jokoski (2012) stresses that the role of the military in these areas has been considerably curtailed, given that in the VRAE their administrative role has disappeared, and in the Alto Huallaga Valley the police in general have retained control of internal order. In addition, the fact that these states of emergency are confined to specific areas would represent a significant lessening of their impact. Nevertheless, our reading is that this use of regimes of exception within the repressive paradigm constitutes a clear continuation of the practice that was established during the 1980s and 1990s. Indeed, it is worth bearing in mind that many of the military officials currently in service in both VRAE and Alto Huallaga Valley were trained during those years (ibid, 14). For her part, the head of a prominent human rights NGO interviewed by the author pointed to a concern for what this meant for democracy for the following reason: "You cannot have a democratic government with pockets of military dictatorship around the country."[59]

Crucially, although the repressive use of regimes of exception connected with remainders of *Sendero Luminoso* and antidrug trafficking operations in the VRAE area are of great significance in Peru in the period under study, there is only one reference to these cases in the opinion columns of the two national newspapers analyzed.[60] Even more surprising, perhaps, is that in that piece, rather than a criticism there is in fact a *demand* for the Armed Forces and Police to retain their privileges, taking into account their difficult working conditions, particularly in areas declared in emergency in the VRAE region. The degree to which the use of repressive regimes of exception in these two areas is managed under a cloak of secrecy is in great contrast to the cases related to protest that were analyzed in the previous section. The lack of debate is attributed to two factors in a personal interview with a key informant: ". . . this type of debate is subject to certain political conditions . . . there is a situation that involved the declaration of a state of emergency which has been overcome, right,[61] and . . . I also think that there is a perception of a sort of re-composition of the political scenario in which the forces that aim to avoid any reform of the armed forces now have the majority in Congress" (Personal interview with prominent human rights lawyer in Lima 2007).

The continuity of military prerogative within regimes of exception can be observed in the outcome of a specific reform. Initially, in 2004, an important step forward occurred when the Constitutional Tribunal ruled that crimes committed by the military and the police in areas declared under state of emergency could not be judged in military courts if there were civilians involved.[62] However, in 2007, Law 29166 once again extended the jurisdiction of the military courts, in the face of complaints that a preoccupation with human rights was hampering the efforts of the fight against insurgency (Jaskoski 2012).

Over twenty years ago, Brian Loveman criticized the historical use of regimes of exception as a mechanism to control internal subversive groups for the following reason: "Even where internal insurgencies continue, their lack of any credible assistance from, or linkage to, hostile external allies will further invalidate any military attempts to interference" (1997, 392). Nevertheless, the use of regimes of exception with the pretext of fighting *Sendero Luminoso* in the 1980s continued into the 1990s and—as shown here—well into and beyond the first decade of the twenty-first century. The fact that a generation of politicians and military officers trained in the 1980s has continued to operate these states of emergency may talk of a personal and not just an institutional path-dependency in this sense. These long-term regimes of exception are in remote, rural areas far away from Lima and do not seem to have captured the imagination or criticism of public opinion in general. As Dreyfus notes (1999, 371), the repeated use of the military in certain parts of the territory can reflect the State's weakness in these areas. The evaluation the scholar made in relation to the conflict of the 1980s and 1990s is still the case in some areas of Peru three decades after its transition to democracy.

The Emergence of a New Paradigm: Disaster Emergency Politics

Although natural disasters have been prevalent throughout Peruvian history—including earthquakes, droughts, and floods—and a constant problem for governments,[63] they have not been written into the history of regimes of exception in the country. Consequently, we know little about how often they have been declared or indeed how they work. A prominent human rights lawyer interviewed by the author[64] suggested that the vast majority of states of emergency had been declared within the repressive paradigm, although the constitution did contemplate natural disasters as a type of "exceptional threat." It is difficult to ascertain how often regimes of exception were declared in the past and how they were used but as a result of the analysis carried out here it is clear that in the twenty-first century they have become increasingly important.

Indeed, between 2000 and 2010, Peruvian presidents issued a total of 79 declarations of regimes of exception within the disaster paradigm. All of these decrees refer to adverse natural phenomena[65] or epidemics and deploy special technical measures or humanitarian aid as a result. The majority of the declarations also refer to the interruption of services and economic sectors and the rehabilitation of these public services and economic sectors. Up until

2004, all of these decrees referred to the exoneration from public contracting procedures although there was a decreasing tendency over time to do so, for reasons that will be outlined later on. In any case, these administrative situations and measures are secondary to the idea of "first aid" reaction in the face of adverse weather or sanitary conditions and consequently the declarations are firmly within the disaster paradigm. Importantly, none of these decrees referred to the suspension of rights or the deployment of Armed Forces, making them totally distinct from the repressive paradigm.

It is also important to note that there was an increasing tendency in time to declare regimes of exception within the disaster paradigm in Peru. Indeed, in 2000 there was no record of this use of states of emergency whereas in 2010 a total of nine declarations of this type were made. Significantly, in 2005 a total of 14 declarations of this type were issued, which corresponds to the effects of an intense period of drought on rural communities revolving around agriculture.[66]

Given that the constitution of 1993 says very little about natural disasters, it is important to point out the parallel legal and political developments regarding this use of states of emergency throughout the period under study, particularly at the start. Indeed, there have been several significant developments regarding the management of natural disasters in laws and regulations that are directly linked to the "state of emergency" provided for in the 1993 Constitution. In this sense, is important to note that, in several decrees issued during the period, the constitutional "state of emergency" is linked to the Decree Law 19338, which is the Civil Defense System Law of 28th March 1972. The purpose of this norm was to offer emergency assistance to affected towns by way of shelter, clothing and the restoration of basic social services (Art 6, c of the Decree Law 19338). Likewise, this decree law provided for the possibility of "exonerations" during a state of emergency, in its final second form.

This secondary regulation of disaster type states of emergency was revised and expanded in 2001, under the interim government of President Valentín Paniagua. Indeed, via DS 058–2001-PCM, the exoneration from public bidding processes for contracts was contemplated within the constitutional state of emergency and in the framework of the Unique Ordered Text of the State Contracting and Procurement Law approved by Supreme Decree No. 012–2001-PCM and its Regulation approved by Supreme Decree No. 013–2001-PCM. As a result, the declarations of regimes of exception within the disaster paradigm during this period have been made within this framework.

Furthermore, in the same year, DS-024–2001-PCM again issued by the interim president Valentín Paniagua, created the National Commission on Emergency to deal with natural disasters, coordinating the public and private sectors. Moreover, it was proposed that works in areas declared in state of emergency should be supervised, referring directly to Article 137 of the 1993

Constitution. The Commission's role was to evaluate and approve recommendations of the declaration of states of emergency and consisted of the President of the Republic, several ministers, and a private sector representative, with the National Institute of Civil Defense as the Executive Secretary. This role would be clarified via DS-058–2001-PCM, which established the necessary procedures to declare a disaster-type state of emergency, as provided in the 1993 Constitution. Indeed, the process involves a series of evaluations by the regional government before suggesting the declaration to the Council of Ministers and, ultimately, the President.[67] This new focus on states of emergency within the disaster paradigm was confirmed by the creation, in 2002, via DS 081–2002-PCM, of the Multi-sectorial Commission for Disaster Prevention and Response, which was given the task to coordinate an appropriate use of resources.

DS-019–2001-PCM is a typical case of a declaration of a state of emergency within the disaster paradigm and this normative framework. Indeed, this decree establishes the possibility of directly adjudicating public contracts to offer humanitarian aid to people affected by floods in different provinces of Puno and to rehabilitate sectors and services there. Three million soles (about $950,000) are also offered to deal with the emergency. Different organisms, including INDECI and several regional level authorities, are called upon to take the measures necessary to deal with the emergency "in favor of the people in the flooded areas in order to help people and protect public and private property" (DS-019–2001-PCM). In very different circumstances—this time an earthquake in Arequipa—DS-077–2001-PCM also established the possibility of directly adjudicating public contracts in order to buy the goods and carry out the actions necessary to offer help to the people affected and rehabilitate sectors and services. Again, different organisms including INDECI and several regional level authorities are called upon to take all measures possible.

At this stage, it is important to describe a long-term application of regimes of exception within the disaster paradigm, mirroring developments within the repressive paradigm. Indeed, after the devastating earthquake that occurred along the Peruvian coastline in 2007, states of emergency were constantly issued and extended to deal with the situation, with the result that from 2007 until the end of 2010 there was a state of exception in place in most of south-east Peru.[68] The initial declaration of a state of emergency (DS-068–2007-PCM) refers to the loss of life and structural damage caused by the earthquake and an emergency of "great magnitude." On this occasion, once again the possibility of the direct adjudication of contracts is referred to and both the INDECI and all of the relevant local authorities are called upon to "carry out the immediate actions necessary to attend the affected population, reduce and minimize the existing damage, and rehabilitate the affected areas," in what appears to be a set phrase for declarations of states of emergency within the disaster paradigm.

Interestingly, after a series of extensions, DS-084–2008 of December 2008 declares a fresh state of emergency and extends it to Lima and districts of Huancavelica, claiming that "the conditions that led to the original declaration of a state of emergency still persist," the same phrasing used in the long-term repressive states of emergency in the VRAE and the Alto Huallaga Valley. Consequently, it appears that the discursive justification to keep states of emergency in place in the long term is passed from one paradigm to the other. Over a year after the original earthquake, it is necessary to ask to what extent the original conditions still existed at that time, given that the exception (as ever) appeared to become the norm.

During the course of the various states of emergency, irregularities transpired regarding aid intended for the victims.[69] In addition, a series of new regulations was issued during this period, which changed how natural disasters were managed in the country.[70] For example Law Nº 28091 was issued on 6th September 2007 and by means of which the tax rate for customs clearance was lifted for donations or humanitarian aid within the context of a state of emergency due to a natural disaster. Likewise, work was made easier for voluntary firemen (DS 017–2007-TR), the dispatching of merchandise for humanitarian aid was controlled (Law 29077), and criteria were established for organizing civil defense warehouses for providing humanitarian aid in disasters (DS 031–2008-PCM). Hence, the legislative emergency politics model appears to assert itself in this case.

In an attempt to increase transparency, in 2007, the RS Nº 272–2007-CG for the Preventive Control Exercise of the National Control System was issued, offering oversight mechanisms in the face of the declaration of a state of emergency due to a natural catastrophe. The appeared objective was to increase transparency although the Controlaría would not interfere directly, only offering recommendations. The type of issues to be scrutinized included the distribution of goods, verification of infrastructure and contracting out of services, using a system of oversight mechanisms. Indeed, according to this resolution, when a "state of emergency" was declared due to a catastrophe, the General Controller would initiate activities of preventive control, setting up oversight mechanisms to identify actions that could have a negative impact on the transparency of the use of resources, collecting the complaints and accusations put forward by the inhabitants affected.

From this incident, therefore, it is possible to draw two key conclusions: first, that by means of declarations and extensions of regimes of exception, a long-term state of emergency (lasting more than three and a half years) was in place because of a natural disaster; second, that the earthquake case could be regarded as an exogenous *shock* which brought with it a change in the normative framework concerning the handling of natural disasters in the Peruvian case, stipulating guidelines over the use of humanitarian aid as well as an important oversight mechanism.[71]

In spite of the numerical importance of disaster type regimes of exception issued in Peru in the period under study, only one opinion column was found in which this type of state of emergency was tackled and rather it is to complain about the lack of preparation in the face of natural disasters and epidemics, suggesting that a state of emergency should be declared to avoid the spread of type A influenza.[72] No evidence was found of a profound, public debate on the use of regimes of exception in the face of natural disasters in the Peruvian case and scarce mention was made of it by key informants interviewed in Peru in 2007 and 2009. Nevertheless, the use of resources, public contracting procedures, and the long-term exception in Pisco make for an interesting discussion on the division of powers and oversight mechanisms that apparently has not been taken up in public or academic debate.

KEY FINDINGS AND ANALYSIS

At this point it is worth highlighting the main findings related to developments in relation to regimes of exception in Peruvian politics between 2000 and 2010. First of all, it is important to note that—despite various developments via secondary legal norms, particularly in relation to the disaster paradigm—the constitutional form of regimes of exception did not change at all during the decade. Indeed, the "state of emergency" and "state of siege" contemplated in Article 137 of the 1993 Constitution remained intact, unchanged, and—largely—un-debated throughout the period studied here. While the "state of emergency" includes situations of natural catastrophe among the extraordinary situations that could lead to a declaration, at the constitutional level both this mechanism and the "state of siege" are placed firmly within the repressive emergency politics paradigm.

In terms of use in practice, given that a total of 115 declarations of states of emergency were issued during the first decade of the twenty-first century, regimes of exception are not just a constitutional possibility but rather a political reality in Peru and one worthy of study. It is important to note that these declarations represent a fraction of a more complex universe of emergency politics in the country, with tendencies toward extensions in time and space, as well as a whole series of emergency mechanisms and organisms at different levels of government. Nevertheless, the study aims to have offered a route in to a better understanding of emergency politics in recent years.

The vast majority of cases that were found fell into two, very different groups. On the one hand were those declarations that dealt with internal protests or violence by suspending certain civil liberties and/or deploying the armed forces for the sake of "maintaining internal order." On the other hand were those declarations that dealt with natural disasters by offering humanitarian aid and/or technical help, as well as more administrative type measures involving the rehabilitation of public services and economic sectors and, on several occasions, the direct adjudication of public contracts. Importantly, there is no relevant use of states of emergency according to an administrative paradigm, despite a handful of attempts to do so.

Although it accounts for fewer cases of declarations of states of emergency than the disaster paradigm, the repressive paradigm is still synonymous with regimes of exception in Peru and clearly has more important implications for democracy. In this study I found a continuity with two historical uses of repressive states of emergency: first to deal with episodes of protest (as had been the case in pre-transition twentieth century) and second to deal with remainders of *Sendero Luminoso* and the illegal cultivation of coca, in two specific regions in the country (as had been the case in several areas during the 1980s and 1990s). As the decade came to a close these two uses remained firm and now constitute a legacy of the use of regimes of exception in Peru during the first decade of the twenty-first century.

In terms of the disaster paradigm, while the sheer number of decrees should speak of a dominant paradigm, its scarce debate in public opinion has meant that it has largely gone unnoticed. Importantly, at the start of the decade in question it was not clear to what extent and how this aspect of states of emergency could be used in practice. Consequently, as of 2001 there was a considerable degree of legal attention to the question of building a normative framework for states of emergency dealing with natural disasters. Indeed, throughout the decade, there were multiple declarations of states of emergency in the face of adverse natural phenomena including volcanoes, earthquakes, floods, and droughts, which aimed to set the wheels in motion of INDECI and relevant regional authorities in order to attend those who were affected and get public services and the private sector going again. The exoneration from public contracting procedures (established in DS 058–2001-PCM) is the most "exceptional" element of these decrees.

One defining and continuing feature of regimes of exception in third-wave Peru is their use as semipermanent rather than temporary mechanisms. This is true both of the repressive paradigm (the regimes of exception declared in the VRAE as of 2003 were still ongoing as of 2010) and of the disaster paradigm (likewise, the regimes of exception declared in Pisco and surrounding areas as of 2007 were still ongoing as of 2010). Consequently, it seems as is if the norm and the exception have a tendency to become blurred in Peruvian emergency politics, in line with the fears of liberal thinkers such as Benjamin Constant that were developed in the first chapter of this volume.

Having established how regimes of exception have been used, it is important to consider how they relate to democracy, given that, three decades into the third wave of democracy, it is the systemic prism in which they must be evaluated. Given the inductive nature of the study, a simple but comprehensive framework was offered in the introduction to this volume with the concept of *democratic governability*. Indeed, democratic governability is concerned about the legitimacy of decisions as well as their efficiency. Consequently, it is a useful framework to evaluate the use of regimes of exception, which we would expect, tip the balance in favor of efficiency rather than legitimacy.

Beginning with repressive regimes of exception, it is important to make a clear distinction between states of emergency issued to repress protest and states of emergency used to control areas in which *Sendero Luminoso* may still be operating alongside the illegal cultivation of coca.

In terms of the former, they are clearly of doubtful *legitimacy* and *efficiency*. As seen in the case studies of May 2003 and May 2009, the fact that the states of emergency intensified the protests rather than putting a stop to them suggests that their application may well be counter-productive. Furthermore, although no excesses appear to have been committed in relation to the suspension of human rights beyond those stipulated by the constitution, there are very few mechanisms of oversight for these declarations and the use of the armed forces to deal with civilian issues is clearly problematic from a human rights perspective. Nevertheless, the role of the Defensoría del Pueblo and criticisms within public opinion point to a degree of openness and accountability that had not been noted prior to this period.

In relation to the repeatedly applied and extended (and therefore effectively permanent) states of emergency in the VRAE and Valle del Alto Huallaga, there is clearly an important issue of *legitimacy* as the suspension of human rights does not respect the principle of temporality established by Despouy (1999). Indeed, the situation reflects the fears of liberal thinkers such as Benjamin Constant about the possibility of the exception becoming the norm. In terms of the conceptualization used here, it would appear that emergency politics blends with discretionary politics in these cases. On the other hand, the very fact that the states of emergency have been in place for years at a time without seemingly solving the problem and returning to a state of normality suggests that as well as of being doubtful legitimacy they are also of doubtful *efficiency*.

Finally, in the case of those the states of emergency declared within the disaster paradigm, the attempt to provide a normative framework for a vague constitutional notion of catastrophe could be seen as a positive step forward in terms of democratic governability. For their part, the creation of oversight mechanisms could likewise be a positive step forward in terms of *legitimacy* and the facility to deploy humanitarian aid and technical measures could conversely constitute a positive step forward in terms of *efficiency*. In terms of how the declarations work in practice, the vast majority seem to be one-off decrees to deal with generally dangerous situations for certain communities and a way of kick-starting the emergency institutions into action. Consequently, these decrees could be seen—provisionally—as broadly legitimate and efficient.

Nevertheless, there are a couple of discordant notes in relation to the disaster emergency paradigm in Peruvian politics. First, there appear to have been misappropriations of resources at certain times, calling into question the real capacity of transparency mechanisms and therefore their legitimacy. Second, and most importantly, the same long-term approach to emergency politics expressed in the VRAE and el Valle del Alto Huallaga was used to deal with the effects of the devastating earthquake in Pisco, although with very different causes and effects. Indeed, the series of declarations and extensions of a state of emergency in Ica, Lima and Huancavelica as of 2007 are of reduced *legitimacy* for the same reason as stated before: the supposedly transitory nature of emergency powers. For the same reason, their *efficiency* is doubtful given that if they had been successful in achieving their aims, the measures should have been lifted and political normality restored within months of their declaration.

These long-term states of emergency continue to define emergency politics in Peru and—as well as Benjamin Constant's concern in the nineteenth century—it is also worth remembering Eguiguren Praeli's comment back in the 1980s: "The longer a state of emergency is used in democracy; it is because the society is not as democratic as it claims to be. When this route is used to resolve with repression what should be overcome via social transformations, the proposal of democracy gradually becomes liquidated" (1989, 286). Undoubtedly, whether it be in order to repress or to avoid public contracting procedures, the reiterated use of regimes of exception is not good news for Peru's democratic consolidation three decades into the third wave.

Consequently, it is clear that states of emergency sit ill-at-ease with democratic governability in Peru, for all of the reasons discussed above. In addition, it is worth reiterating the vagueness and ambiguity of the constitutional form as well as the declarations of states of emergency, which refer to similar, elliptical formulas rather than being clear about the exceptional situations, the justification, and the precise measures to be employed. In these circumstances there is considerable room for improvisation and indeed discretion. Consequently, offering more precise guidelines at both the constitutional and decree levels may contribute to mitigate the extent to which these declarations are at odds with the tents of democratic governability. In the same way, the establishment of meaningful mechanisms of accountability would likewise constitute a real improvement, given that in the different declarations the role for the Congress is minimal (the President merely informs legislators of the decree and the measures taken) and the Constitutional Court effectively nonexistent.

Importantly, none of the key informants interviewed in the course of this study agreed that regimes of exception were intrinsically incompatible with democracy, but rather that they should be subject to stricter controls. In the words of a prominent human rights lawyer: "If you ask me whether the state of emergency should exist because it could be good for a democratic regime I would say that I believe that there are situations that escape constitutional normality and they should be regulated. My impression is that constitutional regulations of states of emergency are currently insufficient" (Personal interview with the author, Lima, April 2007).

NOTES

1. Personal interview with the editor of a national newspaper, Lima, April 2007.
2. The official register is available at www.elperuano.com.pe. The search was carried out online and according to the nomenclatures used in the constitutional regime of exception, in this case "estado de emergencia" and "estado de sitio." As well as collecting the declarations, other relevant information including extensions in time or into different territories was also collected.
3. These laws will be highlighted throughout the text and were found thanks to help from interviewees (see following note) and an analysis of the declarations of regimes of exception.
4. In 2007, interviews were carried out in Lima with a prominent human right's lawyer, the head of an important human rights NGO, a constitutional law expert, and the editor of a national newspaper. In 2009, interviews were carried out in Cusco with the leaders of two peasant unions, the leader of a public trade union, the head of an important local human rights NGO, and representatives of the national Human Rights Ombudsman. Likewise, in the same year an interview was also carried out in Lima with a legal expert on the sociopolitical dynamics of the *cocalero* farmers. In 2011, an additional interview was carried out with an indigenous leader from the Amazon region during a visit to Spain. These interviews were conducted taking into account the methodological approach of Miguel Valles for qualitative interviews (2009) and according to a snowball technique. The texts of these interviews—which in most cases were tape recorded but in another cases were more akin to informal conversations—are on file with the author.
5. These reports will be highlighted throughout the text, but two are worth highlighting from the outset, the Reportes Mensuales de Conflictos Sociales (monthly reports of social conflict) published by the Defensoría del Pueblo (2004–2010) and

the important report drawn up by the Coordinadora Nacional de Derechos Humanos (2004). Likewise, data from the Economic Commission for Latin America and the Caribbean (http://www.cepal.org/en) are also referred to in order to support observations and findings.

6. The electronic archives of two of the main national newspapers were consulted between 2000 and 2010: El Comercio (www.elcomercio.pe) and La República (www.larepublica.pe).

7. It is worth mentioning Law 20820 of 1974 in which harsh penalties were introduced for attempts to carry out political assassinations. Permanent Councils of War were also created, which had the capacity to try civilians under military jurisdiction.

8. May and August 1978; January, March, June, and August 1979.

9. On the use of this mechanism in Peru see the chapter by Gregory Schmidt in the volume of Carey and Shugart (1998).

10. Regarding the military's influence over the 1979 Constitution, see Rubio Correa (1989).

11. There was an important debate about the idea of restricting guarantees rather than the rights. Ultimately it was decided that rights but not guarantees could be suspended, in line with international law (García-Sayán 1989).

12. Law 24150 of 1985 established that the Armed Forces could replace civil authorities during regimes of exception, below the authority of the president (Correa Rubio 1989, 245). Nevertheless, in theory, military justice could not try citizens, according to Article 282 of the constitution (García Saýan 1987, 113).

13. On this issue, see Clutterbuck 1995 and Eguiguren Praeli 1989.

14. Rubio Correa notes how at the start of the 1980s there were constant references to and fears of "golpes de estado" (1987, 244–45), pointing to concerns over the fragility of democracy.

15. Information from personal interview with prominent human rights lawyer in Lima, April 2007.

16. Information from Power Manchego Muñoz (1989, 272–80). It is important to note—as García Sayán (1989,114) does—that during this time other states of emergency were applied to deal with labor or social conflict. According to his calculations, 10 such decrees were declared by President Belaúnde alone.

17. Indeed, the epicenter of *Sendero Luminoso* was Ayacucho, a region with particularly poor socioeconomic indicators (García Sayán 1987b, 115).

18. It is important to ask—as Correa Rubio does (1987, 245)—whether members of the Armed Forces are best placed to replace administrative authorities, given that their training is for a different purpose: eliminating the enemy. Eguiguren Praeli notes that these commands were often established in areas where the State had little presence (1989, 263).

19. García Sayán (1987b, 119) calculates that between 1983 and 1984 at least 1,500 forced disappearances took place.

20. See Tanaka (2005, 262).

21. Interestingly he called his government a "gobierno de emergencia y reconstrucción nacional"—a government of emergency and national reconstruction—(Comisión de la Verdad y Reconciliación 2003).

22. Interview with prominent human rights lawyer in Lima, April 2007. The lack of a secondary law on regimes of exception adds to this ambiguity, see also Eguiguren Praeli (1989).

23. See García Sayán 1989; Eguiguren Praeli 1989 Advisory Opinion OC-9/87 of the Inter-American Commission on Human Rights in relation to the application of *habeas corpus* during regimes of exception. The argument is the following: although the enjoyment of rights may be suspended, the guarantees of these rights must remain in place in order for arbitrary suspensions to be avoided and to determine whether the right suspended is related to the exceptional situation.

24. Later on, a ruling from the Inter-American Court of Human Rights in 2005 confirmed that this amnesty could not be upheld (Jaskoski 2012).

25. Personal interview, Lima, April 2007.

26. Personal interview, Lima, April 2007.

27. Interview with prominent human rights lawyer, Lima, April 2007.

28. For example, García-Sayán 1987b; García Sayan 1989; Eguiguren Praeli 1989; and Power Manchego-Muñoz 1989.

29. Information from interview with the representative of an important human rights' NGO, Lima, April 2007.

30. Personal interview with a prominent human rights lawyer, Lima, April 2007.

31. The trauma of the armed conflict, with around 70,000 deaths, multiple human rights violations, and side-effects on levels of social capital and political mobilization in Peru have been widely documented. See the final report of the Comisión de la Verdad y Reconciliación (2003), Hagopian and Mainwaring (2005), and Burt (2007).

32. Personal interview in Lima, 2007.

33. Declarations of regimes of exception are understood as those decrees in which the President—referring to the relevant articles of the Constitution—declares a "state of emergency." Importantly, in five decrees the reference was implicit rather than explicit but given that a "state of emergency" is declared they are included in this recount. In this sense, we are following the precedent established by Ferreira Rubio and Goretti (1998) in their analysis of the decrees of necessity and urgency in the Argentinian case.

34. The vast majority of decrees—112-state a specific time limit but in practice the extensions that are easily given to the President make this time limit irrelevant. For instance, the following declarations—all of which are within the repressive emergency paradigm—were renewed at least once: the DS-016–2007-PCM was prolonged for a further fifteen days by means of the DS-030–2007-PCM; the DS-067–2006-PCM was prolonged for a further nineteen days by means of the DS-087–2006-PCM; the DS-082–2004-PCM was prolonged for a further sixty days through the DS-089–2004-PCM; and DS-015–2000-PCM was prolonged for sixty more days by means of the DS-022–2000-PCM. All these examples are decrees of exception which include the suspension of human rights.

35. For example, the DS-019–2001-PCM was extended from several districts of Puno to cover the whole Puno Department by means of the DS-025–2001-PCM; the DS-071–2004-PCM was extended to the districts of Ollachea and Ayapata by means of the DS-072–2004-PCM; and the DS-027–2009-PCM was extended to the whole of the Amazonas Department by means of the DS-035–3009-PCM.

36. Opinion expressed by the editor of an important national newspaper in a personal interview carried out in Lima, April 2007, and shared by a prominent human rights lawyer in a personal interview carried out in Lima, April 2007.

37. Power Manchego-Muñoz (1989, 272–80).

38. In a personal interview with head of a human rights NGO in Lima, April 2007, she asserted that under both Toledo and García this mechanism had been widely used.

39. This finding was highlighted in a prepublication, see Wright (2014a).

40. See for instance Graham (1992, 132).

41. A reduced analysis of this episode was included in a prior publication (Wright 2013b).

42. A chacra is an area of land cultivated by peasants.

43. This covenant has been a key legal mechanism for defending indigenous peoples' rights, particularly to consultation, in Latin America. On this issue in Peru see Wright (2014b).

44. These decrees were DL1073 and DL1090. 65º Reporte de Conflictos Sociales, julio 2009, Defensoría del Pueblo de Perú, www.defensoria.gob.pe.

45. "Perú: estado de emergencia contra los pueblos amazónicos," published on 13th May 2009 at www.servindi.org.

46. "Perú: Amazónicos intensifican lucha tras estado de excepción," published on 11th May 2009 at www.servindi.org.

47. See for instance, Amnistía Internacional "Perú, Bagua seis meses después" (2009) and "Informe Final" Comisión Especial para Investigar y Analizar los Sucesos de Bagua" (2009), available at www.servindi.org.

48. Data from Amnistía Internacional 2009.

49. For instance Carlos Reyna "Protesta invisible, Constitución suspendida" opinion column published in la República, 11th May 2009; Augusto Álvarez Rodrich "¿Hay un ruido raro en Chuncholandia, no?" opinion column published in la República 13th May 2009; Chachi Sanseviero "Atila del oro verde," opinion column published in la República 13th May 2009; Javier Diez Canseco "Estado excluyente e insurgencia" opinion column published in la República 18th May 2009; Nelson Manrique "El estado contra los pueblos amazónicos" opinion column published in la República 20th May 2009; Carlos Castro "La ley de la selva," opinion column published in la República 24th May 2009; Alberto Adrianzén M. "En la selva sí hay estrellas," opinion column published in la República 6th June 2009.

50. Alberto Adrianzén M. "En la selva sí hay estrellas," opinion column published in la República el 6 de junio del 2009.

51. Editorial "Ni intransigencia ni incomunicación en paro minero" published in El Comercio 6 de abril del 2010.

52. Cajamarca 2011 (DS-093–2011-PCM), Espinar 2012 (DS-056–2012-PCM), and Cajamarca 2012 (DS-070–2012-PCM) are recent examples. These episodes are analyzed in Wright 2013a.

53. DS-077–2003-PCM, DS-093–2003-PCM, DS-027–2006-PCM.

54. DS-098–2005-PCM, DS-056–2007-PCM, DS-019–2008-PCM, DS-060–2009-PCM, DS-055–2010-PCM.

55. Information from an interview with legal adviser to cocalero farmers, Lima, February 2009.

56. In the 1980s, this valley produced 60% of the world's coca (Kruijt 1996).

57. Personal interview held with a representative of a human rights NGO held in Lima in April 2007; personal interview with a legal adviser to cocalero farmers, held in Lima, February 2009; personal interview with indigenous leader, personal interview held in Bilbao, May 2011.

58. For the Institut Internacional de Gobernabilitat de Catalunya (2005), the two key problems in the Peruvian continue to be insecurity and the cultivation of coca.

59. Data from personal interview held in Lima, April 2007.

60. Editorial "The state's debt to the Armed Forces and the National Police," published in El Comercio, 27th September 2010.

61. Clearly, I do not agree with this aspect of his evaluation.

62. Information from Jaskoski (2012).

63. As pointed out in Chapter 2, there is nothing new in this situation: during the nineteenth century, Peru's rulers dealt with different types of natural disaster which were affecting both the people and agricultural production. (Carcelén Reluz 2011).

64. Carried out in Lima, April 2007.

65. According to data from the ECLAC. In the period under study, Peru had been struck by a very wide range of adverse natural phenomena, including 6 earthquakes, 1 volcano eruption and 23 adverse weather incidents.

66. See for instance DS-025–2005-PCM declared in several provinces in Apurímac, DS-020–2005 declared in several provinces in Lambayeque, or DS-019–2005 declared in several provinces in Piura.

67. Information from Instituto de Defensa Civil de Perú, www.indeci.gob.pe.

68. The state of emergency was initially declared in Ica and gradually extended to Lima and Huancavelica. The initial declarations are: DS-068–2007-PCM, DS-084–2008-PCM, DS-061–2009-CM, and DS-060–2010-PCM, together with a whole series of extensions.

69. See for example Ministerial Resolution N° 564–2008-VIVIENDA of 15th September 2008.

70. For example the Law N° 28091 of 6th September 2007 by means of which the tax rate for customs clearance was lifted for donations or humanitarian aid within the context of a state of emergency due to a natural disaster; or the DS 155–2007-PCM "Regulation of the Law N° 29081—a Law which excludes from taxes the importation of goods arriving for humanitarian aid as a result of the declaration of a state of emergency" dated 5th October 2007.

71. Peru has suffered the human, economic and social effects of earthquakes for several centuries. See Pérez-Mallaína Bueno (2000; 2005).

72. Sandra Bellido "What a headache!" opinion column published in La República, on 18th July 2009.

Chapter 4

Bolivia

The Disaster Paradigm

Looking through the archives of *El Deber*, a Santa Cruz daily, I found a rather curious editorial piece from 2008 on changes in the repertoire of protest. What caught my attention specifically was the following sentence: "Well, what used to be called a simple road-block, is now known as a 'social state of siege.'"[1] This idea of a "social state of siege" rather eloquently reflects the degree to which a historic, decidedly repressive regime of exception became politicized in Bolivia. Indeed, as an ex-police chief explained in a personal interview with the author in Sucre, in April 2007: "the experience that the Bolivian citizen has of states of siege is that they have only helped to kill, they were decreed and people were killed. Given that Bolivians have this understanding of states of siege it has to be removed (from the Constitution)." This chapter charts and analyzes the processes behind the widespread, public rejection of this mechanism of emergency politics as well as the shift in focus in both the regulation and use of regimes of exception, away from the repressive paradigm and toward a framework of risk management.

The primary material used in the following pages are the declarations of regimes of exception issued between 2000 and 2010,[2] together with the relevant legal frameworks, identified as the "state of siege" established in the Constitution of 1967, the figures of "disaster" and "emergency" established in Law 2140 for the Reduction of Risks and Attention of Disasters of 2000, and the "state of exception" established in the Constitution of 2009. While the focus of the study is decidedly political, it is important to take into account these normative developments, given that they have necessarily shaped the use of regimes of exception and at the same time reflect new opinions and agreements about the nature of emergency politics in Bolivia. A whole wealth of sources are used to complete the analysis, including reports and bulletins,[3] in-depth interviews with key-informants,[4] and newspaper articles.[5]

The chapter is structured as follows: first of all, a starting point is established, in which historical tendencies and relevant normative frameworks prior to 2000 are identified; next, an in-depth analysis is offered of regimes of exception as they have been used in practice in Bolivia between 2000 and 2010; and finally, an ending point is established, offering an overview regarding developments in regimes of exception in practice and changes or continuities at the formal level. The final section also offers some reflections on the relationship between regimes of exception and democratic governability in Bolivia, taking into account possible trade-offs between legitimacy and efficiency.

THE STARTING POINT: HISTORICAL USE AND LEGAL FRAMEWORKS PRIOR TO 2000

The intended contribution of this chapter is its analysis of the period between 2000 and 2010, given that it is possible to piece together considerable knowledge about the historical use of regimes of exception in Bolivia from other secondary sources. In order to contextualize the study nevertheless it is important to offer an overview of developments relating to the constitutional form and use of regimes of exception prior to the twenty-first century, particularly in the post-transition period. Consequently, in this section, more distant historical precedents and legal figures are briefly analyzed (both in the nineteenth and twentieth centuries), before summarizing developments in the first twenty years after Bolivia's transition to democracy. In this way I hope to offer a historical path and starting point from which to begin the in-depth empirical study that constitutes the core contribution of this chapter.

The political history of Bolivia has been characterized by the presence of the military and persistent political instability. With the military coup of the 16th July 1809, a tendency was started that would not come to an end until 1982 (Whitehead 2001, 24). Until the War of the Pacific with Chile in 1879, the armed forces dominated the country's political life, taking over the State apparatus via a series of coups and counter-coups. Indeed, between 1840 and 1849 alone, there were 65 attempts at overthrowing the government (Bonilla 1987, 270). Consequently, the foundation of the Bolivian Republic is linked to a constant, violent redistribution of power and political instability, with aborted reforms, coups, assassinations, and transitory executives (Loveman 1993). In this context, regimes of exception were swiftly introduced into the country's constitutions—in line with the general pattern in Latin America according to Aguilar Rivera (1996)—including those of 1826, 1831, 1834, 1839, 1843, 1851, 1861, and 1868 (Gargarella 2005, 132). The paragraphs that follow aim to chart the constitutional and political developments regarding regimes of exception during this period, drawing largely on the seminal work by Brian Loveman (1993).

The first regime of exception after Independence was included in the 1826 constitution, foreseeing the suspension of constitutional formalities under extraordinary circumstances by either the Congress or the President. Importantly, the declaration included an explicit timeframe, in line with the tenets of Republican exceptionalism. When Santa Cruz came into power, the 1826 constitution was derogated and in 1831 a new constitution was drawn up, giving the executive and military greater powers and establishing a similar regime of exception. In this case, in the face of war, internal commotion or (unspecified) "extraordinary danger" or threats, the President would have limited power. During his time as President—which lasted until 1839—Santa Cruz repeatedly referred to these clauses to deal with invasions and internal uprisings (ibid, 141).

In 1839, a new constitution came into being that reduced executive power and increased that of the legislative, in a reaction against Santa Cruz's ten-year reign. The charter established specific powers for the president, thereby reducing their scope. Indeed, it was not possible to expel, exile, or punish citizens, deprive them of property or liberty, interfere in court proceedings, or impede elections. Likewise it was not possible to prevent those elected from taking office, dissolve congress, or suspend its sessions. Moreover, the power of the military was also limited (ibid, 242). Nevertheless, Articles 79–81 of the constitution included a regime of exception in which clear powers were outlined, although no clarity on circumstances was offered. These powers included: increasing the size of the National Guard, financing the military, arresting subversives and bringing them before a judge within 72 hours, naming generals, and declaring amnesties and pardons for political crimes (ibid, 243). Importantly, the President would have to report to Congress on the measures used. Despite these greater checks on executive power, General Velasco was unable to implement the constitution in the face of several invasions and uprisings, going into exile in 1842 (ibid, 244).

In the same year, Ballivián took control of the Bolivian State and—true to form—drew up a new constitution in 1843, once again giving more power back to the president and army and establishing that, in case of danger or threat (understood as internal commotion or external danger), the executive could take whatever measures necessary, in what amounted to an extralegal model of accommodation, with no congressional review. As Loveman rather eloquently notes: "Ballivián had thus surpassed Bolívar and Santa Cruz; unilateral presidential determination of the existence of external danger or internal commotion suspended all civil liberties and rights, including the long list of *garantias* commencing with liberty, security, property, and equality before the law. . . ." (ibid, 244). These provisions were clearly the broadest in postindependence Bolivian constitutionalism, offering full powers to the president, and were used repeatedly by Ballivián.

In a move toward a *decisionist* understanding of the norm and the exception, when Belzú assumed the presidency, he suspended the 1843 constitution and assumed full powers. In 1851 another constitution was drawn up, with a regime of exception that was very clear in that rights and guarantees would be suspended. If the *patria* was in danger (via an internal commotion or external war), broad powers could be offered to the executive. For his part, when General Córdova was designated president in 1855, he repeatedly used regimes of exception to deal with revolts. In the face of this political instability, Linares became de facto president in 1857 and declared martial law in 1858. As Loveman (1993) points out, he did not base his emergency powers on the constitution simply because he did not see any reason to do so. After his exile, elections were called in 1861 and again a new constitution was drawn up. Importantly, this constitution prohibited extraordinary powers for the President although the "estado de sitio" or "state of siege" was introduced, permitting the suspension of guarantees. These previsions were used widely to imprison opposition supporters.

The 1861 constitution was suspended by Mariano Melgarejo who came to power in 1864, ushering in another decisionist era of politics in Bolivia. Given that he had little popular support, the President relied on the army and drew up a new constitution in 1868 for reasons of legitimacy rather than political conviction (Loveman 1993, 254). While the 1868 constitution offered a list of rights, it also contemplated provisions for emergencies, internal commotion, danger to the State, and for constitutional dictatorship. Crucially, in 1870 Melgarejo was ousted and General Morales marched to La Paz, suspending the constitution and declaring a state of siege in opposition areas. The following year, Melgarejo fled and a new constitution was drawn up, in which congress could give president powers to expand the armed forces, increase the budget, and protect the internal security of the Republic.

For its part, the constitution of 1878 stood the test of time, remaining in place until 1938. In relation to regimes of exception, it sought to limit extraordinary powers under the "estado de sitio" or "state of siege." Articles 26–30 outlined powers to conserve public order, including special financial measures and the suspension of guarantees, including internal exile, arrest, voluntary external exile, the censorship of correspondence, travel restrictions, etc. As Loveman (ibid) points out, these clauses constitute the basis of the regime of exception that would be established at the normative level immediately before, during, and after Bolivia's transition to democracy, which culminated in 1982. Importantly, all of Bolivia's—civilian—Presidents of the 1880s and 1890s would declare states of siege to deal with political opponents and uprisings, based on the provisions of the 1878 constitution. Consequently the history of regimes of exception in eighteenth-century Bolivia is ample in both military and civilian hands, in a context that oscillated between a clear division between then exception and the norm, *Republican Exceptionalism*, and a more permanent exception, in line with the ideas of *decisionism*.

These oscillations between temporary and permanent exceptions continued into the twentieth century, when regimes of exception were crafted and used within a predominantly repressive paradigm. Indeed, the regime of exception established in 1878 is the basis for the regimes of exception contemplated in the constitutions of 1938, 1945, 1947, and 1967, which underwent only cosmetic changes. It is also important to note that the political instability that characterized postindependent Bolivia continued into the twentieth century, with a series of military coups and authoritarian regimes between 1939 and 1953 and then again between 1964 and 1978. Even when the country was going through its transition to democracy, there were a series of new coups by the military, which clearly reflects the predominance of "anti-politics" in the country.

In line with Brian Loveman's seminal analysis (ibid), in the first decades of the twentieth-century liberal governments replaced the conservative ones and state of siege mechanisms were still regularly used. For instance, in 1914 Ismael Montes' government declared a state of siege to repress opposition by carrying out arrests, forcing internal exile, and making deportations. While Bolivia's Republican Party proposed to restrict the framework and use of the state of siege, upon reaching power in 1920 it made no changes whatsoever. In 1923, President Bautista Saavedra repressed a miners' strike, killing several dozen miners and members of their families. For his part, President Hernando Siles—in power between 1924 and 1928—used a state of siege to control political opponents, strikers, teachers, student demonstrations, and uprisings by indigenous people. Undoubtedly, during this period the use of states of siege as a mechanism to repress the opposition—even by democratic governments—became consolidated.

Although the 1967 Constitution was promulgated by the democratic government of General René Barrientos Ortuño, it was enacted during a period of political and social instability, with frequent *golpes de estado*. It was, in fact, General Barrientos himself who had participated in the overthrowing of Víctor Paz Estenssoro only a couple of years earlier, in 1964. Furthermore, Barrientos was to be elected president in 1966 in a problematic election, which saw Víctor Paz Estenssoro vetoed because he was the only candidate other than Barrientos who had any real chance of winning.[6] Against this backdrop of dubious democracy and the latent militarism of the president, the constitution was drawn up, wherein the armed forces were made primarily responsible for maintaining internal order. Importantly, the constitution of 1967 survived the transition to democracy and indeed until 2009. Consequently the "state of siege" established in Articles 111–115 is worth describing in some depth here given that it offers a key normative background for the analysis carried out later on in this chapter.

With regard to emergency situations, Article 111 establishes that the state of siege could be declared in the face of an "internal commotion or international war." Again, we come across the term "internal commotion" which is particularly ambiguous. While the source in Latin refers to the idea of a rebellion or violent altercation (Molina 1987, 164), in Bolivia it was generally interpreted as being related to internal disorder (mobilizations or protests) and in some cases in relation to natural disasters.[7] For many analysts, the great danger of the mechanism lies in the ambiguity of the nature of the emergency situations itself, rather than the type of measures that can be employed.[8]

For its part, Article 112 establishes the measures that could be taken against "people who have been found to be scheming against public order."[9] These measures include: i) increasing the number of members of the Armed Forces; ii) imposing anticipated taxes; iii) the suspension of guarantees and rights of "those persons found to be scheming against pubic order"; iv) the arrest of those mentioned above by the legitimate authority (which could be a local executive rather than judicial authority[10]), while respecting *habeas corpus* by placing them before a judge within 48 hours; v) the confinement of the detained to different provinces; vi) and—only in case of international war—the censure of correspondence and media. Undoubtedly, Article 112 of the constitution of 1967 offers important resources that are primarily repressive but also administrative in nature, specifically in relation to the imposition of taxes.

After a maximum of ninety days the state of siege would automatically expire, with the exception of situations of ongoing civil or international war. However, this exception meant that in theory the permanent application of the state of siege was possible. According to the constitution, it was not possible to declare more than one state of siege in the same year unless Congress was in favor of doing so, offering an important limitation mechanism. Once the state of siege was over, citizens could be freed, except in those cases in which a trial had begun in the competent tribunals, which—as we have already highlighted—could be chosen directly by the Executive. Curiously, reprimands could only be imposed on those who were "carrying out orders," and not on those who issued them.

It is important to note that, despite its "democratic" origins, the state of siege written into the 1967 constitution became synonymous with an authoritarian form of government due to its repeated use by military regimes to repress internal disturbances in the 1970s (Loveman 1993). For their part, several key informants interviewed in Bolivia explained that the state of siege in the Bolivian social psyche is synonymous with twentieth-century military regimes due to the repeated use given to them during the 1970s. According to a prominent human rights defender: "The military used many states of siege . . . for long periods because they had the country under complete control but as soon as something happened there was always the state of siege to resort to and the state of siege gave them even more free rein to do as they liked" (Personal interview with the head of a human rights NGO in Laz Paz, April 2007). For his part, a former police chief observed that: "Bánzer was a tyrant when he was in power in the 1970s, he governed with the state of siege" (Personal interview carried out in Sucre, April 2007). Finally, an advisor at the Constituent Assembly made the following assessment: "Given that we are a country with an authoritarian, dictatorial past, generally the state of siege is associated with this dictatorial past, the military, the armed forces etc." (Personal interview carried out by the author in Sucre, April 2007).

Consequently, it is clear that the constitutional form of and use given to regimes of exception in the twentieth century follows on from their use in the nineteenth. In that sense, they were created, thought of and used as mechanisms of repressive emergency politics, throughout the century and particularly during the military dictatorship of the 1970s. However, it is important to remember that elements of both disaster and administrative emergency politics are written (rather awkwardly)[11] into the state of siege in all of Bolivia's twentieth-century constitutions, there is no record of regimes of exception being used in accordance with either of those two paradigms. Rather, paralegal attempts at declaring "emergencies" within both the disaster and administrative paradigms are scattered throughout the 1970s.

For instance, within the disaster paradigm, the DS16295 declared by President David Padilla, of the Military Junta, on 21st March 1979 refers to landslides near a tin manufacturing plant La Palca in the Department of Potosí that have interrupted the activities of the plant, consequently "putting in danger the very structure of this important industrial complex of the State mining system." Faced with this situation, the immediate contracting of technicians and specialists to prevent further risks is permitted. Although the decree has no clear legal basis, it refers to a "situation of emergency" and consequently can be considered an expression of paralegal emergency power. In the same way, President David Padilla returned to this type of extralegal mechanism via DS16794, in order to buy machinery and equipment for the development of the Province of Punata in 1979 within an administrative paradigm.

It is not clear how widespread these paralegal emergency powers were during the twentieth century and certainly prior to Bolivia's transition to democracy, regimes of exception were synonymous with repression. Nevertheless, the decrees mentioned before point to a search for another type of emergency politics, within the disaster and administrative paradigms, and which at this stage was expressed in extralegal terms. This is an important observation that will be taken up when discussing developments after 2000.

Bolivia's (long and interrupted) transition to democracy began in 1978 and was subject to a series of military coups and declarations of states of siege (Loveman 1993). With the elections of October 1982, democracy was ushered back in and Bolivia (like Chile, Argentina and Uruguay) maintained its old constitution rather than calling up a constituent assembly and during up a new charter (Loveman 1997). As already highlighted, the 1967 constitution included broad regime of exception provisions, clearly within the repressive emergency politics paradigm and no reforms to the relevant articles were made during the period. Furthermore, it has been noted that the "state of siege" was the preferred measure for Bolivian military governments to impose order, particularly in the 1970s. The evaluation of a prominent Bolivian historian with regard to its use during the turbulent period between 1978 and 1982 is particularly interesting:

> "The state of siege has the same characteristics as other constitutional mechanisms that refer to the privileges of the transition period from a dictatorship to a democracy. It is a legacy of an authoritarian past in the constitution of democratic countries. . . . I would say that the mechanism was used in the transition from authoritarian governments to democracy precisely because democratic institutions were not firmly established." (Personal interview with the author in Sucre, April 2007).

It is important to highlight that at the time of the transition, there was considerable criticism of the design and use of regimes of exception. For his part, Molina (1987, 162–165) confirms the firmly repressive (and on occasion preemptive) nature of the state of siege, claiming that the penal code should be sufficient to deal with protests and strikes. Likewise, he establishes that the threats of violence and internal commotion in the 1967 constitution are extremely vague. Referring to the use of states of siege in Bolivia's past the scholar offers a reading that reflects the tenets of securitization theory: "We all know how easy it is for a government to suggest that there may be an attempted plot of something; with a small, selfish tendency and a certain inclination for abuses and excess, it is possible to create a plot that seems to be true in order to carry out persecution, confinement and human rights violations" (Molina 1987, 164).

This reading of regimes of exception remained valid in the first years after the transition to democracy. Indeed, four states of siege were declared between 1982 and 1999 in order to deal with massive social unrest in the form of strikes and protests against the neoliberal adjustment plans implemented during those years[12] (Alenda 2003). In this sense, regimes of exception in Bolivia at the time became synonymous with repression of those opposed to neoliberal measures (Domingo 2006, 236) and in fact as a means to introduce them (Nolte 1994, 15; Klein 2007). Indeed, in a personal interview carried out in Sucre in April 2007, a representative at the Constituent Assembly argued that the state of siege was a key mechanism for restricting workers' rights in Bolivia during the 1980s and 1990s. "From my point of view, at least, it has been used to limit the demands made by the working classes. So, until now at least, it has been used by the dominant, powerful classes."

Crucially, these declarations were made in the framework of the "Pact for Democracy" which gave rise to a degree of political stability but on the other implied the exclusion of the poorest and most marginalized sectors of the country.[13] Indeed, the main actors affected by the declarations of states of siege were miners and the important union Central Obrera Boliviana (COB). Of the four declarations of repressive regimes of exception that occurred between 1982 and 1999, DS21069 declared by Víctor Paz Estenssoro was the most shocking as in effect it was a mechanism to repress opposition toward his new economic policy that had been unilaterally declared by another, executive decree (DS20160). The strike called by the COB was referred to as "internal commotion" and thus the state of siege found a vague but constitutional justification. Nevertheless, as Molina (1987) points out, during the state of siege, the Prefectures of La Paz and Police Commands issued notices of the restriction of other freedoms other than those constitutionally established (arrest, confinement and censorship), including the freedom of assembly or to formulate petitions. In this sense, the DS21069 was also a case in point about the "imagined" powers under the regime of exception being much broader than those established formally by the constitution. Likewise, it is important to note that during these states of siege the army was put in control of internal order (Gamarra and Morón 1996).

Consequently, in the first two decades after the transition to democracy—rather than a multifaceted regime of exception—the "state of siege" had become known due to both its constitutional and historical use as a clearly—and uniquely—repressive measure, used at specific moments as a last resort by the governing elite against the massive mobilizations of the sectors excluded from the "Pact for democracy." For this reason, by the year 2000, the "state of siege" had already become a bad word, evoking traumas of the worst kind of governmental repression within the collective subconscious.[14] As an ex-police chief explained in our personal interview in Sucre in April 2007: "The experience we Bolivian citizens have is that states of siege have only served to kill more."

Finally, despite the possibility of natural disasters being understood as a cause of states of siege, as pointed out in several personal interviews in Bolivia,[15] and the presence of administrative powers within the constitutional framework, it is important to note that, in the first twenty years after Bolivia's transition to democracy, states of siege were not declared within the disaster or the administrative paradigm. Again, I have found several supreme decrees referring to emergencies related to natural disasters[16] or emergency administrative programs,[17] but these appear to be an extralegal expression of emergency politics with no clear reference to formal regimes of exception as they are understood in this volume.

EMERGENCY POLITICS IN BOLIVIA 2000–2010

As outlined at the start of this chapter, the intensive, original empirical research that forms the real contribution of this chapter on Bolivia is the collection of information relating to the declarations of regimes of exception by Presidents in the first decade of the twenty-first century. Indeed, fieldwork was carried out by the author in Bolivia in 2007 to perform in-depth interviews with key informants, consult the databases of the official State Bulletin, and collect secondary information including reports and newspaper articles from two national dailies, *El Diario* and *El Deber*. Further fieldwork was carried out in 2012 in line with the information gathered during the analysis within an emergent methodological approach.

The main aim of the study is to understand how regimes of exception have been used in Bolivia in recent years and chart any changes, continuities, or developments in that sense. A secondary aim is to understand how these uses can be understood in relation to democracy, specifically according to the conceptual prism of democratic governability, with its two pillars of legitimacy and efficiency. In the previous section, it was noted that throughout history, regimes of exception in Bolivia have been used according to a repressive paradigm throughout history, and since the transition to democracy, much more sporadically than in the case of neighboring Peru. In this section my findings suggest that this historical use of regimes of exception within the repressive paradigm has been very much circumscribed in Bolivia in recent years, in sharp contrast to the case of Peru. Rather, there is broad evidence of the use of regimes of exception according to the disaster paradigm during the period, representing a break or change in direction from the previous historical path. In the same way, a rather sporadic—and legally clumsy—use of regimes of exception according to a broadly administrative paradigm has emerged throughout the first decade of the twenty-first century, in contrast to the case of Peru, where this paradigm has been decidedly absent.

Before offering an in-depth analysis of how the repressive emergency paradigm gave way to the disaster emergency paradigm in Bolivia, it is important to highlight that our analysis of declarations issued in the *Gaceta Oficial del Estado* revealed that the use of regimes of exception in general has been considerable, although much more limited than in Peru. During the eleven-year period, only two declarations of regimes of exception were made by Presidents with direct reference to the constitutional regime of exception, with a further 63 declarations based (either explicitly or implicitly) on a regime of exception within an entirely new legal, framework that will be discussed below.[18] In contrast to Peru, these declarations very rarely established an explicit time limit and yet on very rare occasions were extended in time or space.[19] It is also interesting to observe a sharp increase in the use of regimes of exception until the end of 2005, just before Evo Morales became President.[20] Afterward, during Morales' government (2006–2010), there is a lesser tendency to use regimes of exception. This observation is of particular contextual importance given the crises of governability that came to a head the year before he came into power.

The sections below describe the different uses given to regimes of exception, as well as significant legal developments, focusing on the shift from repressive to disaster emergency politics, and the tentative emergence of an administrative paradigm.

The End of an Era? Repressive Emergency Politics

Having identified a broad use of regimes of exception within the repressive emergency politics paradigm throughout Bolivian history, and a sporadic use to deal with opposition to structural adjustment reforms in the 1980s and 1990s, in this section I analyze how regimes of exception have been used within this paradigm in the first decade of the twenty-first century. In the paragraphs below I refer to important normative and political changes in relation to this type of emergency politics, to a great extent a result of the critical juncture of the *Guerra del Agua* in 2000, which is discussed in some depth. On the face of it, the fact that two repressive states of siege were declared during this period suggests continuity with the sort of use given to the mechanism in the first years of the transition to democracy. Nevertheless, the degree of debate and criticism surrounding the use of states of siege as a mechanism of repression during this period are truly unprecedented in Bolivian history and have undoubtedly instigated important changes at both the normative and political levels. These events and discussions are highlighted throughout the following paragraphs, which begin with the important events that occurred in the year 2000.

The events leading up to the *Guerra del Agua* are well known and have been covered in other works.[21] Nevertheless, it is important to briefly recall the events that occurred between January and April 2000. Indeed, during this period a series of protests took place in the city of Cochabamba in opposition to the decision to sell the distribution of water in the city to "Aguas del Tunari," a multinational consortium. Despite various rounds of negotiations, a general strike was carried out on the 4th and 5th of April in Cochabamba, together with road-blocks by *campesinos* (peasant farmers), that affected six of the country's nine departments. This episode seemed to open a window of political opportunity as other protests occurred, including a hunger strike by police in the capital city La Paz, which extended to various activists and social leaders of the COB. In this context, by 7th April the social conflict in Bolivia was at a critical moment.

In this context, President (and ex-military dictator) Hugo Bánzer declared a "state of siege" throughout the national territory for a period of nintey days, via DS25730. Two reasons were given to justify the declaration: the impact of the events in Cochabamba on the "normal functioning of citizens' activities" in the rest of the country, and the fact that some sectors of the population had claimed to be representatives of the popular will—referring to the *Coordinadora del Agua*—which undermined the position of the authorities elected in democratic processes.

The first measure ordered by the government was the detention of 22 of the most important trade union and peasant leaders who were confined in the remote tropical city of San Joaquín. This measure was carried out on 7th April, the day before the state of siege was formally declared. In opposition to this, several violent clashes took place in Cochabamba, between the protestors and the security forces. For its part, the army tried to raise the road-blocks, causing two deaths and various injuries in Achacachí, near to La Paz. Enraged by these measures, a mass of citizens carried on rising up in strikes and protests. At the same time, the riot police were ordered to force their way into the COB in La Paz in order to detain the protestors, who were on hunger strike. However, a group of the riot police revolted and consequently the measure was totally inefficient. Clearly, the repressive measures employed under the state of siege served to create further tensions and polarize an already complicated conflict. In terms of victims, there were 5 dead and 48 injured.

Given that the conflict could not be resolved with measures of force, the government established talks with the different social actors. Although the main conflicts were channeled toward dialogue after a few days, the students carried on protesting and the armed forces continued to be present on the streets of La Paz and Cochabamba, reflecting the continuing tension. Finally, on 20th April the state of siege was lifted and all of the detained were freed with no charges. It was the shortest state of siege in Bolivia's democratic history and a process which explains the state of discredit in which the constitutional mechanism finds itself today in the country. Rather than solving a grave conflict to protect democracy the state of siege of April 2000 showed the incapacity of a government to deal with social demands and the power of citizens when making demands outside institutional channels.

An important aspect of the *Guerra del Agua* in relation to the use of the state of siege specifically were the criticisms made by important political actors, including the Congress of the Republic and—importantly—the Human Rights Ombudsman (Defensoría del Pueblo). Indeed, it is possible to speak of an element of horizontal accountability, as understood by Guillermo O'Donnell (2007) in a moment of great tension and repression.

For its part, the Bolivian Congress established an important debate on the declaration of the state of siege. As Deputy Diez Vaca of the Movimiento de la Izquierda Revolucionaria (Movement of the Revolutionary Left—MIR) noted during the debate: "I would like to salute the fact that the treatment {. . .} of a constitutional measure of exception, as is the state of siege, is carried out in this environment, in an environment of calm, reflection, analysis, criticism, before the people via Bolivian television, a truly democratic atmosphere Mr President," this is all the more important "because we cannot forget the previous state of siege {. . .} when we debated {. . .}, they turned off the lights and dissolved the Session and we could never finish our consideration of or approval of that State of siege" (Congreso de Bolivia 2000).

Likewise, the debate was an opportunity to vent opinions for and against the use of the state of siege. The analysis of a minister of CONDEPA is particularly interesting in that sense: ". . . people are livid, that is why the state of siege is not respected, before, the day after a state of siege was declared the workers' mobilizations and actions would grind to a halt but that's not happening now" (Congreso de Bolivia 2000).

Nevertheless, the most significant criticism over the use of the state of siege came from the Human Rights Ombudsman (Defensor del Pueblo), an organization of horizontal accountability that was created in 1999. On 10th April 2000, the ombudsman put forward and won a resource of habeas corpus, in the name of various citizens detained the night before the state of siege was declared. Referring to international human rights treaties such as the Inter-American Covenant of Human Rights, it was argued that the detentions of the peasant leaders on 7th April were illegal because it was the eve of the declaration and publication of the state of siege and consequently the measures were not yet in force.

Furthermore, the peasant leaders were taken to the Department of Pando, in itself a questionable decision from a humanitarian point of view, as a key informant who "followed the events very closely" explained in a personal interview with the author: "The issue was taking them to that little town in Pando, Pando is a tropical area where the temperature rises to 40 or 42 degrees so you are taking people from La Paz where it is cold, so the journey, the difference in climate, people were affected as a result, they had skin allergies, insect bites, the sun etc. . . . surely that affects their right to health?" (Personal interview with an advisor at the Constituent Assembly in Sucre, April 2007).

In the same way, referring to the individuals detained in La Paz, Cochabamba and Patacamaya, after the state of siege was officially declared, the Ombudsman pointed out that there was no order of arrest from a legitimate authority and they were not brought before a judge. Consequently, as the basic requisites were not met in both cases, the Defensoría del Pueblo claimed that the detentions were illegal (Recurso de Hábeas Corpus, 10th April 2010).

The resource was upheld, a decision that was ratified by the Constitutional Tribunal in its sentence 439/2000. According to the sentence: "the authorities have acted with an excess of power and abuse of authority, attacking the rights and guarantees that the Constitution consecrates even in cases of states of exception." It was the first time in the democratic history of Bolivia that a tribunal had established damages for illegal actions carried out during a state of siege. According to the ombudsman's report before congress in 2001, it constitutes a "historic moment in the country's constitutional life" given that, since then, "this exceptional measure is no longer synonymous with dictatorship or human rights violations, but rather it has limits and constitutional rules. . . ." (Defensoría del Pueblo 2001, 180).

The state of siege declared in 2000 in the context of the social conflict known as the "Guerra del Agua" undoubtedly marked a qualitative change in the use of states of siege in Bolivia as a mechanism of repressive emergency politics. In this sense, the presence of the ombudsman can be understood as a crucial mechanism of horizontal accountability. Ana María Romero, the first Defensora del Pueblo in Bolivia, cites a conversation with President Hugo Banzer in which she explained to him that a state of siege could not be managed in that way: "He responded, very annoyed, that all of his predecessors had acted in the same way. I explained serenely that at that time there was no Defensor del Pueblo but now there was" (Romero 2006, 127). The words of a former police chief echo the idea of the episode of the *Guerra del Agua* marking an end of an era: "It became clear then that people didn't want any more harsh measures, tough measures that go against the enjoyment of individual rights, they wanted more peace, more tranquility and the Guerra del Agua has shown that the Bolivian population is not in favor of harsh ways of governing, dictatorial ways of governing, particularly with Bánzer" (Personal interview in Sucre, April 2007).

Not only did the critical juncture of 2000 represent a change in terms of the way in which a state of siege was managed, normed, and understood, it also made it very difficult for other presidents to use the mechanism. Indeed, in the aftermath of 2000, it was deemed pretty much impossible that another President would declare this mechanism to repress a protest or a strike. For their part, all of the experts interviewed in Laz Paz and Sucre in 2007 stated that it was very unlikely for a President to declare a state of siege. Below I offer some interpretations on the reasons behind this and the consequences for Presidents faced with episodes of mass mobilization in the following years.

The first reason why, in the aftermath of the critical juncture of 2000, it seemed impossible for a President to declare another state of siege is due to an intense politicization of the mechanism itself. Its link with the authoritarian governments of the twentieth century became accentuated and there appears to be a general rejection of it within a democratic framework. Furthermore, due to the live television debate in congress in 2000, the public became acutely aware of the state of siege, which meant that citizens became much more critical of it.[22] This politicization produced a kind of collective aversion to "states of siege," the name and everything that it entailed. Consequently, any government would have to think twice before declaring it. This concern over its past use and possible use in the future is reflected in the country's newspapers in the first years of the decade.[23] As a representative of an important national human rights NGO commented in our personal interview in La Paz in 2007: "This government would commit suicide if it declared a state of siege. As I say, it is a bad word."

The second reason does not exclude the former but is more related to the correlation of forces in the country that became apparent as a result of the critical juncture described above.[24] According to this vision, the *Guerra del Agua* in April 2000 was the first moment that the pacted model of democracy had been seriously undermined by the popular movement led by Evo Morales. Before, it had been possible for governments to inhibit less powerful actors, has had been the case with the states of siege declared in the 1980s.[25] However, in the context of the *Guerra del Agua*, the result was not the overthrowing of the popular movement but rather a series of criticisms of the government and the model of democracy itself, given that people remained on the streets in protest. As a representative of the Defensoría del Pueblo explained in our personal interview in Sucre, Bolivia, in April 2007: "It is not so easy to dictate a state of siege when the social movements are protagonists and contestatory and mobilize over any problem or irregularity."[26]

In any case, this generalized rejection of the state of siege as a mechanism of democratic politics undoubtedly served as a factor that restricted its use. On several occasions in 2003 and 2004 newspaper articles expressed fear that a state of siege would be declared to deal with the intense social conflict that characterized those years, externalizing what could be equated to an expression of collective paranoia.[27] Consequently, Presidents avoided declaring states of siege and generally looked for dialogue. Nevertheless, on three occasions Presidents dealing with episodes of intense conflict resorted to a figure of "emergency" loosely written into the Law of the Armed Forces or the Law 2140 (which will be described more fully in the following section), in order to avoid the much-maligned constitutional mechanism but nevertheless put a forceful end to protest and conflict.[28]

For instance, when the *Guerra del Gas* broke out in October 2003, President Sánchez de Lozada hesitated in using a state of siege[29] and declared an "emergency" with DS27209. In this case, the emergency situation is framed as the transport and supply of gas, which has been interrupted by massive protests. The deployment of the armed forces to deal with the situation raised serious concerns among human rights organizations. As an advisor at the Constituent Assembly explained in a personal interview in Sucre in April 2007, "The question we were asking in October (2003) was: under what juridical figure the military were sent out on to the streets? The military are not meant to maintain public order, that's what the police are for, but if you use the state of siege there are other possibilities."

In fact, the decree of "emergency" was made with reference to Law 1405 of 1992 on the Armed Forces, and the deployment of the military on the streets of el Alto led to the massacre of 65 civilians. Tragically, this figure is much higher than the outcome of the infamous state of siege declared in 2000, during which time five people were killed (Assies 2003, 14), and therefore could be considered a much worse outcome in terms of the cost to human lives. As well as the stigma surrounding the state of siege at the time, there was a general idea among key informants that the political moment within the conflict had gone beyond the limits of this mechanism. For a representative of the Defensoría del Pueblo interviewed by the author in Sucre, April 2007: "In this conflict everything came together at once . . . (the government) had already committed political errors and they were going to pay a very high price . . . this provoked a series of strikes, the population was protesting peacefully, the military were up in arms, so it was very difficult for them to declare a state of siege." Likewise, an adviser at the Constituent Assembly noted: "I believe that the state of siege has a moment. If the government lets the social convulsion go beyond what is controllable it creates another problem because at that time, with people in the streets, massive hunger strikes, who are you going to detain with the state of siege? I think it has a contextual moment" (Personal interview with the author, Sucre, April, 2007).

It is worth pointing out that almost immediately after the declaration of DS27209, President Sánchez de Lozada made his historical exit from the country by helicopter (Salman 2007, 121) and consequently it also had disastrous results for his government. This episode—together with the *Guerra del Agua*—represents a real rupture of Bolivia's pacted model of democracy (Domingo 2006) and galvanized the social movements that would take Evo Morales' MAS party to power.

For his part, President Carlos Mesa decreed DS28120 in May 2005, again putting the military in charge of internal order after months of protests and roadblocks demanding a new hydrocarbons law.[30] In this case referring to the regulations of Law 2140 (which is described in some depth in the following section), an "emergency" is again declared in order to protect the transport and supply of petrol. In this case, the army is deployed to oversee the safe travel of the fuel through the country, protecting border areas and decommissioning petrol that had been unlawfully gained. To a certain extent presented as an administrative type emergency, it is best understood as a declaration of a regime of exception within the repressive paradigm, given the context of massive protests and the deployment of the military, as was the case with DS27209 declared in the case of the *Guerra del Gas*. This declaration was rather uncharacteristic of his administration, which—despite serious protests—looked for dialogue, as a former police chief explained in a personal interview in Sucre, in April 2007, "he didn't dictate a state of siege because he was between a rock and hard place so he preferred to leave things as they were, let the social convulsion progress." Not long after the declaration of "emergency," President Mesa would submit his definitive resignation.

For his part, when Evo Morales came to power in 2006, he consolidated the rupture of the pacted (and exclusive) model of democracy that had operated since the transition. Having experienced first hand, the disastrous state of siege of April 2000, Morales had publicly and famously declared that he would never declare one as President.[31] In an interesting move in June 2006, President Morales issued DS28736, by which the process of agrarian reform was declared a "national emergency." The decree refers to a lack of mechanisms to implement the planned reform (which had been drawn up ten years previously), leading to conflict and tensions in rural areas and which (according to the decree) endangered people's lives. Crucially, the first measure contemplated in the decree is implementing the reform and hence there is clearly an administrative aspect to this particular declaration of emergency. Furthermore, social organizations are called upon to help with the process. Nevertheless, the use of coercive measures with the help of the "public force" (i.e. the police and armed forces) in the face of social conflict places the decree firmly within the repressive emergency politics paradigm. Interestingly, the declaration is made with a discourse of risk management, repeatedly referring to "threats," "risks'" and "proportionality." However, behind this discourse there lurks a mechanism of repressive emergency politics that in previous years might well have been expressed via a "state of siege."

For an ex-police chief, these emergency decrees correspond to a real fear over using the state of siege as a mechanism of repressive emergency politics: "I don't think for the moment a government will try another one (state of siege) because in the collective imagination, the collective subconscious the idea that it is to kill still lingers."[32] In all three cases, the decrees are used to protect important economic sectors or processes from social conflict, including the transport of gas (in 2003 and 2005) and an agrarian reform (in 2006). Furthermore, the decrees essentially cloak the repressive measures as an expression of "fast-track" administrative intervention, which must be supported by the use of coercion, particularly by the army. My reading of these decrees is that they are rather awkward expressions of emergency politics, avoiding the constitutional mechanism without finding a suitable normative framework.

Despite all the criticisms surrounding and degradation of the state of siege mechanism, these declarations of "emergency" were rejected by the key informants interviewed during fieldwork in Bolivia, according to the following logic: "On some occasions it is worth referring to an exceptional legal measure rather than putting the military onto the street and causing a confrontation because ultimately, the state of siege—beyond formal issues and questions—is an exceptional measure acknowledged in the State's political constitution . . . it is better to use a legal measure than acting outside the law" (Personal interview with an advisor at the Constituent Assembly, Sucre, April 2007).

Despite his public declarations not to do so and the paralegal declaration of emergency in 2006, President Evo Morales returned to the constitutional mechanism of emergency politics and declared a state of siege in 2008. Throughout that year, there had been episodes of severe tension over the impending referendum on the new constitution—culminating in a series of protests in Sucre, where the draft constitution had been drawn up—as well as actions by political figures from the region of the *Media Luna*.[33] The situation came to an apparent head in the town of El Porvenir, in the Department of Pando, where in September 2008 violent clashes between opponents and supporters of Evo Morales led to the deaths of several peasant farmers and further protests in the area. At that time, President Morales was in talks with the Prefect of Tarija, Mario Cossío, on how to move the political stalemate forward. In a rather surprising move, he declared a state of siege via DS29705. Seemingly aware that the measure would be highly controversial, Morales was keen to justify the use of the measure to the press, reminding them that he was still against the use of states of siege but in this case it was "A state of siege to defend life."[34]

The decree itself, issued on 12th September, emphasizes the need to protect lives and order, referring to the violence stirred up by "racist and criminal groups" who—according to the decree—killed people, damaged State buildings, interrupted internal order, and, thus, created an "internal commotion." Furthermore, as "the public is already aware," the situation has got out of the police's hands and in order to protect life and the country's economic interests, a state of siege is declared throughout the Department of Pando. Importantly, the decree establishes precise measures which are to be taken, including: the prohibition of carrying firearms, the prohibition of organizing political meetings and protests, a partial curfew, arrest of those who are involved in acts against public order or security, and the deployment of the military. The fact that the specific measures to be taken are described in a list undoubtedly goes a long way to making the measure more transparent, rather than an invitation to a free reign for the executive and/or the army.

Despite the application of the state of siege, there were still a few isolated protests but the violence certainly subsided. In any case, the measure was in place for two and half months and, understandably, subject to much criticism and debate.[35] Those who opposed MAS and the constitution saw it is a despotic measure and criticized, particularly, the deployment of the army in an isolated area of the Amazon and the detention of citizens, including the Prefect of Pando (and key opponent of Morales) Leopoldo Fernández. On the contrary, those who supported MAS saw it as a clearly justifiable measure to deal with extreme acts of violence and which had been used with restraint. Indeed, according to some analysts the episode served to consolidate Morales' power.[36] When the measure was lifted—prior to the referendum on the constitution—there was great jubilation in Pando with people flocking to the main square to celebrate, although the army did not immediately leave. A commission from Unasur was sent to investigate the acts of El Porvenir and the state of siege itself, which certainly represents a move toward greater accountability/transparency although many questioned the neutrality of the report.[37]

In this sense, an extract from a personal interview with an ex-police chief back in 2007 becomes rather prophetic, when he commented on the need for a future government "to issue a State of Siege as it should be, restricting certain rights, for instance the right to free transit, managing it in a much more democratic way, without violence, without deaths then people would understand that it a State of Siege is there for other reasons not just killing. That is what a government should do" (Personal interview, Sucre, April 2007).

While the state of siege declared in 2008 showed considerable respect for constitutional limitations, it is likely to be Bolivia's last. Indeed, with the new Constitution of 2009 a different regime of exception has been created and—significantly—with a new name, the "estado de excepción" (state of exception), doing away with the "bad word" of the state of siege. While those interviewed in Laz Paz and Sucre in 2007 noted that there was little debate over the mechanism in the Constituent Assembly, interestingly the Permanent Secretary of the Supreme Council of Defense (Consejo Supremo de Defensa) declared that one of his priorities was for no regime of exception to be included in the new charter, reflecting the degree to which the mechanism had been tainted.[38]

Nevertheless, although it explicitly established natural disaster as a possible cause of a state of exception, the mechanism designed in Articles 137–140 of Bolivia's new constitution remains firmly within the repressive emergency politics paradigm, referring again to external and internal threats as well as "internal commotion" and the suspension of civil rights. Crucially, the declaration of a state of exception now depends on the *prior* approval of the Plurinational Legislative Assembly. It is also up to this body to decide the measures to be taken. In this way, Bolivia's constitutional regime of exception is no longer the exclusive instrument of the Executive, as the Congress now also has an important role to play.

Furthermore, there is clarity over restrictions on the limitations of human rights: "in no case can the guarantees of rights, nor fundamental rights, nor the right to due process, the right to information, and the rights of those persons deprived of their liberty be suspended" (Article 137). The issue of due process and the protection of rights remind us of the disastrous management of the "state of siege" declared in April 2000. Likewise, there is no explicit reference to deploying the Armed Forces, which—without explicitly prohibiting it—represents a shift in terms of the historic prerogative under states of siege. In any case, between 2009 and 2010 no states of exception were declared in Bolivia.

To sum up my analysis of regimes of exception within the repressive paradigm in Bolivia, suffice it to reiterate the significant changes that have occurred throughout the decade under study. Indeed between 2000 and 2008 particularly, Bolivia's state of siege mechanism became highly politicized, debated, criticized, and feared in a way that in Peru, for instance, it has simply not occurred. Consequently, this type of political culture in its broadest sense creates a mechanism of social control or accountability that has served to inhibit the use of repressive regimes of exception. Interestingly, during this period various social movements declared themselves in states of siege or exception, in a clear attempt to subvert the language of constitutional dictatorship,[39] according to the logic of infrapolitics (Scott 2003). In the same way, there appears to have been a search for a new institutional framework in order to express repressive emergency politics. The state of exception of the constitution of 2009 offers a new normative framework for repressive emergency politics in Bolivia, that constitutes a clear departure from the state of siege mechanism that had survived constitutional change largely intact since 1878, and is a clear step forward in terms of the compatibility of regimes of exception with democratic governability.

A New, Dominant Paradigm: Disaster Emergency Politics

In order to chart the shift from repressive to disaster emergency politics in Bolivia, it is important to describe Law 2140, which was promulgated on

25th October 2000 by General Hugo Bánzer Suárez and created an entirely different normative framework for and conceptualization of regimes of exception.[40] In the past there had been clear attempts to find some sort of legality or institutionality to deal with natural disasters, something that the historic "state of siege" did not really deal with, despite disasters being considered a possible cause for its declaration. It is clear that Law 2140 offers a new, relevant normative framework very much within the risk management model.

Revising the text of the law, several key elements appear from the start: first, the idea of preventing risks; second, that risks are seen as both social and economic; and, third, that the threats are widened so as to include risks brought about by natural, technological, and/or human causes. Indeed, in this first clause the main objective of the norm is stated: "To regulate all activities in the ambit of the reduction of risks and attention to disasters and/or emergencies and to establish an appropriate and efficient institutional framework faced with disasters/and or emergencies, to attend to events caused by natural, technological and man-made threats in an opportune and effective manner" (Law 2140 of 25th October 2001, Article 1).

Interestingly, certain principles are invoked, including collective interests and obligations; the right to the protection of physical integrity, productive infrastructure, goods, and the environment; the responsibility of both public and private institutions as well as individuals; planning and both public and private investments for sustainable development; and, the principle of decentralized management, wherein the municipal governments are given primary responsibility of intervening in the case of disaster or emergency.

Consequently, the idea of the exception has become much more diverse than the previously dominant repressive paradigm that had been dominant in Bolivia. Indeed, an exceptional event is seen as being a risk for the country's economic or social stability and can be caused by nature, technology, or human beings. There are two emergency situations that can be declared by the President in the framework of this law, "disaster" or "emergency": the former being "a situation of serious harm or alteration of the normal living conditions in a determined territory caused by natural, technological or man-made phenomena and which can cause losses of human life, or material, economic, or environmental losses, and which need special attention by State organisms as well as other entities that are humanitarian or social in nature, either public or private in nature" (Article 4f); and the latter "a situation that is created before the real or imminent presence of a phenomenon that puts in danger the normality of life in a specific territory" (Article 4h). Consequently, the concept of the exceptional threat proposed by this law is more relative than absolute, given that it is a question of the government's capacity to respond rather than the intrinsic nature of the event itself.

The measures established in the law are very broad, including first aid, administrative intervention, and even the use of force, without explicitly permitting the restriction of human rights. What is of interest for our study is that fact that Law 2140 establishes that "a regime of exception established in the relevant legislation will enter into force" (Article 27). Importantly, there is no specific mention of what this regime of exception involves in practice but DS26739—the regulations on the reduction of risks and attention to disasters and/or emergencies—clearly states that the regime of exception in question is established in the Normas Básicas del Sistema de Administración para Bienes y Servicios (DS25964, Article 61, paragraph e) and the Norma Básica para Inversión Pública (Resolución Suprema 216768, Article 30). In both norms, the regime of exception implies an exemption from ordinary public contracting processes. Furthermore, in the case of Emergency, a risk reduction plan is referred to (Article 40, incision 1) and in the case of Disaster a response plan (Article 50, incision 1).[41]

Law Nº 2140—in Article 6—also creates an emergency organism, the Sistema Nacional para la Reducción de Riesgos y Atención de Desastres y/o Emergencias (National System for the Reduction of Risks and the Relief of Disasters and/or Emergencies—SISRADE). The SISRADE is made up of civil society institutions and organizations at the national, departmental, and municipal levels and is headed by El Consejo Nacional para la Reducción de Riesgos y Atención de Desastres and/or Emergencias (National Council for the Reduction of Risks and Attention to Disasters and/or Emergencies) CONARADE. For its part, the CONARADE is headed by the President of the Republic and made up of the Ministry of National Defense, the Ministry of Finance, Ministry of the Presidency, Ministry of Sustainable Development and Planning, and the Ministry of Government. Importantly, CONARADE is established as the key body for dealing with disasters and emergencies.[42] Undoubtedly, the exceptional measures offered in Law 2140 offer a great deal of discretion to this organism. Indeed, once the disaster or emergency situation has been declared (Article 23), CONARADE will point out the measures to be taken, "in relation to the expropriation, occupation and demolition, imposition of tasks and solution of conflicts, incentives and other actions of rehabilitation and reconstruction," a very broad group of competences, from the use of force to administrative powers.

Undoubtedly, the regimes of exception contemplated in Law 2140 have offered a new normative framework for and impulse to a dominant disaster emergency politics paradigm, giving rise to a total of 50 declarations of emergency or disaster[43] issued between 2000 and 2010, and a handful of declarations of emergency or disaster using the nomenclature of the law without specifically referring to it. For the representative of the Vice-Ministry of Security interviewed in La Paz in 2012, the regime of exception contemplated in Law 2140 has always been used to deal with natural disasters and his evaluation of the mechanism is highly favorable.[44] Although our research suggests that the law has been the basis for the declaration of other types of regime of exception (including several cases of administrative emergency politics, discussed in the following section) there is clearly a particularly strong link between this law and disaster emergency politics.

Many exceptional situations are referred to in the declarations, all of which include reference to what could be considered an adverse natural phenomenon, including heavy rains, droughts, the effects of climate change, water shortages, and epidemics, including influenza and dengue. In all cases, these situations are presented as having a negative impact on the population, whom the government has a responsibility to protect. Nevertheless, in the majority of cases there is also a reference to administrative problems in sectors or services that have arisen as a result of the adverse natural phenomenon, including the interruption in the activities of public services or economic activities or low production levels in the agriculture sector. Consequently, while all of the declarations have a focus on protecting people from the negative impacts of adverse natural phenomena, many also focus on protecting the economy from it, something that will be returned to a little later on.

In terms of the exceptional measures included in the declarations, it is equally important to note that they follow a generally elliptical pattern that makes them rather difficult to analyze. Indeed, in many decrees, we simply read: "According to what is established in Articles 26 and 27 of Law 2140, it is permitted to take the actions established in that Law and Supreme Decree Nº 26739 of the 4th of August 2002, General Regulations of the Reduction of Risks and Attention of Disasters and/or Emergencies" (DS26810 of 2002). I have already established that in the legal framework of Law 2140, the following measures are included: expropriations,[45] a technical response plan, conflict resolution, and the exoneration from ordinary public contract bidding processes. Consequently, it is clear that all of these measures can be used, according to CONARADE's analysis of the situation. According to an expert on Bolivian constitutional law,[46] the key measure is permitting the exoneration from public contracting procedures and the use of technical contingency plans. For the Coordinator of the Vice-Ministry of Citizen Security, in contrast, the most important aspect is a reply in the framework of specialized units: "The key change in the past decade is that via Law 2140 units of risk management are created, in ministries, public entities, private organizations, municipalities, governments. How has this helped? By offering a reply to the emergency via these units at the national, departmental, or municipal level . . . before, during, and after the emergency" (Personal interview with Ana Soliz Landivar, carried out in La Paz, January 2012).

In the same interview, the representative of the Vice-Ministry of Civil Defence explains that—in the framework of the law 2140—improvements have been made regarding transparency: "Civil Defense must account for these resources to CONARADE and SISRADE, which in turn do so to the President, so everything is managed with transparency . . . if there is an act of corruption there is a whole process. . . .” He noted that in the past there were actions of corruption but claims that this is now under greater control: “This happened many times before: resources were given and there was no accountability so people who should not have been benefitted were benefitted but with Law 2140 this is being stopped.”

It is difficult to ascertain in practice how transparently resources are used and contracts are adjudicated, given that the whole process occurs within the risk management system and executive branch. Nevertheless, the awareness of and regulations surrounding this issue suggest an awareness of and concern over transparency that is a considerable step forward.

Given my interest in understanding how extraordinary situations and extraordinary measures fit together, at this stage it is worth observing some declarations of regimes of exception within the disaster paradigm are orientated toward helping citizens in danger or need; while others are orientated toward offering first aid to rehabilitate sectors or services. Typical cases of the first type involve: first aid for people who have seen their homes and health affected by forest fires (DS26326 of 2001), technical intervention to mitigate the devastating effects of landslides on communities (DS27844 of 2004), and help for people affected by floods caused by intense rains due to climate change (DS29425 of 2008). In terms of the latter type, representative cases include the reconstruction of central sections of highway damaged by rain (DS 28430 of 2005), and extra resources and technical help offered to farmers to deal with the negative effects of drought (DS29770 of 2008).

It is also important to note that the use of coercion has—sporadically—been contemplated in declarations of emergency or disaster within the disaster paradigm. The Coordinator of the Vice-Ministry of Citizen Security declared that force had not been used in the framework of the Law 2140.[47] However, according to our analysis, in six decrees[48]—the majority of which were issued by President Evo Morales—the use of force is employed in order to deal with the natural disaster situation. On one hand, there are decrees which call upon the Armed Forces to carry out the technical and administrative measures necessary to overcome the emergencies caused—typically—in the country’s road system (DS27301 of 2003) and agricultural sector (DS29021 of 2007). On the other hand, there are declarations in which force is used to avoid the spreading of an epidemic, as was the case in 2009 with the declaration of DS0104, allowing the Armed Forces took over control of border crossings and took those affected to health centers. As well as concerns over transparency with exemptions from normal procedures for public bidding for contracts, the (sporadic) use of the armed forces in relation to natural disasters raises potential concerns over the protection of human rights as well as military intervention in civilian politics.

Finally, it is important to note that despite the considerable number of declarations of regimes of exception within the disaster emergency politics paradigm in the case of Bolivia—and the political importance of Law 2140—there does not seem to have been an important political or academic discussion about these measures. When revising national press, debates in congress, and personal interviews with experts on the issue, there seems to be little knowledge or awareness of this type of regime of exception. Indeed, the fact that they are largely technical events, administrated and employed at the subnational level may have something to do with this. However, it must be acknowledged that all of the decrees imply some sort of administrative measure, in many cases exoneration from ordinary contracting or budgeting procedures. This presents a new challenge to democratic governability given that it offers lesser transparency with regard to public resources and contracts and great power to CONARADE. Likewise, several decrees have facilitated the deployment of the Armed Forces, a measure that—I suggest—should be subject to debate due to its implications for civilian control over the military.

Creativity in the Face of Conflict: Administrative Emergency Politics

In the first section of this chapter, I pointed out that there had been no clear normative basis for or historical tradition of declaring regimes of exception in Bolivia within the administrative paradigm. The "state of siege" established in the 1967 Constitution did indeed contemplate various administrative type measures, although they were established within a more repressive paradigm. For its part, Law 2140 of 2000 also facilitates various administrative type measures, although in this case they were mainly established and used within a disaster paradigm. Nevertheless, in the decade under study I also discovered ten declarations of broadly administrative type regimes of exception, in the form of "emergencies" and with explicit or implicit reference to the Law 2140. Interestingly, they appear to cross-over with (and to a certain extent subvert) the repressive paradigm, in the sense that they are mainly used with the justification of dealing with social conflict (as indeed established in Law 2140). All the same, in essence they address what are considered to be exceptional administrative situations by employing exceptional administrative measures, particularly direct purchases and contracting processes.

First of all, several regimes of exception were declared within the administrative paradigm to repair the structural damage created by violent protests. Interestingly, two of the episodes in question relate to cases of repressive emergency politics referred to above. For instance, DS27233 was issued in

2003 to deal with damage to buildings after protests in the cities of La Paz and El Alto after the *Guerra del Gas*. As a result of this decree, an emergency is declared for ninety days, during which time, money is transferred to cover the costs of rebuilding, original documents can be replaced with photocopies, and any outstanding administrative procedures can be extended. In a similar way, in 2008 President Morales issued DS29837 in the aftermath of the "state of siege" declared in Pando (see DS29705). The decree refers to the government report that discovered material damage to roads and routes and an emergency plan to reconstruct the damage caused. Consequently, the specific exceptional measure offered by the declaration of this administrative type regime of exception is direct purchasing and contracting, in line with Law 2140. Several other decrees of this type were found, including DS29678 declared in 2003 to deal with the damage to buildings and loss of public information that was caused by the protests of 12th and 13th February of the same year; DS28986 of 2006 to repair damage to buildings after clashes between citizens in various town in the Department of Santa Cruz; and DS29025 to deal an interruption in mining activities after clashes between miners in the Department of Oruro.

On the other hand, in some cases the justification of the declaration of a regime of exception within the administrative paradigm is to prevent a social conflict occurring through the use of social aid and employment programs. For instance, in 2001 DS26317 declared an emergency in order to facilitate the elaboration of a national emergency plan to deal with unemployment; in 2001 DS26406 declared an emergency to implement plans to regenerate the mining sector in Potosí and Ururo and thus create new jobs; and DS27332 was issued in 2004 declaring an emergency in "lower-income areas," calling upon the Red de Protección Social to implement a plan to create jobs, permitting the use of special resources and direct purchases. What is interesting about these decrees is that they appear to give way to legislative-type emergency powers, in the form of vague instructions to create plans or policy.

Consequently, while these declarations of regimes of exception or "emergency" are essentially administrative, that fact that their justification is to prevent social conflict or to "clear up the mess," points toward the historical idea of internal commotion and turns the way in which conflict or violence is dealt with on its head. Indeed, although the decrees refer (either explicitly or implicitly) to Law 2140, there is a sense that they constitute a rather innovative and largely isolated attempt to deal with social conflict, again avoiding the traditional repressive mechanism of the "state of siege." It is also important to note that the bulk of these decrees were issued in 2003. Importantly, this year was the peak of the crisis of the "pacted" form of democracy, with a confluence of social conflicts[49] based on ethnic, class, and regional divisions.[50]

According to several analysts, the slowness of replies on the part of the government appeared to create further tension, frustration, and disappointment at the functioning of democracy.[51] Therefore, it is important to interpret this sudden creativity with regard to regimes of exception as a mechanism to deal with a very difficult social context and political pressures in a "fast-track" way.

Although none of these declarations of administrative regimes of exception were commented upon in the media, it seems as if at times the national media supported administrative and economic powers for the executive in order to regenerate economic sectors and avoid future conflict. Indeed, several opinion articles published in 2003 and 2004 called for this type of powers,[52] although the Constitution of 1967 expressly forbids it. For instance, one columnist states that is necessary to make radical changes and reforms, proposing "a regime or state of exception and national emergency and a cabinet of national salvation integrated by independent, honest and non-ambitious citizens, designated via competition of social organizations."[53] Other articles imagine rather an economic-type state of exception in order to face this sort of crisis.[54] In any case, this public call for an administrative type of regime of exception again speaks of the crisis of "ordinary politics" in the Bolivian political system between 2000 and 2005 and a search for a new institutionality that is not found either in the constitution or the Law 2140.

KEY FINDINGS AND ANALYSIS

Several years ago now, upon trying to schedule an in-depth interview with a former Bolivian president, I explained that the topic of my research was the use of regimes of exception in Bolivia. The prompt reply was that his agenda was full but in any case that regimes of exception "are a great topic for a *historical* study." The idea that regimes of exception, synonymous with the state of siege, belong to a rather painful past is widespread and pervades the collective imagination in Bolivia. Nevertheless, the study carried out here has showed that these mechanisms continue to be relevant up until the present day although—crucially—are no longer synonymous with repression but rather with managing natural disasters within the framework of risk management.

In contrast with Peru, in Bolivia there have been profound transformations within the legal framework during this decade. In 2000, Law 2140 was drawn up, orientating emergency politics toward the risk management model and bringing regimes of exception largely within the disaster emergency politics paradigm with the two figures of "disaster" and "emergency". Later on, in 2009, a new constitution did away with the "state of siege," creating the "state of exception," maintaining its primarily repressive nature but explicitly considering natural disasters as an exceptional situation and letting Congress decide on which measures—including the suspension of rights—could be employed. This elimination of the "state of siege" with all of the negative connotations it involved can be evaluated as a massive step forward for Bolivian democracy and seems to address the concerns of Molina back in the 1980s: "Conserving this institution in our constitution, in the political practice of our people, has meant and continues to mean turning the Executive Power into a Constitutional Dictatorship, with the functioning of the Legislative Power reduced to impotence and the complete paralysis of the Judiciary" (Molina 1987, 181).

While Law 2140 has provided the basis for the vast majority of declarations of regimes of exception during the decade in question, it is important to note that no declarations of "states of exception" based on the 2009 constitution were issued during the decade. In any case, a total of 65 declarations of regimes of exception based (explicitly or implicitly) on constitutional and legal norms were made by Bolivian Presidents between 2000 and 2010, a much lower number than in neighboring Peru. Likewise, the case of Bolivia is in clear contrast to that of Peru, given that repressive emergency politics has been of very little relevance in comparative terms and the disaster paradigm has been clearly dominant, in a new framework of "risk management." Finally, a nascent administrative paradigm has also emerged, although it has struggled to find an adequate legal framework.

From the perspective of democratic governability and in relation to repressive emergency politics, while the use of the "state of siege" in April 2000 was undoubtedly rather disastrous in terms of *legitimacy* and *efficiency*, the legal intervention of the Defensoría del Pueblo (Human Rights Ombudsman) and open, public criticism offered a possibility of social control of the mechanism. While the state of siege declared in Pando in 2008 was clearly polemical and divided public opinion, it was a much more tempered use of this type of power. This evident desire to control the use of repressive regimes of exception is clear in the "state of exception" mechanism included in the 2009 Constitution which gives a very important role to the Congress and is clear about which rights must always be protected, in the light of the mistakes made in April 2000. This limited use, public oversight, and normative developments are undoubtedly good news for the compatibility of regimes of exception with democratic governability in Bolivia.

Despite these improvements, it is also important to point that the three declarations of "emergency" loosely based on Law 2140 and the Law of the Armed Forces and thinly veiled as administrative type regimes of exception throw up considerable concerns from the perspective of democratic governability. Indeed, the deployment of the Armed Forces to safeguard the petrol industry from protests and conflict on one occasion had even more disastrous consequences than the "state of siege" declared in April 2000. In what appears to be a fumble to declare a state of siege without officially declaring one, the emergency declared in the face of the *Guerra del Gas* was the mechanism put the military in control of El Alto and ultimately facilitated the massacre of dozens of people. In this sense, I would argue than rather than reaching beyond the law or to secondary laws, the constitutionally defined "state of exception" would be more adequate for this type of situation, in line with the arguments of Despouy (1999).

In relation to disaster emergency politics, specifically, Law 2140 has undoubtedly aimed to provide a normative basis for their use and this must be seen as a positive step forwards toward democratic governability bearing in mind that in the past, in practice measures were taken to deal with natural disasters via informal political practices of para legal emergency decrees. Law 2140 shows a concern for and responsibility toward risk management and a multifaceted approach to threats beyond the national security paradigm, with ideas of multilevel and effective governance. This is surely an important achievement.

In terms of the *efficiency* of emergency politics within the disaster paradigm in Bolivia, it would be necessary to offer an in-depth analysis of CONARADE and how it works in practice. Beyond the positive evaluation offered by an interviewee in La Paz in 2012 that specific, in-depth study goes beyond the scope of this volume. Nevertheless, it is important to note that the declarations are generally one-off and restricted to the sub-national level rather than repeated or indeed permanent events means that they could be considered relatively efficient. In terms of their *legitimacy*, the majority of declarations were based on adverse natural phenomena rather than truly catastrophic events and hence it would be important to ask to what degree the threat faced is *exceptional* as such and therefore subject to emergency politics. Even more importantly, the ease with which public contracting procedures are suspended and funds can be transferred is concerning from the perspective of accountability. Despite considerable attention to oversight mechanisms, they are internal to the national emergency system and no public debate on the use of these mechanisms was found during the period under study. Although the Armed Forces have been called upon to support episodes of disaster emergency politics very rarely, there is also a potential for human rights abuses and this should not be ruled out.[55]

Finally, the sporadic use of regimes of exception within the administrative paradigm is an interesting development but does not find a firm normative basis either in the Constitutions of 1967 and 2009 or in Law 2140.

The justification of dealing with social conflict is interesting given that it would appear to bring the old idea of internal commotion within the framework of risk management. However, given that the social conflict is either potential or has already passed it would be important to ask what the real exceptional threat is and whether the justification is purely discursive and a way of legitimizing what should be done via other means, in line with the tenets of securitization theory. The possibility of direct purchasing and contracting is troubling for accountability for the same reasons as discussed in the previous paragraph and the occasional nod to drawing up plans and policy is suggestive of emergency powers to legislate, something that had been expressly forbidden in Bolivian constitutionalism. Hence, the use of administrative decrees in Bolivia is troubling from the perspective of *legitimacy*. In terms of their *efficiency*, again the fact that they were one-off events and appear to have diffused certain situations of tension (particularly during the tumultuous year of 2003) would suggest that they offered an important emergency valve to Bolivian presidents. Consequently, in order to make these decrees more compatible with democratic governability, it would be interesting to bring them within a specific normative framework and establish strict oversight mechanisms.

In summary, three decades after the transition to democracy, regimes of exception have constituted a sporadic mechanism of government in Bolivia, in line with the tenets of *Republican Exceptionalism*. Likewise, the locus of concern regarding regimes of exception has moved from protection of human rights to the need for transparency and accountability on the use of public resources and offering swift replies to difficult situations, in line with use in practice. Importantly, the number of annual declarations has decreased since 2006, when President Evo Morales took up the Presidency, reflecting a distinct move away from the exception. Both developments should be seen as clear progress in the history of regimes of exception and democratic governability in the Bolivian case.

According to Molina (1987, 162), since Independence there have been two prevailing ideas relating to emergency politics in Bolivia: on the one hand, that it is impossible to regulate powers under a regime of exception, according to a more decisionist vision of politics; on the other, that it is important to regulate regimes of exception and say exactly what effects a regime of exception may have, limiting executive power. Notwithstanding several shortcomings or concerns that have been highlighted above, three decades after its transition to democracy, Bolivia has taken important steps in the latter direction. Indeed there has been a search for a new conceptualization and regulation of emergency powers at the normative level, which should be understood as the result of very public and heated debates, in other words: a *political* variable.

NOTES

1. Editorial published on 5th April in the Santa Cruz daily *El Deber*.

2. These declarations are available at Bolivia's Official Gazette, http://www.gacetaoficialdebolivia.gob.bo/. The search was carried out online and according to the nomenclatures used in the relevant normative frameworks of regimes of exception, in this case "estado de sitio," "estado de excepción," "emergencia," and "desastre." As well as collecting the declarations, other relevant information including extensions in time or into different territories was also collected.

3. These reports will be highlighted throughout the text, but two are worth mentioning here, both of which are related to episodes of social conflict: Laserna & Villarroel (2008) and Amnistía Internacional (2000). Likewise, data from the Economic Commission for Latin America and the Caribbean (http://www.cepal.org/en) are also referred to in order to support observations and findings.

4. Fieldwork was carried out by the author in La Paz and Sucre in 2007 and—with the help of Ana Soliz Landivar—additional interviews were carried out in La Paz and Santa Cruz in 2012. Those interviewed included representatives from the Defensoría del Pueblo (Human Rights Ombudsman), from a National Human Rights NGO, an ex- Police Chief, an advisor at the Constituent Assembly, a Constituent Assembly Representative, a prominent historian (in 2007), and a representative of the Citizen Security Vice-Ministry and a constitutional law expert (in 2012). The interviewees were selected according to the findings discovered throughout the study and according to the snowball technique, according to the guidelines of Valles (2009). The identity of the interviewees is not revealed here in order to protect their opinions and comments and because what is of interest is their sociopolitical function and perspective, rather than their personal identity.

5. The electronic archives of two of the main national newspapers were consulted between 2000 and 2010: *El Deber* based in Santa Cruz (www.deber.com.bo) and *El Diario* (www.eldiario.net).

6. On René Barrientos, see Mesa, Gisbert, and Gisbert (2007, 512).

7. Data from personal interview with a prominent Bolivian historian carried out in Sucre, April 2007 and personal correspondence with a constitutional lawyer, October 2011.

8. Personal interview with prominent Bolivian historian (Sucre, April 2007) and an advisor at the Constituent Assembly (Sucre, April 2007).

9. Constitution of 1967, Article 111, Paragraph 3.

10. An advisor at the Constituent Assembly (Sucre, April 2007).

11. As has been pointed out, disaster is considered a possible cause for the declaration of a state of siege and considerable administrative measures are contemplated.

12. 1985, 1986, 1990, and 1995.

13. On this issue, see Alcántara (1999), Barreda (2006), Domingo (2006), Institut Internacional de Gobernabilitat de Catalunya (2004), Mayorga (2005), Morales (1992), Pachano (2007), and Romero Ballivián (2006).

14. Interview with ex-police chief, Sucre, Bolivia, April, 2007 and the representative of human rights NGO, La Paz, Bolivia, April 2007.

15. The ex-police chief interviewed in April 2007 and the constitutional lawyer interviewed in January 2012.

16. Decrees such as DS19515 declared by President Siles Zuazo in 1983, which made it possible to buy equipment and tools necessary to resolve the drinking water problem in Potosí or DS19525 of the same year which allowed for direct acquisitions for the agricultural sector.

17. In 1983 President Siles Zuazo decreed an emergency plan to "construct 300 houses of social interest, for workers of the nationalized and privatized mining sector of the country . . ." (DS19830). Also in 1985 an Emergency Work Creating Program was created via DS20631, with the aim of dealing with problems in Bolivia's labor market. During the same year—in the framework of the neoliberal adjustment measures and during the state of siege declared by DS21060—the Emergency Social Fund was created. During the 1990s, at the same time that neoliberal reforms were being introduced without consulting the population, various social emergency measures were also introduced. For instance, in 1997 Hugo Bánzer created the "Plan de Emergencia para combatir la pobreza en la ciudad de el Alto" via DS24929. On the (lack of) efficiency of these programs see Salman, 2007.

18. Declarations of regimes of exception are understood as those decrees in which the President—referring to the relevant articles of the Constitution or legal framework—declares a "state of siege" "state of exception," "emergency," or "disaster." During this time, 2 "states of siege" were declared, 52 cases of "emergency," and 11 cases of "disaster." Importantly, in 14 of these decrees, the reference to the relevant normative framework was implicit rather than explicit but given that the same terminology is used, they are included in this figure. In this sense, we are following the precedent established by Ferreira Rubio and Goretti (1998) in their analysis of the decrees of necessity and urgency in the Argentinian case.

19. In a total of 51 cases there is no reference to how long the declaration is to last for although the relevant constitutions and legal frameworks do establish time limits.

20. Interview with member of the National Human Rights Ombudsman in Sucre, Bolivia, April 2007. For an analysis of the importance of Morales coming to power and the sociopolitical crisis of the years before 2006, see Salman (2007) and Kohl and Farthing (2009).

21. The information in this section comes from the following sources: Amnesty USA, 2000; Defensor del Pueblo, Recurso de hábeas corpus, 10th April 2000; and Congreso de Bolivia 2000. For a contextual understanding of this episode, the following works are highly recommended: Assies (2003); Assies and Salman (2003); Rodas (2006); and Romero (2006). It is also interesting to watch the film that was inspired in the protests over the privatization of water, called *También la lluvia* (2010). A reduced analysis of this episode was included in a prior publication (Wright 2013b).

22. Data from personal interview with member of human rights NGO in La Paz, April 2007 and "Octava Sesión Ordinaria de Congreso Nacional Miércoles 12 de abril 2000," the text of which is available at www.congreso.gov.bo.

23. On its use in the past see for example Floren Sanabria G. "El golpe de Todos Santos" opinion piece published in *El Diario* on the 1st of November 2004; Santiago Berríos Caballero "Falacias Parlamentarias" opinion piece published in *El Diario* on

the 16th of May 2004; Angel Torres "*El Diario* confirma su decanatura de la Prensa con la de joven centenario," opinion piece published in *El Diario* 8th May 2004. On concerns over its future use, see: Samuel Mendoza "La democracia en peligro," opinion piece published in *El Diario* 23rd January 2003; Francisco Justiniano Suárez "No logran restituir el orden" opinion piece published in *El Deber* 13th December 2003; and Juan Carlos Fernández Bowles "El estado de sitio sería un triunfo para Evo," opinion piece published in *El Deber* on the 23rd January 2001.

24. Opinion of prominent historian and an advisor at the Constituent Assembly, personal interviews carried out in Sucre, April, 2007.

25. Data from personal interview with a prominent historian, Sucre, April 2007. In a personal interview with an the ex-police chief carried out in Sucre, April 2007, a similar conclusion was reached. For contrasting analyses on the effects of the relocalization of miners via the DS21060 see Gill 1997 and Paramio 2006. On the miners' resistance see Sanabria, 2000.

26. On indigenous mobilizations between 2000 and 2005, see Albro 2006.

27. See: Samuel Mendoza "La democracia en peligro," opinion piece published in *El Diario* 23rd January 2003; Francisco Justiniano Suárez "No logran restituir el orden" opinion piece published in *El Deber* 13th October 2003; and Juan Carlos Fernández Bowles "El estado de sitio sería un triunfo para Evo" opinion piece published *El Deber* el 23rd January 2003.

28. A full analysis of the law will be offered in the section on disaster emergency politics.

29. Opinion expressed by an advisor at the Constituent Assembly in a personal interview in Sucre, April 2007.

30. On this episode, see Spronk and Webber 2007; Romero Ballivián 2006.

31. Data from interview with ex-police chief, Sucre, April, 2007.

32. Personal interview, Sucre, Bolivia, April 2007.

33. Several Departments (including Santa Cruz, Tarija, Beni and Pando) that formed a considerable opposition to Morales' project of political transformation, even proposing some form of political autonomy from the rest of Bolivia. On the importance of the Media Luna, see Assies (2006), Eaton (2007), Kohl (2010), and Humphreys Bebbington and Bebbington (2010).

34. Quoted in "Evo justifica intervención militar e insiste en su CPE," article published in *El Deber* 14th September 2008.

35. For instance, "Acciones de defensa y Estados de Excepción," editorial published in *El Diario* 27th December 2008; "Referendum con estado de sitio en Pando?" Editorial published in *El Deber* 24th November 2008; "Pando despues del Estado de Sitio," editorial published in *el Deber* 24th November 2008.

36. See Kohl and Bresnahan (2010, 7).

37. "Pando despues del Estado de Sitio," editorial published in *el Deber* 24th November 2008.

38. Information from personal interview with ex-police chief carried out in Sucre, April 2007.

39. References of this type were found in a series of articles throughout the decade including Armando Aquino Huerta "El Referéndum y sus preguntas" opinion piece

published in *El Diario* 3rd May 2004; Paulovich "En estado de emergencia" opinion piece published in *el Deber* 5th October 2005; "Seguridad Jurídica" 25th May 2006; Francisco Justiniano Suárez "Bebiendo de su propia medicina" opinion piece published in *el Deber* 23rd August 2006; "Bloqueando la democracia," opinion piece published in *el Deber* 5th April 2008.

40. This law is analyzed in some depth in two other studies: Wright and Soliz Landivar, 2013a and Wright and Soliz Landivar, 2013b.

41. In the regulations there is emphasis on the different levels at which the declaration of emergency can be declared: national, departmental, or municipal, the difference being who is responsible for the measures: the Minister of Development, Prefect, or Mayor, respectively.

42. It is important to point out that CONARADE is not the first organism created in Bolivia with the aim of dealing with natural disasters. For instance, via DS08274 of 1968 President René Barrientos created the "Comité Permanente de Emergencia Nacional con el objeto de prestar auxilio y ayuda inmediata a las poblaciones del país que en cualquier tiempo pudieran sufrir calamidades públicas, inundaciones y otro género de siniestros." In fact, in the past the typical reaction faced with natural disasters seemed to go through the creation of a specialized committee for each case, such as DS08669 of 1969. Later on, in 1974 General Hugo Bánzer issued DS11362 to create the Comités Permanentes de Emergencia Nacional in the capitals of Bolivia's 9 departments. Even in 1983, Siles Zuazo created the "Comité Ejecutivo del Plan Agrario de Emergencia" via DS19528.

43. It is worth noting that more cases of emergency (which entails imminent danger) than disaster (which entails a real crisis situation) were declared during this period.

44. Data from personal interview with Ana Solíz Landívar in La Paz, January 2012.

45. In a personal interview carried out by Ana Soliz Landivar in La Paz in January 2012, the representative of the Vice-Ministry of Citizen Security stated that expropriations may help to prevent catastrophes such as landslides.

46. Personal correspondence, November (2011).

47. Data from personal interviews carried out by Ana Soliz Landivar in La Paz, Bolivia, January 2012. Our analysis of the declarations of regimes of exception suggests that this is not entirely accurate.

48. DS27301 de 2003; DS29021 of 2007; DS29040 of 2007; DS29892 of 2009; DS0104 of 2009; DS0560 of 2010.

49. Personal interview with representative of the Human Rights Ombudsman in Sucre, April 2007. See also Salman (2007, 121) and Domingo (2006, 236).

50. Webber 2010, 51.

51. See Salman (2007, 113), Institut Internacional de Gobernabilitat de Catalunya (2004, 34) and Morales et al. (2010, 142)

52. Rafael Morató "Imperativo: Estado de Excepción y Gabinete de Salvación Nacional," opinion piece published in *El Diario* 13th February 2003; Rolando Alegría "Cobranzas en tiempo de crisis" opinion piece published in *El Deber* 21st October

2001; Erika Brockmann Quiroga "Poder real para Mesa: a cambio de decisiones," opinion piece published in *el Deber* el 29th March 2004.

53. Rafael Morató "Imperativo: Estado de Excepción y Gabinete de Salvación Nacional," opinion piece published in *El Diario* 13th February 2003.

54. Erika Brockmann Quiroga "Poder real para Mesa: a cambio de decisiones," opinion piece published in *el Deber* 29th March 2004.

55. The danger of enabling military authorities to deal with natural disasters has been pointed out by Claudia Heiss in the case of Chile, see http://www.cooperativa.cl/noticias/pais/sismos/que-es-el-estado-de-excepcion/2014–04–02/193000.html.

Chapter 5

Ecuador

The Administrative Paradigm

In a personal interview carried out by the author in Quito in July 2010, a political economist referred to a duality in the nature of regimes of exception in Ecuador: "In Ecuador, the state of emergency has been used . . . with different visions: a fiscal vision to overcome contracting procedures for public works and another vision to control conflict."

With this duality in mind, the following pages are dedicated to revising the use of regimes of exception in Ecuador in recent years, charting how the repressive emergency politics paradigm has in this case been surpassed by the administrative emergency politics paradigm. As will become clear, this constitutes a tendency that began toward the end of the 1990s and which became firmly established in the context of President Rafael Correa's *Revolución Ciudadana* or "Citizen Revolution."[1] As a result—and as will be demonstrated throughout this chapter—the locus of concern over the impact of regimes of exception on democratization efforts has moved largely from the protection of civil rights to the need for transparency over the use of public resources and the adjudication of public contracts, as well as the continuing role of the military in the face of important questions of political legitimacy.

The primary sources used in this study are the declarations of regimes of exception issued between 2000 and 2010,[2] together with the relevant legal frameworks: the Constitution of 1998 with its "state of emergency" and the Constitution of 2008 with its "state of exception." Crucially, these legal developments are of secondary interest to the study and are important to the extent that they help to shape the use of regimes of exception in practice and indeed reflect new opinions and agreements about the mechanisms. One of the justifications for the empirical approach in this volume is that the imagined powers of regimes of exception can be just as important as those powers formally established in normative frameworks. Finally a whole wealth of sources is used to complete the analysis, including reports and bulletins,[3] in-depth interviews with key-informants,[4] and newspaper articles.[5]

The chapter is structured as follows: first of all, a starting point is established, in which historical tendencies and relevant normative frameworks prior to 2000 are identified; next, an in-depth analysis is offered of regimes of exception as they have been used in practice in Ecuador between 2000 and 2010; and finally, an ending point is established, offering an overview regarding developments in regimes of exception in practice and changes or continuities at the formal level. In parallel with the chapters on Peru and Bolivia, this final section offers some reflections on the relationship between regimes of exception and democratic governability in Ecuador, taking into account possible trade-offs between legitimacy and efficiency.

THE STARTING POINT: HISTORICAL USE AND LEGAL FRAMEWORKS PRIOR TO 2000

As established in Chapter 2, the processes of independence from colonial rule in Latin America were fraught with violence, conflict, and antipolitics led by soldiers and *caudillos* (Loveman 1993). Similarly to the political development of Peru and Bolivia, while constitutional discussions raged between liberals and conservatives throughout the nineteenth century, the political situation of the emerging State bore more resemblance to discretional rather than ordinary or even emergency politics. Indeed, as Loveman (ibid) points out, the first years of independence in Ecuador were marked by the rule of *caudillos* who came to power after military uprisings. Indeed, General Juan José Flores (1830–1845). General José María Urbina (1845–1860), and Dr Gabriel García Moreno (1860–1875) dominated postindependence politics in Ecuador. In this context, the possibility of suspending citizen guarantees and offering Presidents emergency powers was included in every charter in place during this period, including the Constitutions of 1830, 1835, 1843, 1845, 1852, 1861, 1869, 1878, 1884, and 1897. In the following paragraphs—which yet again owe a great deal to Brian Loveman's seminal work of 1993—I shall briefly highlight the context in which these provisions were included, their main features, and their use in practice.

Although Ecuador did not become a fully independent State until 1830, the 1821 Bolivarian Constitution for Colombia (of which Ecuador formed part) already included comprehensive regimes of exception (Loveman 1993, 183). Consequently, when Independence was finally declared in 1830 and a Constitution was drawn up in the same year, a whole list of liberal rights was accompanied with emergency powers for the President in times of internal commotion or foreign invasion. The first chartered case of a regime of exception is when, faced with a liberal uprising in 1833, President General Juan José Flores requested extraordinary powers. The liberals, in turn, produced a pamphlet called "Las Facultades Extraordinarias" criticizing these extraordinary powers (ibid, 184) and—I might add—politicizing them. Although Flores sent members of the group into exile and censored their publications, his emergency powers did not prevent a full-scale uprising.

In this context, negotiations were held and in 1835 Vicente Rocafuerte became President with Flores as the military "defender of the constitution." A new constitution was drawn up in the same year, with the military given a permanent duty to protect internal order and the congress was authorized to concede the President whatever extraordinary powers were deemed necessary in the face of an internal commotion or foreign invasion (ibid, 186). Other extraordinary powers included collecting taxes in advance, increasing the size of the military and ordering the arrest, interrogation, banishment, internal and foreign exile, or temporary dismissal from public employment of those suspected of conspiring against the government. Although President Rocafuerte had originally opposed these powers, he made ample use of them to deal with opponents. Interestingly, emergency powers were used to deal with issues other than conflict or violence including fiscal crises, epidemics, and corruption. Although Loveman (ibid) does not offer an analysis of what sort of powers were used to deal with these situations they undoubtedly suggest expressions of disaster or administrative emergency politics, something that had not been recorded in either Bolivia or Peru at the time.

When the 1843 Constitution was drawn up, General Flores had been back in power for several years and sought to create a type of constitutional monarchy. Although he failed to do so, the Constitution offered up even greater emergency powers and rather than a fullyfunctioning Congress, a permanent commission of five senators was to make laws and concede powers to the president when the *patria* was in danger. Again, these extraordinary powers offered a combination of administrative and coercive measures very much in keeping with those that had been included previously. It was also possible for the President to transfer the government's location when the capital was under threat. At this time conflicts raged and Ecuador was plunged into civil war. Defeated by rebels in Peru, Flores was exiled, ushering in a six-year period of civilian governments between 1845 and 1851.

In reaction against Flores' predilection for concentrating power, a new Constitution in 1845 reduced powers for the president, increased sessions for congress and prohibited emergency powers to legislate. Nevertheless, the list of emergency powers remained largely unchanged, although Congress would determine the grave danger and had to give the President permission to control the armed forces. In 1851, military government returned and two constitutions were drawn up in quick succession, offering even broader emergency powers in the face of internal commotion, foreign invasion, sedition, and rebellion. The military had the permanent role of maintaining internal order and ensuring the execution of laws,[6] reflecting a predominantly *decisionist* type of politics. In any case, it is important to note that all of Ecuador's governments at that time (both military and civilian) used regimes of exception to deal with crisis and conflict (ibid, 191).

In the context of conservative government, the two constitutions in place between 1861 and 1875 contemplated more comprehensive regimes of exception and extraordinary powers than before (ibid, 192). The 1861 constitution reversed previous liberal reforms with congress meeting only once in every two years for sixty days, unless an extraordinary session was called by the President. In line with previous constitutions, the President was given special powers to deal with emergencies or subversion but emergency powers could also be delegated to subordinates. In the face of liberal opposition to these reforms, there was widespread repression including banishment and exile, although they were banned by the constitution. After a two-year period of acute political instability, a military coup was staged and another, essentially theocratic constitution was drawn up under the watchful eye of President García Moreno in 1869. Ordinary and extraordinary powers of the executive branch were increased and the figure of the state of siege was introduced to deal with actual or threatened internal commotion or foreign attack, allowing the government to suspend all guarantees. As well as measures that had been contemplated previously—including increasing the size of the armed forces and imposing taxes—this mechanism made it possible to search residences, exiling or confining people in different parts of the Republic, confiscating literature, prohibiting meetings that could incite disorder, and—crucially—subjecting those deemed to be responsible for the emergency to military law.

After President García Moreno was assassinated in 1875, interim President Antonio Borrero y Cortázar was in power for a year. Interestingly, although he initially rejected the use of extraordinary powers, in 1876 he declared a state of siege for four months throughout the Republic. There was conflict over the lack of a new constitution and, when General Ignacio de Veintemilla became supreme chief of the nation, he was given full extraordinary powers and the 1861 constitution was reinstated. With these extraordinary powers and using martial law provisions to deal with conservative opponents, Veintemilla oversaw a new constitution in 1878. While including a full list of liberal rights, the constitution offered extensive extraordinary powers in cases of internal commotion or foreign invasion in limited places, times, and purposes. Despite certain limitations, the new powers could essentially create military government, with suspects being detained for ten days without a court appearance, and public funds being used at discretion. President Veintemilla continued to use emergency powers, called congressional elections under a regime of exception in 1880, and staged an *autogolpe* to become an outright dictator in 1882.

Another coup was staged by military officers in 1883 and President Veintemilla went into exile. True to form, a new constitution was drawn up in 1884 ushering in a period of civilian rule. More power was given to the Congress and less to the President although extraordinary powers were contemplated in cases of internal commotion or foreign invasion. The regime of exception established in the 1884 Constitution was the most restrictive to date (ibid, 200), although a typically broad interpretation by the executive in practice saw new President Caamaño executing opponents under military law. Despite continuing political strife and the use of extraordinary powers, the Constitution of 1884 lasted until 1897 and was consequently the great survivor of nineteenth-century constitutionalism. However, in 1895, a military coup was staged by General Jose Eloy Alfaro Delgado and a new Constitution that was drawn up in 1897 maintained emergency powers. His government and constitution would be in place until 1901, drawing the nineteenth century to a close.

Consequently, nineteenth-century Ecuadorian politics moved frequently between discretionary and emergency politics, with military governments punctured by civilian ones. At the same time, despite a few, very interesting pointers to administrative and disaster emergency politics, the regimes of exception established at the constitutional level were conceived of and used firmly within the repressive paradigm. The twentieth century would see a continuity of this dynamic with periods of rule by caudillos such as Plaza and Velasco Ibarra (1901–1947) and then both civilian (1948–1960) and military (1960–1979) governments. All of the Constitutions in force during this period—that is to say those constitutions of 1897, 1906, 1925, 1938, 1945, 1946 and 1967—reproduced the extraordinary powers and regimes of exception established in the nineteenth century. Perhaps rather surprisingly, the information available points to a rather limited use of these provisions during this period, albeit firmly within the repressive emergency politics paradigm.

The regimes of exception established at the constitutional level to a large extent reproduced the powers already established in the aftermath of Independence and which have been described above. In that sense, the constitution of 1967 with its state of siege is an interesting case in point as it is a clear model for the regimes of exception that would be in force during the third wave. Furthermore, it offered several institutional controls and was very explicit about the types of extraordinary powers that could be given to the President. A state of siege could be declared in the face of external conflict or internal commotion and the President could be given powers to suspend constitutional guarantees, arrest or confine those charged with being responsible, mobilize the military, raise taxes, spend resources budgeted for other purposes, change the government's location, censor the press, open and/or close ports, and declare amnesties. Importantly, both the Congress and the Tribunal of Constitutional Guarantees could revoke the declaration at any time. The state of siege also contemplated the possibility of natural disasters (including earthquakes, floods or fires) or events that could affect a community's social or economic life (Dávalos Muirragui 2008, 154). Importantly, only some of the aforementioned powers could be used in this case, specifically mobilizing the military, declaring a security zone and/or spending resources budgeted for other purposes.

The few existing studies on the use of regimes of exception in Ecuador are not entirely clear on how often (or indeed how) they were actually used in practice during the twentieth century, prior to the transition to democracy, which culminated in 1979. Loveman's seminal work of 1993 focuses almost exclusively (albeit very comprehensively) on the nineteenth century, stating in general terms that constitutional regimes of exception and use in practice legitimated tyranny at the start of the following century. For his part, Durán Díaz (1987, 70–71) notes that despite persecution of political opponents and window-dressing to whichever constitution was in place at the time, the military governments of the twentieth century did not employ a systematic strategy of human rights abuses with or without regimes of exception, in contrast with the authoritarian regimes of the Southern Cone. Likewise, he claims that the states of emergency declared in Ecuador were always in place for a brief period of time and the measures used were typically arbitrary imprisonment, censorship, and infringements of the rights to the inviolability of the home and the secrecy of correspondence (ibid, 67). While Dávalos Muirragui (2008, 149) cites a report by the Inter-American Commission of Human Rights that refers to a long history of declarations of states of emergency to deal with social and economic problems, as well as crime, it is not clear where the early years of the twentieth century fit into this history.

Despite this apparent "knowledge gap," a very useful report was carried out by the NGO Inredh, delving into the use of regimes of exception in Ecuador between 1924 and 1997.[7] According to this report, nine declarations of regimes of exception were made between 1924 and prior to Ecuador's entry into the third wave of democracy in 1979. It gives several examples including President José Luis Tamayo who used emergency powers in the face of an armed internal commotion (1924); President Alfredo Baquerizo who declared an emergency to deal with alterations of public order in 1931 and again in 1932; and President Federico Páez who used emergency powers to censor the press and correspondence in 1937. While clearly within the framework of repressive emergency politics, nine declarations in over five decades are in fact much fewer than those made during the first two decades after the transition to democracy, as will be described in the following sub-section.

In post-transition Ecuador there was no apparent debate on the use of regimes of exception, in contrast to Bolivia (Chapter 4) and Peru (Chapter 3), likely given their rather sporadic use in the twentieth century. Nevertheless, at that time they were clearly synonymous with the suspension of constitutional guarantees (Durán Díaz 1987, 66) and a generalized national security paradigm that survived the transition (Dávalos Muirragui 2008, 157). As Loveman puts it "As elsewhere in Spanish America, Ecuador's nineteenth-century foundations of constitutional dictatorship legitimised twentieth-century political repression" (1993, 203). In the following paragraphs I highlight an interesting development during the first twenty years after Ecuador's transition to democracy: what can only be described as an avalanche of regimes of exception declared between 1979 and 1997 and the emergence of both the disaster and the administrative paradigm.

As in the case of Peru, a new constitution was adopted in Ecuador's transition to democracy. The constitution of 1978 included in its Article 103 (on the President's general faculties), incision n, the "state of emergency." In terms of emergency situations, the Constitution identifies four: "imminent external aggression, international war, grave internal commotion, or natural catastrophes." Clearly, these circumstances incorporate both political violence and disasters, but the idea of "grave internal commotion" is deliberately ambiguous, in line with other constitutional frameworks (Valadés 1974).

In terms of extraordinary measures, the state of emergency facilitates various powers, which resemble to a large extent those included in the postindependence charters. These measures include: i) decreeing the anticipated collection of taxes; ii) investing public funds destined to other causes; iii) moving the government's location; iv) establishing security zones; v) censuring the media; vi) limiting or suspending certain rights; vii) using the armed forces; viii) ordering mobilizations and requisitions according to the law; and ix) closing or opening ports. Again, the measures involved are both repressive and administrative in nature and resonate with those established in the nineteenth century. Importantly, the Congress or the Constitutional Tribunal could revoke the decree and so both the legislative and judicial powers (in theory) had much greater power over declarations of regimes of exception than in Bolivia or neighboring Peru at the time.

It is worth saying more about point (viii) the mobilization of Armed Forces and requisitions according to the law. Specifically, the law referred to is the Ley de Seguridad Nacional (Law of National Security) of 1979, which in its Article 146 establishes that the President can delegate extraordinary faculties to both civil and military authorities. Furthermore, Article 147 establishes that when a state of emergency is declared infractions will be judged according to the Código Penal Militar (Military Penal Code), given that ordinary citizens become mobilized, and consequently subject to military authority and jurisdiction. As highlighted in the following section, in 2007 the Constitutional Tribunal declared the unconstitutionality of this article given that it represented an invasion of military control over civilians, a key precept of democracy. It is important to highlight that the Ley de Seguridad Nacional of 1979 does not refer to the role of the Armed Forces in states of emergency declared for "natural disasters" specifically, although no restrictions are placed on their role either by that law or the "state of emergency" established in the Constitution of 1978.

Importantly, regimes of exception were generally considered synonymous with the suspension of guarantees and repression during this period (Davalos Muirragui 2008; Durán Díaz 1987). Indeed, for the representative of a national trade union interviewed by the author in Quito in July 2010, there was a broad use of the measure in the 1980s to stop protests when "governments found themselves in critical conditions of political and juridical instability." In the same way, for an ex-leader of the indigenous organization CONAIE[8] who had been on the receiving end of a state of emergency declared in 1994, states of emergency constituted the classic reply from the government whenever there had been mass mobilizations and protests against unpopular laws. In his own words: "given that the city was surrounded as well as the sites, the places where the most important powers are located, the National Congress, obviously the first thing the government did was to dictate a state of emergency, right?" (Personal interview with the author, Quito, July 2010).

Conversely, other key informants felt that the use of regimes of exception during the period was related to one-off incidents rather than a political strategy. However, for the ex-president of an important union of workers of the petrol sector,[9] its use against trade unions during the 1980s was not particularly noteworthy. For his part, a prominent sociologist believed that it had been a very extreme measure saved for important crisis occasions: "I don't think that there have been abuses in the use of states of emergency here, I don't think so, but rather they have been resorted to when things have got really complicated." (Personal interview with the author, Quito, July 2010).

According to a study carried out by the human rights NGO Inredh,[10] since the return to democracy in 1979, the "state of emergency" established in 1979 was used repeatedly,[11] with 54 states of emergency being declared between 1979 and 1997,[12] a much higher number than the nine declarations recorded in the pre-transition twentieth century. The way in which it was used is considered briefly in the following paragraphs.

In the context of a clear tendency to declare states of emergency within the repressive paradigm, the Presidency of Sixto Durán Ballén is a case in point, given that he made ample use of them in the undeclared war with Peru during the 1990s. He also used them to deal with vandalism and internal commotion, leading to a highly debated case in 1992. Via Decree No. 86 President Durán Bellén declared a state of emergency in Guayaquil and ordered a massive police and army operation that culminated in what was effectively the extra-judicial execution of various citizens. In 1994 the case was taken to the Inter-American Commission of Human Rights and finally in 2006 it came before the Inter-American Court of Human Rights. Fifteen years after the events took place, a sentence was handed down to Ecuador in which various criticisms were made, including the use of military force to deal with internal order, the disrespect for a time limit, the lack of clarity of the declaration itself, and the need to define the territorial application of the measures (Dávalos Muirragui 2008).

Crucially, however, the report carried out by the human rights NGO Inredh also points to the use of regimes of exception (and other extraordinary powers) beyond this repressive paradigm. Indeed, as well as internal commotion, public order, and external aggression, the extraordinary situations referred to during this period also included crime, natural disasters and administrative issues such as contraband, economic crisis and the poor functioning of public services. Indeed, referring to regimes of exception, and other extraordinary powers between 1979 and 1997, the study discovered an increasing category of "other" types of declarations, including administrative and economic difficulties for public institutions. What is not clear, however, is which measures were used to deal with these different types of extraordinary situations. These findings are vital for our study given that they suggest that the use of regimes of exception in Ecuador, in the period immediately prior to the twenty-first century, was much more varied in political terms than in neighboring Peru or Bolivia.

To conclude the observations in relation to this very interesting report on the use of regimes of exception in twentieth-century Ecuador, it is also important to mention that as of 2001 two thirds of the declarations were effectively still in place given that previous Presidents had not taken care to lift the measures once the emergency was over. For his part, the representative of a human rights NGO interviewed by the author in July 2010 pointed out another historical shortcoming: "They say that as soon as a state of emergency is declared it should be notified to both the Secretary General of the OEA and the Secretary General of the United Nations. This has never happened in Ecuador and it is something that we checked, they have never transmitted a notification to either of the organisms with regard to states of emergency. So Ecuador has received some international criticisms about that." This lack of formality with regard to the declarations appeared to continue well into the twenty-first century, as will be pointed out in the following section.

In this context of a widespread use of regimes of exception—much broader, indeed, than before the return to democracy in 1979—Ecuador's Constitution of 1998 repeated the mechanism of the "state of emergency" which is almost identical to that of 1978 in terms of the extraordinary situations and the extraordinary measures offered as a result. Nevertheless, Dávalos Muirragui (2008) points to several, mainly formal differences that constitute clear improvements. The first is that in the Constitution of 1978 the only limits to the restriction of rights had been not suspending the right to the inviolability of life and personal integrity, not expatriating Ecuadorian nations, and not confining people in areas outside of provincial capitals or of the region in which they lived. In contrast, the Constitution of 1998 specifies the only rights (not guarantees) that can be suspended or limited and thus adds more clarity.[13] In the same way, Dávalos Muirragui (2008) points to the fact that the Constitution of 1978 includes the state of emergency within a long list of presidential faculties whereas that of 1998 offers a whole chapter on the mechanism (Articles 180–182) and therefore gives the regime of exception the importance that it deserves. It is also important to note that none of the rights it establishes as subject to derogations are at odds with the standards set at the international and regional levels (Article 181.5), a clear time limit of sixty days is established (182), and the Congress (although not the Constitutional Tribunal) can revoke the declaration at any time (Article 182).

Consequently, as a result of this revision of other, secondary sources, it is clear that by the year 2000, regimes of exception had become firmly established as mechanisms of emergency politics within Ecuadorian political history. Both in their constitutional form and their political usage they are synonymous with the repressive paradigm of emergency politics, although the early and decisive inclusion of natural disasters as extraordinary situations and an emerging administrative paradigm sets them apart from the cases of both Peru and Bolivia.

Bearing in mind these observations, my attention now turns to the use of regimes of exception during the first decade of the twenty-first century, in an effort to identify possible changes and continuities from this broad starting point.

EMERGENCY POLITICS IN ECUADOR, 2000–2010

In the previous section, it was noted that since Independence regimes of exception in Ecuador have been synonymous with the repressive emergency politics paradigm, although their use was much more widespread after the transition to democracy than beforehand. Furthermore, natural disasters and administrative measures have been incorporated in Ecuadorian constitutions since the nineteenth century and there are clear indications of the increasing presence of both disaster and administrative emergency politics throughout the first years after the country's transition to democracy. In this section our findings suggest that while this historical use of regimes of exception within the repressive paradigm has made itself present at certain junctures between 2000 and 2010, its use appears to have been curtailed in recent years in the light of debate and politicization. Furthermore, while there has been frequent use of regimes of exception to deal with natural disasters, what is clearly distinctive in the case of Ecuador is the declaration of states of emergency firmly within an administrative paradigm, something that has been captured in the collective imagination.

Before offering an in-depth analysis of these important developments in Ecuador, it is important to highlight that a total of 112 declarations of regimes of exception were made during this period, a figure that is much higher than in Bolivia (65) and very similar to that of Peru (115).[14] Consequently it is possible to speak of a widespread use of these constitutional measures during the first decade of the twenty-first century, much more so even than in the first two decades after the transition to democracy. Furthermore, there appears to be an *increasing* tendency for Presidents to declare regimes of exception in Ecuador. This situation is again similar to Peru and in contrast to Bolivia, which showed a decreasing tendency in this sense.

Before proceeding, it is important to highlight a significant problem that was found in this case. In the analysis of official registers, references were found to 10 declarations of regimes of exception[15] but yet the actual text of the corresponding declaration could not be found online, during fieldwork, or with the help of local researchers. According to the representative of an important human rights NGO, there has been a problem in relation to the publication and storage of official registers and decrees, which could explain the existence of what appear to be phantom cases. He also explains that there could be confusion over dates, given delays in publishing declarations: "The executive did not feel that it had an obligation to publish them, but the legislative had to wait for the declaration (to oversee the measure). What happened is that the state of emergency was published a month late so there was no control" (Personal interview with the author in Quito, in July 2010).

Despite all of my best efforts, these decrees simply could not be found and potentially never existed. On the other hand, there is also a possibility that there are typing or factual errors. In any case, these errors highlight a degree of informality with which regimes of exception have been treated during the first decade of the twenty-first century, in line with the observations made in the abovementioned report in relation to an apparent oversight in lifting previously declared states of emergency.

Political Crises and Repressive Emergency Politics

Chapters 1 and 2 established that regimes of exception have generally become synonymous with a repressive paradigm of emergency politics, characterized by the suspension of certain civil liberties and/or the deployment of the military to deal with unrest or political violence. Indeed, this emergency paradigm had been dominant in Ecuador since Independence and, although in numerical terms fewer declarations were made according to this paradigm than in the disaster or administrative paradigms during the first two decades after the transition to democracy, the constitutional form and social representations still placed regimes of exception firmly within the repressive paradigm. With a total of 14 declarations of repressive type states of emergency or exception between 2000 and 2010, it is evident that they have been used more frequently than in Bolivia, but considerably less so than in Peru. Nevertheless, there is a clear tendency for declarations of this type to decrease over time, after a considerable increase in 2005 and 2006, for reasons that will be discussed below.

In any case, it seems that the historical, "circumstantial use" of this measure as a means to repression[16] has continued in the first decade of the twenty-first century. Although regimes of exception have been rather sporadic, the analysis made by experts is that their use during this period has intensified existing crises and—more importantly—criminalized social movements, reducing their capacity to participate in politics and have their say in legal changes, and obliging them to remain in clandestinity during important moments. Indeed, as the representative of a human rights NGO noted in a personal interview with the author in Quito in July 2010: "Generally, it ends with the criminalization of social protest. Politically what happens, what has happened with the state of emergency is that, rather than eliminating the conflict, it is not eliminated, it becomes more intense."

To understand the political implications of this evaluation more fully, it is important to analyze several key cases in which Presidents sought to deal with political instability and protests that directly challenged their governments. Importantly, all of these declarations brought about criticisms in the written press, indicating the degree to which this repressive use of regimes of exception became politicized.[17] Crucially, for Presidents Mahuad Witt and Gutiérrez the disastrous use of a regime of exception would ultimately lead to their downfall. These episodes are of particular transcendence in recent Ecuadorian political history and constitute the backdrop to the presidential interruptions and political instability referred to in recent volumes by Pérez-Liñan (2007) and Llanos and Marsteintredet (2010).

For his part, President Jamil Mahuad Witt was in power between 1998 and 2000, being forced out three weeks into the year. With increasing protests against his government throughout the country, at the start of 2000 he issued a repressive decree of exception via DE1674. In the declaration itself he refers to a context of the "internal commotion" caused by these mobilizations, their negative impact on the State's economy and security and the need to declare "extraordinary measures." These measures include the declaration of a security zone throughout the country, the army being placed in control of internal order (including military jurisdiction over ordinary citizens), and the four civil rights contemplated in the 1998 constitution are suspended. However, in the aftermath of this highly repressive decree, protests led by the CONAIE continued in Quito against the dollarization of the economy and President Mahuad was forced to resign.[18]

Just a year later, in the aftermath of the massive mobilizations that had overthrown President Mahuad and a very difficult economic situation, President Noboa faced further protests by the CONAIE in the context of considerable social tension.[19] In this context, he declared DE1214 in February 2001 declaring a state of emergency throughout the Republic. The extraordinary situation referred to in the decree is related to threats and protests that have destabilized the country's internal order, producing a "grave internal commotion." Again, the extraordinary measures include the declaration of a security zone throughout the country, the army being placed in control of internal order (including military jurisdiction over ordinary citizens), and the enjoyment of the four civil rights contemplated in the 1998 Constitution is suspended. Although several peasant farmers were killed and scores of soldiers and civilians injured, negotiations were established and President Noboa remained in power.

Four years later, Lucio Gutiérrez—who had led the rebellion against President Jamil Mahuad Witt—decreed a state of emergency via DE2752 in the face of massive protests known as the "Rebelión de los Forajidos."[20] Both the reasons for and the measures established in this decree are particularly interesting and include the following:

> There are political and social groups interested in de-stabilizing the democratic system with violent protests that go beyond the control of the Public Forces. . . . The National Congress via Resolution 25–181 of 9th December 2004 . . . resolved to dismiss the magistrates of the Supreme Court of Justice, who were in their roles and the Honorable National Congress until now has not resolved on the dismissal of the [interim magistrates of the] current Supreme Court of Justice. . . . [It is decreed to] Article 1 Declare the Metropolitan District of Quito in a state of emergency. . . . Article 2. Dismiss the magistrates of the current Supreme Court of Justice. . . . Article 5 Limit the civil rights established in Article 23 numerals 9, 12, 13, 14 and 19 of the Political Constitution of the Republic. Article 6 Dispose that the Public Force via the Joint Command of the Armed Forces control and maintain order. . . .
>
> DE2752 issued on 15th April 2005.

Without a doubt, this is a multifaceted decree given that it uses force to repress protest over an unpopular decision in relation to the replacement of the interim magistrates of the Supreme Court of Justice. Likewise, the decree itself seeks to implement the decision and over-rule Congress. The idea that protestors are de-stabilizing the democratic system reminds us of the constitutional doctrine of the "exceptional threat," but also of Presidents traditionally using regimes of exception to save their own skin rather than the democratic system per se. This decree was the last, desperate act of government carried out by Lucio Gutiérrez, who fled the Presidency due to the continued protests of the *forajidos*.

Another case which seemed to attract considerable press attention and which the President used to defend his government, was the "state of exception"[21] declared by President Rafael Correa on 30th September 2010 in order to deal with several police abandoning their position in protest or—as at the time was claimed—in an attempted coup.[22] In the decree itself (DE488) the government attributes itself a responsibility to uphold national, citizen, and human security[23] in the context of an internal commotion produced by the police rebellion. Without referring explicitly to the suspension of civil rights, the Armed Forces and Police are mobilized and put in charge of internal order. Importantly, Article 5 states that notification must be given to the National Assembly, the Constitutional Court, the Organization of American States, and the United Nations, in a clear attempt to respect Leandro Despouy's principles (1999). Apparently, what most concerned public opinion in this case was the censorship that was imposed during the state of exception, although this is not clearly stated in the decree. Furthermore, questions are raised about its duration and its negative impact on the country's image as a tourist destination.[24] Within a short period of time, normality returned and President Correa remained firmly in the Presidency.

Interestingly, despite the disastrous results for two Presidents and considerable public debate, these cases were not enough to produce a real change in the way "states of emergency" were viewed or indeed normed in Ecuador.[25] In any case, the episodes are roughly comparable to the cases of the *Guerra del Agua* or the *Guerra del Gas* in Bolivia due to the public attention, anger and sense of "rebellion" they aroused. Nevertheless, these events in themselves were not sufficient to bring about a change in the use of repressive states of emergency in Ecuador. Rather, this happened in a very different context: the use of regimes of exception to deal with indigenous protest over natural resources, a pattern that occurred both prior to and after 2000.

The logic behind this specific use given to regimes of exception is similar to that in Peru, in Chapter 3. Indeed, according to the literature on extractivism, disagreements over the use of natural resources have often led to conflict that, in some cases, has turned violent or involved the use of repression (Bebbington and Humphreys Bebbington 2010). Ecuador has not been the exception in this sense, with a series of social conflicts since massive exploration and exploitation began in the 1970s (Fontaine 2003). The presence of the military in these areas has undoubtedly constituted a source of violence and polarization of these conflicts (ibid) and there has been a sort of abandonment on the part of the State—in line with O'Donnell's concept of brown areas (2004)—and a scarce, generally indigenous population.[26] As the representative of a human rights NGO explained in a personal interview with the author in Quito, in July 2010, in these areas "there is no State presence and there is a minimal presence of the national police, sometimes those who take on the role of the State are the military . . . this is a time bomb, together with great social unease due to the lack of basic services, uncontrollable petrol activity, increasing pollution, extremely high levels of cancer in the region, and particularly the State's abandonment of a social policy."

In this context, between 2000 and 2010, I discovered six declarations of regimes of exception in order to deal with protests that have affected the petrol industry, particularly in the provinces of Sucumbíos y Orellana. What is of most concern is the disposition that sanctions will be in accordance with the Law of National Security, permitting military jurisdiction over civilians. Furthermore, in the text of the decrees the importance of maintaining the activity of the economic sector is established as the primary justification and cause of the "internal commotion" as is clear in the extract from the DE162 issued by President Alfredo Palacio:

> There has been a situation of conflict provoked with clear intentions of vandalism by groups interested in causing chaos, destabilizing the normal development of activities in the provinces of Sucumbíos and Orellana, with the threat of and subsequent occupation of petrol installations, as well as attacking the public forces, causing irreparable damage to the national economy and putting the security of the State in grave danger, which creates a grave "internal commotion". . .
>
> DE162 of 25th May 2005

There was considerable debate in the media in relation to the use of these decrees. On the one hand, some columnists were in favor of declaring repressive states of emergency, particularly when the protests or strikes affect the country's economy, as is the case of these decrees to protect the petrol sector from protest.[27] On the other hand, there is a specific concern over the use of this mechanism in the Amazonian areas of Orellana and Sucumbíos, given the series of declarations mentioned above.[28] For instance, after a state of emergency was declared in this context 2001, two indigenous protestors were killed. In this context, a columnist comments that the application of a state of emergency "requires a cool head, otherwise the risk is creating further commotion, as was the unfortunate case yesterday."[29] For his part, a political economist interviewed by the author in Quito in July 2010 noted that: "when there have been indigenous mobilizations they have decreed the state of emergency but finally these processes have been negotiated politically, the state of emergency has not been of any use. Rather, the state of emergency has prevented negotiations."

Nevertheless, these considerable criticisms yet again did not amount to a widespread debate on states of emergency or a change in their use or legal form. It would take the critical juncture brought about by the conjunction of the case of Dayuma and the Constituent Assembly in 2007 to do that.

In a different political context from the declarations mentioned above, another state of emergency was declared to protect petrol installations from protest, this time by President Rafael Correa in Dayuma, within the province of Orellana, via DE770 issued on 29th November 2007.[30] The decree—following the precedent set by President Palacio—refers to the State's inalienable property of natural resources, an "internal commotion," acts of sabotage, damage to public and private property, and the daily loss of approximately three million US dollars in petrol revenue. In reply, a Security Zone was established, the enjoyment of human rights related to the freedom of movement and association was restricted, military jurisdiction over civilians was established, and again an unknown quantity of resources was offered for an unknown purpose. In this context, an observer who was taking photographs was detained, *habeas corpus* was refused, and he was tried by a military authority.

Following these events, the conflict gradually subsided and negotiations were established, the correlation of forces between the citizens of Dayuma and the government had changed. As the representative of a human rights NGO interviewed in Quito in July 2010 explained: "Of course at that time, just after the social mobilization and the repression, the State is all-powerful, it is a different kind of approach, not based on respect . . . the State had shown its force, it had demonstrated that 'you people (the protesters) won't achieve much, with your ideas and demands.'"

This case is particularly important because it gave rise to a very public and heated debate about states of emergency, particularly military jurisdiction over civilians.[31] Crucially, it coincided with the meetings of the Constituent Assembly, provoking further discussion of the issue.[32] Ultimately the Plenary of the Assembly issued an amnesty for the crimes that had been committed, both by civilians and members of the Armed Forces.[33] Noting that this was not an isolated case but rather symptomatic of the kind of abuses that occur under states of emergency,[34] NGOs exerted pressure over the Constitutional Tribunal to declare Articles 145 and 147 of the Law of National Security unconstitutional. Indeed, these articles disposed that any infractions committed when a "mobilization" is declared may be judged by military rather than civilian authorities.[35] The sentence of the Constitutional Tribunal on 10th June 2008[36] accepted the demand for unconstitutionality. This constitutes an important step forward for the democratization of regimes of exception in Ecuador, particularly within the repressive paradigm.

Another important development in the aftermath of Dayuma was the creation of a new regime of exception: the "state of exception" mechanism, included in Articles 164–166. In terms of exceptional situations, they are very similar to those established in the "state of emergency" of the constitution of 1998, specifically: "international or internal aggression or armed conflict, grave internal commotion, public calamity or natural disaster." Rather than clearing up the ambiguity of the "internal commotion," the 2008 constitution adds to it with the equally vague idea of a public calamity. In terms of exceptional measures, Article 164 maintains precisely the same ones included in the state of emergency of 1998, that is to say: anticipated tax collection, use of public funds for other ends, moving the headquarters of government, censorship, security zones, armed forces, opening/closing of ports, airports and border controls, mobilizations and requisitions, and the suspension of several human rights, including the right to the inviolability of the home, the inviolability of personal correspondence, freedom of movement, freedom of association and reunion, and freedom of information.

Firmly within the repressive paradigm, this regime of exception appears to be much more in keeping with the tenets of international and regional human rights norms: as in the constitution of 1998, the rights it establishes as subject to derogation are permitted at both the international and regional levels (Article 165); it also refers to several of Despouy's principles, including legality, a time limit, proportionality and concordance with international treaties and introduces other principles including necessity, territoriality, and reasonability[37]; as well as the Congress, the Constitutional Tribunal is once again given an explicit role to check the constitutionality of the decrees (Article 166); and the national security law which is referred to no longer establishes military jurisdiction over civilians (Article 165). Consequently, the "state of exception" established by the Constitution of 2008 fulfills many of the formal recommendations regarding regimes of exception established at the international and regional level.

As well as these significant changes with regard to the normative framework, it is important to note that, in the aftermath the case of Dayuma, there appeared to be a decreasing tendency to declare repressive regimes of exception in Ecuador, with no cases in 2008, one case in 2009 to deploy the army in the face of organized crime[38] and another in 2010, the case of the police revolt against President Correa in 2010 which was analyzed at the beginning of this section. This is not comparable to the situation in Bolivia but undoubtedly represents a clear change. Nevertheless, this did not mean the end of military force in the context of regimes of exception, as will be highlighted in the following section.

Getting Things Done: Administrative Emergency Politics

In contrast with Peru and Bolivia, administrative emergency politics has become synonymous with regimes of exception in Ecuador and, in practice, constitutes the dominant paradigm. This development is superbly reflected in a personal interview with a political economist carried out in Quito in July 2010: "Over the past years, the figure of the state of emergency or state of exception has been used fiscally, that is to say the government has declared an emergency in order to reduce fiscal procedures for public contracting because contracting involves a very long process, it takes a really long time. So over the past years, to avoid this red-tape and to be able to assign works, governments have declared states of emergency."

This duality of regimes of exception reminds us of the two types of Roman dictatorship, established by Rossiter (2002): a dictatorship to suppress insurrections and a dictatorship to get things done. As pointed out in previous sections of this chapter, although Ecuador's past regimes of exception have not framed emergency politics within a distinctly administrative paradigm, as of the nineteenth century they have offered considerable administrative powers including a discretional use of the budget, the capacity to raise taxes, the temporary opening and/or closing of ports, and the possibility of moving the location of government. For its part, the report by the human rights NGO Inredh discovered a tendency between 1979 and 1997 to declare regimes of exception to deal with contraband, economic crisis, and the poor functioning of public services. Consequently, administrative emergency politics in Ecuador is nothing new. The apparent novelty is the extent to which they have been used in the first decade of the twenty-first century is apparently unprecedented in Ecuadorian history and is worthy of attention and analysis.

In my review of official registers, a total of 47 administrative-type regimes of exception were declared in sectors, activities or services by Ecuadorian Presidents between 2000 and 2010, with a clear peak in 2007—corresponding to the first year of President Correa's "Citizen Revolution"—and an increase over the decade. In general terms, the declarations share some interesting features. Crucially, the state of emergency or exception is declared in a specific activity, service or sector rather than in a territory, something that challenges the traditional conceptualization of a regime of exception applying to a specific geographic area. All of the decrees refer to the possibility or presence of an internal commotion as a justification for the declaration, perhaps because of the fact that administrative problems themselves are not included in the constitutional framework of 1998 or 2008 as a cause for the declaration of the regime of exception. Furthermore, all of the decrees refer to situations in which economic activities or public services are interrupted and in the vast majority, poor management is seen as the reason for this. In a few cases, adverse natural phenomena are also referred to as a problem, but this is secondary to the administrative difficulties that are faced.

In terms of the extraordinary measures, in various cases a complete administrative or management overhaul is decreed but the key administrative power here is the facilitation of public contracting.[39] In a personal interview with a political economist,[40] this particular measure must be interpreted in the light of the fact that "contracting implies a very long process of asking for permissions, bureaucracy, procedures, it takes ages, so governments—particularly recent ones—to avoid these procedures and assign works directly have declared a state of emergency."

Beyond this overview of administrative-type declarations of regimes of exception, it is important to offer a contextualized reading of two important trends. In the paragraphs below I analyze two key uses given to decrees within this administrative paradigm: on the one hand, cases which are of a purely administrative nature, and on the other, cases which include an element of coercion by handing over the reins of the petrol industry to the Armed Forces. It is important to analyze these two groups separately as they have very different implications for democratic governability.

A total of 32 decrees were found in which the extraordinary situations and measures are overwhelmingly administrative. The idea of doing things "fast track" ("por la vía rápida") permeates these decrees and offers a helpful way to think of them. Importantly, various sectors are affected by these fast-track administrative emergency decrees, including (but not limited to) the General Direction of the Civil Register, the energy sector, the road system, the cultural heritage system, the penitentiary system, and even the Constituent Assembly in 2007.

One particularly interesting trend is the decidedly non-fast-track, long-term use of regimes of exception to deal with cash-flow problems between Ecuador's national electricity and petrol companies. Indeed, seven, very similar declarations of states of emergency or exception were declared by Ecuadorian presidents between 2000 and 2010 in order to resolve this problem.[41] The decrees all follow a similar model. First, the supply of electricity is identified as of national interest and the state is deemed to be responsible for covering the basic necessities of this commodity to satisfy Ecuador's "socio-economic development." Next, the economic crisis affecting electricity companies and the increase in international prices of fuels is identified as responsible for defaults in prepayments to Petrocomercial. In the case of DE244 of February 2010, it is claimed that the situation could lead to an "internal commotion" and a problem for "citizen security." In the face of this repeated situation, an "electric state of emergency" is declared throughout the country seven times between 2004 and 2010, with various extensions during this period.[42] Consequently, this fast track administrative intervention should be understood as essentially a long-term intervention that does not respect the idea of temporality implicit in a regime of exception.

As well as this significant, long-term application of regimes of exception to deal with a permanent difficulty within two important state energy companies, there is also a clear link between fast-track administrative type states of emergency and the start of Rafael Correa's "Revolución Ciudadana" (or Citizen Revolution), in 2007. Indeed, in that year a total of 14 declarations of regimes of exception were declared, with the vast majority firmly within the administrative paradigm. A few of the situations appear to be one-off administrative headaches, including the situation of Ecuadorian migrants returning from Spain (DE89), and productivity in the agriculture sector (DE153). However, the majority relate to structural problems including the national highways (DE147); education (DE188); the prison system (DE441 and DE807); cultural heritage (DE816); and true to form, the electricity sector (DE525A and DE683). Particularly interesting are two decrees related to the police force (DE675 and DE761), which is said to be unprepared to deal with a context of increasing insecurity. Rather than passing control to the armed forces or suspending human rights (in a repressive model), the exceptional measures employed in this case are of an administrative nature, in order to improve infrastructure and equipment.[43]

One of the most striking examples of the use of administrative regimes of exception is the declaration of a state of emergency to begin the Constituent Assembly in 2007. Indeed, from an administrative point of view this key moment was carried out in a totally exceptional framework. The importance of the constituent moment cannot be underestimated in Ecuadorian political history and consequently this is a key finding of the study.[44] The declaration itself offers the following justification and measures:

> Considering . . . That the National Constituent Assembly will be installed at the end of November 2007 and consequently the National Constituent Assembly runs the risk that if the building, offices, computers and other items are not installed on the date that has been set aside, it could cause a commotion in the country. . . [I hereby decree to] Article 1—Declare a state of emergency due to the grave commotion that the non-installation of the National Constituent Assembly could cause in order to take the necessary measures to provide the necessary infrastructure, furniture, computers and other running costs that may be necessary. . . . Article 3 The necessary procedures to carry out the works, acquire the goods and offer the services—including consultancy—that are necessary to resolve the emergency are subject to the exceptional contracting

procedures foreseen in the Ley de Contratación Pública [Law of Public Contracting] and Ley de Consultoría [Ley of Consultancy], respectively.

DE752, 15th November 2007

The use of these decrees makes perfect sense if we take into account Correa's minority government and urgency in beginning with his political transformation.[45] As Freidenberg explains, (2008, 95) during this period there were events that violated the Rule of Law and respect for democratic institutionality and—I would add—this use of regimes of exception would undoubtedly be symptomatic of this context of political abnormality. In a personal interview with the author in Quito in July 2010, the representative of a human rights NGO explained that with President Correa the number of declarations of regimes of exception had increased exponentially: "there are declarations of states of emergency in various sectors in the country, of course it helps the State suppress fundamental rights but also to skip over public contracting procedures which ultimately can lead to problems of corruption. We have seen all of these uses of states of emergency."

These administrative type decrees were subject to an intense public debate and undoubtedly reflect a new awareness of regimes of exception within the administrative paradigm in Ecuador. It is striking that the greatest concern over states of emergency in opinion columns in Ecuadorian newspapers during the period under study is in relation to this type of fast-track administration rather than the repressive model.[46] There are heated discussions over their use in penitentiary systems, the energy sector and the road system. One journalist makes a particularly incisive point: "The government introduced the modality of these declarations in several areas supposedly to facilitate the flow of resources and free the execution of works from slowness and bureaucracy, despite the fact that as a result it was distorting the constitutional figure of emergency, which is exceptional and transitory in nature." Despite a generalized concern in public opinion, there are differences over what the real problem is. On one hand, there are complaints about the inefficiency of the measures used and the lack of a long-term solution (as is the case of insecurity mentioned above).[47] On the other hand, there is concern over the lack of transparency in the use of financial resources and the way that contracts are adjudicated. These concerns reflect the two pillars of democratic governability.

Among the declarations of regimes of exception by Ecuadorian Presidents between 2000 and 2010 I also discovered a considerable number of cases (15) in which the administrative paradigm turns potentially violent: in these cases, states of emergency or exception are declared to resolve an administrative problem by getting the military involved and/or declaring security zones, together with standard exceptional measures regarding public contracting procedures. This development is interesting as there is no reference to social upheaval, protest, or disturbances, rather the importance of protecting economic development. Conceptually this is different from the repressive emergency politics paradigm given the lack of social "disorder" but given the militarization of administrative processes, the logic is rather similar. Furthermore, the implementation of administrative changes via force and without the participation of the opposition is more in line with authoritarian regimes than democratic ones (Neuhouser 1996, 636). Interestingly in our analysis of regimes of exception in nineteenth-century Ecuador it was established that the military could be called upon to implement political decisions and hence this phenomenon would appear to have clear historic roots.

While these declarations were made throughout the first decade of the twenty-first century, there was a sharp increase after 2007, again when Rafael Correa came to power. Importantly all but one of these decrees are related to the management of strategic natural resources, including the electricity sector (DE1956 of 2001; DE1348 of 2008; DE124 of 2009),[48] water supplies (DE230, DE292A and DE460 of 2010), and the transportation of gas (DE1442 of 2004, DE254 of 2007, and DE1033 of 2008).[49] Nevertheless, the key tendency in these declarations of regimes of exception is to offer a military intervention in the state petrol company, Petroecuador. Indeed, several declarations[50] of this type facilitated a structural and semipermanent intervention of the military in the petrol sector, causing great debate in the media.

The decrees in question all follow the same basic structure: first of all, there is a reference to previous governments and their poor management of Petroecuador leading to a lack of income in the sector; next, Petroecuador and its different departments are declared in a state of exception; and finally several measures are established including economic and military mobilization, as well as the direct participation of the Naval Force in the management of the national petrol company. The first decree of this type, DE766 reads as follows:

> Considering . . . that it is the aim of the National Government to recuperate the operative capacity of the Petroecuador system to detain the progressive and intense process of reduction of efficiency in the areas of: exploration and production; industrialization; commercialization and transport of petrol that directly and negatively effects the Ecuadorian people; that it is necessary to intervene urgently throughout the Petroecuador system to protect national interests. . . . In exercise of the faculties given in article 180 of the Political Constitution of the Republic; and Articles 52 and following of the Law of National Security, I hereby decree: Article 1 To declare an emergency in the State Company Petróleos de Ecuador, PETROECUADOR. . . . This emergency extends throughout the so-called Petroecuador sytem. . . . Article 2. . . . It is

disposed that the Ministry of Defense, via the General Commander of the Naval Force, should authorize the participation of personnel of this branch of the Armed Forces in the management of the State Company Petróleos de Ecuador, PETROECUADOR, and its permanent subsidiaries, with the aim of overcoming the situation of emergency.

DE766, 29th November 2007

The use of states of emergency and exception to facilitate military intervention in Petroecuador became a key issue of interest for the media during this period.[51] Indeed, it seems as if these decrees were politicized in a similar way to the "state of siege" in Bolivia.[52] The most frequently referred to concerns are the illegitimacy of military intervention, the possibility of corruption, and the lack of money and productivity in the sector. Moreover, when—in line with its new oversight measures established in the "state of exception" of the 2008 Constitution—the Constitutional Court ruled that this type of decree was indeed correct and constitutional, in 2009, a journalist made the following complaint: "It is very, very serious that the declarations of states of exception, situations that due to their transcendence require the maximum levels of prudence and responsibility, are taken so light-heartedly in Ecuador."[53] Clearly this is the most scandalous use of regimes of exception for public opinion but the debates do not appear to have worked as a mechanism of social accountability as the executive continued to use them throughout the period under study.

In a personal interview with a representative of a human rights organization interviewed by the author in Quito in July 2010, the informant explained that the reason behind these declarations is simple: the military act as representatives of the State in the Amazonian region and have signed contracts to collaborate with the petrol plants installed in the area. His vision is that the use of states of emergency to put the army in charge of the petrol sector is both "strange" and a clear violation of the constitutional form of states of emergency and exception, because "the word itself 'mobilization' in relation to the army means moving troops in a defensive strategy but he (the President) understood that he could move them from one place to another so that they can take charge of this sector. That is a perverse understanding of the constitution."

Undoubtedly, the use of the military to carry out administrative changes and control certain industries or sectors is still a reality in many Latin American democracies, constituting a threat to democratic consolidation (Martínez 2006). Nevertheless, the discovery that regimes of exception can offer a means to facilitate the military's administrative and economic influence over the long term and in a democratic context, stresses the importance of bringing these mechanisms under great scrutiny. The fact that President Correa shows a clear tendency toward the use of these measures reflects a concentration of power in the executive and reliance on the military that could be considered a key and troubling characteristic of the *Revolución Ciudadana*.[54]

An Emerging—but Secondary—Disaster Emergency Politics Paradigm

While regimes of exception have never been synonymous with disaster emergency politics in Ecuador, it is worth noting that—in contrast to Bolivia and Peru—since the constitutions of the nineteenth-century natural catastrophes have been explicitly established as a possible cause for the declaration of a regime of exception. Furthermore, in the report by the national-level Inredh, the vast majority of the many states of emergency declared between 1979 and 1997 were related to adverse natural phenomena including flooding, earthquakes, and epidemics. What is not clear, however, is what exceptional measures have been used to deal with these situations, given that the constitutional forms of 1978, 1998, and 2008 all refer to both coercive and administrative measures but not specifically to technical or humanitarian aid. Importantly, the Ley de Contratación Pública (Law of Public Contracting) of 2001 offers in its Article 6 exceptional contracting procedures in the face of damage caused by events—implicitly—related to natural disasters within the framework of states of emergency.

In numerical terms, a total of 51 declarations of states of emergency or exception were declared to deal with natural disasters or adverse natural phenomena in Ecuador between 2000 and 2010. Importantly, this represents less than half of the declarations of regimes of exception issued by Ecuadorian presidents during that period. This finding offers a contrast with the case of Bolivia, where the disaster paradigm has become clearly dominant, and with Peru where—although the repressive paradigm is still predominant in practical and symbolical terms—well over half of the declarations made during the same period were done so within the disaster paradigm. Consequently and categorically, it is clear that the disaster paradigm is relevant but has not been dominant in recent political processes in Ecuador.

Typical cases of declarations of regimes of exception within the disaster paradigm include: technical works to mitigate the effects of flooding (DE1729 of 2001), technical works to repair the structural damage and resolve sanitation problems caused by flooding (DE2492 of 2002), technical measures to deal with pollution in a land-fill site (DE281 of 2003), technical measures to protect people from a landslide (DE1572 of 2006), special funds and plans to deal with epidemics (DE175 of 2007), technical measures to safeguard the population on Ecuador's coast from a particularly harsh winter season (DE900 of 2008), and technical measures to deal with droughts affecting the population and agricultural sector DE254 (2010). In line with the comments made by a political economist in a personal interview with the author,[55] in these situations, fast-track budgeting and contracting measures prove to be particularly useful.

Although the majority of the declarations appeared to be one-off events, two situations gave rise to what in effect became semipermanent or reiterated regimes of exception, throughout the decade. The first is to repair the damage to the road network caused by heavy rains. Indeed, the different declarations made throughout the decade were connected by several extensions in time, meaning that they constituted a semipermanent state of emergency or exception in the country's road system, facilitating the long-term, direct adjudication of contracts to carry out technical work. DE 2454 is a case in point and points to previous declarations and a need to decree a new state of emergency:

> Considering . . . that Executive Decree 2015-A published in the Official Register No. 415 of 7th September 2004, renewed the declaration of a state of emergency in the roads of the provinces of Orellana, Sucumbíos, Napo, Pastaza, Morona Santiago and Zamora Chinchipe, an emergency declared via Executive Decree No. 1790 published in Official Register No. 364 of the 25th June 2004. . . . That it is the duty of the Ecuadorian state, faced with the recurrence of the danger that threatens this region to adopt the necessary measures. . . . That the Ministry of Public Works and Communications, given that the causes that motivated the declaration of emergency in the provinces previously mentioned, asks for the state of emergency to be declared again. . . .
>
> DE2454 5th January 2005

As a result, direct contracting procedures are offered up to the Ministry of Public Works and Communications, as established in the following excerpt:

> Article 1 A state of emergency is declared in the roads of the provinces of Orellana, Sucumbíos, Napo, Pastaza, Morona Santiago and Zamora Chinchipe, which are determined as a zone of priority attention, and, as a result, it is disposed that the Ministry of Public Works and Communications is in charge of carrying out the necessary processes and procedures established in the Law of Public Contracting and its regulations required in these cases, in order to carry out the necessary works in order to deal with the roads, paths, and bridges and to solve the events caused by nature and the imminent danger that undoubtedly poses a threat to this important and strategic region.
>
> DE2454 5th January 2005

In the same way, a semipermanent or repeated application of regimes of exception was used to offer technical and administrative responses to eruptions of the Tungurahua volcano throughout the decade. In the course of my research I discovered several initial declarations of states of emergency or exception in relation to volcanic activity in the area[56] but as in the case of the road system they need to be understood in the context of a whole series renewals and new declarations, as is clear in the case of DE1914 issued on 11th October 2006. Indeed this decree refers to an initial declaration of a state of emergency via DE1424 of 2004, a renewal for a further sixty days via DE1655, and another renewal for a further sixty days via DE2333 and DE210. Next it refers to a new declaration of a state of emergency via DE952 in 2005, which was renewed in 2006 first via DE1195, then via DE1415, and then via DE1682. Finally, DE1777 extends the decree throughout the provinces of Tungurahua, Chimborazo, and Bolivia, over a year after the specific declaration (DE952) was issued. In this context the decree states: ". . . to date, the situation that caused the original declarations and renewals of states of emergency which have been referred to has not disappeared but rather it has got worse" (DE1914, 11th October 2006).

This reiterated or permanent use of regimes of exception to deal with a specific threat over time may be considered roughly parallel to the situation in a large part of Southern Peru following the earthquake of Pisco in 2007. Volcanic certainly constitutes a disaster or catastrophe rather than a natural adverse phenomenon and there were frequent eruptions of Tunghurahua between 2000 and 2010. Nevertheless, it is important to ask whether this semipermanent state of emergency is more akin to discretionary or decisionist rather than emergency politics, given that a long-term exception seems to have arisen.

Before concluding this section, it is important to mention a sporadic but significant tendency to call upon the military to implement the measures decreed within the disaster paradigm, via the use of force, or the suspension of certain rights.[57] Indeed, between 2000 and 2010, several declarations of this type were issued, mirroring developments in Bolivia. To understand how the use of force is employed in a disaster type emergency, DE1693, signed on 29th April 2009, is a case in point. In this case, the threat of swine flu is identified as a possible cause of "internal commotion" throughout the Republic. Hence, a state of exception is declared, permitting the mobilization of the military and public resources. Likewise, the health sector is called upon to prevent and contain the virus. Crucially, human rights may be subject to suspension as Article 1 states "The freedom of movement and assembly of those living in Ecuador may be limited in line with the evolution of the possibility that the swine flu virus reaches the country and provokes an outbreak of swine flu." It is interesting to note in this case that declaring a regime of exception was Ecuador's immediate reaction to a potentially global threat and is presented as the government's responsibility toward both Ecuadorian citizens and the global community.

In a personal interview carried out in Quito in July 2010, the idea of suspending rights in the framework of disaster emergency politics was talked of quite naturally. There was concern, however, over potential abuses: "If rights are to be limited, there should be a degree of certainty. . . . Otherwise you don't know whether in a state of emergency where you have to flee the region because of a natural disaster they are going to confiscate my property. So this creates considerable uncertainty, that is one of the dangers."

Importantly, there does not seem to be much debate in Ecuador about the use of regimes of exception within the disaster paradigm.[58] Nevertheless, a few articles were found in the press in which brief discussions were established.[59] The main preoccupation is that the reiterated use of emergency decrees to resolve problems of natural disasters would not constitute a satisfactory long-term reply or policy, in the case of, Tungurahua and the road system. In any case, there is an apparent de-politicization of regimes of exception within the disaster paradigm in Ecuador, mirroring the situation in both Bolivia and Peru. Nevertheless this use is by no means innocuous given that three potentially concerning features have become apparent in the case of Ecuador: the use of resources and adjudication of public contracts, semipermanent or reiterated declarations of regimes of exception, and the occasional use of military force and/or suspension of human rights to deal with epidemics and natural disasters.

KEY FINDINGS AND ANALYSIS

In a personal interview with the author, carried out in Quito in July 2010, a political economist observed that states of emergency have been used sporadically in Ecuador and that they "have not formed part of a strategy, they have not formed part of a dynamic of the political system." While this may be true of regimes of exception used within the repressive paradigm, it certainly is not true of regimes of exception within the administrative paradigm, which came to characterize a style of government during the first years of President Rafael Correa's *Revolución Ciudadana.*

One of the other key findings of this study is the transformation of regimes of exception at the formal level. Indeed, as in the case of Bolivia, a whole new normative framework was established in Ecuador with a new Constitution, in this case in 2008. In the context of a very repressive and polemical declaration of a state of emergency at Dayuma, there was considerable debate in the Constituent Assembly and the figure of the "state of exception" was introduced.[60] For the principal purpose of this study, the new normative framework for the regime of exception is not so very different in terms of the extraordinary situations (external/internal aggression, internal commotion, calamity, and natural disaster) and extraordinary measures (military intervention, the suspension of several human rights, and various administrative or budgeting powers) that it completes. Nevertheless, there have been considerable formal changes and limitations put on executive power in the framework of this mechanism, including the explicit mention of Despouy's principles (1999), details of the information that must be included in every declaration, and an important oversight power for the Constitutional Tribunal. These changes were made in the light of a very public ruling in 2007 by the Inter-American Court of Human Rights and the national Constitutional Tribunal in 2008 in relation to military control over civilians in the framework of states of emergency.

Beyond these formal developments, regimes of exception continue to be a political reality in Ecuador. Indeed, over one hundred declarations of states of emergency or exception were made by Ecuadorian Presidents between 2000 and 2010, a considerably higher number than in Bolivia and a very similar number to that of neighboring Peru. While various declarations were made within the repressive paradigm, and a considerable number within the disaster paradigm, what is particularly interesting is the higher number of declarations within the administrative paradigm. As the representative of a human rights NGO explained in a personal interview in Quito in July 2010, "A state of emergency is declared if there is an energy crisis, a food shortage, an education crisis. States of emergency are declared for any reason." This development appears to be an Ecuadorian innovation or, if you like, "speciality."

Furthermore, the degree to which this use has become linked to one President—Rafael Correa—and politicized in the press means that in recent years the administrative paradigm has come to dominate how regimes of exception are thought of and practiced in Ecuador. States of emergency or exception are equivalent to intervening in sectors, implementing decisions with the justification that if they are not done so in a fast-track way, an (unspecified) internal commotion will occur.

Next, it is important to evaluate what these developments mean for the compatibility of regimes of exception in Ecuador with its consolidation as a democracy. In a personal interview with the author,[61] the representative of a national-level human rights NGO identified four main shortcomings with regard to the use of regimes of exception in Ecuador: a lack of formality in declaring the decrees,[62] a lack of effective oversight (even with the new role of the Constitutional Tribunal as of 2008),[63] situations that are not really emergencies as such, which I would add is in line with the tenets of securitization theory, and an overuse of the idea of "internal commotion" as an umbrella to justify unnecessary declarations. All of these observations have been corroborated in this chapter.

More specifically, in terms of the use of regimes of exception within the repressive emergency politics paradigm, it would be accurate to evaluate their use in general as not particularly *effective*. Indeed, according to the interviewees and the cases revised here, the use of states of emergency to repress indigenous protest over natural resources and mobilizations that threatened the government had two main, negative consequences from this perspective: first, rather than putting a stop to the conflicts and protest the declarations actually radicalized them, and second because—in the cases of President Mahuad and President Gutiérrez—the unpopular application of a state of emergency ultimately lead to their downfall. The only real exception to this could be the state of exception declared by President Correa in 2010 as it certainly put an end to the protests and served to consolidate his power, in a similar way to the case of President Morales and the state of siege declared in Pando in Bolivia in 2008.

In the same way, regimes of exception used within the repressive paradigm have not generally been considered *legitimate*, given that they have offered a way to criminalize protest by disadvantaged groups in society. According to the analysis of an ex-leader of CONAIE, Ecuadorian governments have declared states of emergency "first to try to repress and scare people and second to avoid any changes in a law that is drawn up according to their interests" (Personal interview with the author, Quito, July 2010). Likewise, although they have considerable power at the formal level, Congress and later the Constitutional Tribunal have not proved effective in overseeing these measures. As the representative of a human rights NGO explained in a personal interview in Quito in July 2010: "I am of the impression that [the Tribunal] has responded quickly but it has never responded negatively and that is also some suspicion because the court is allied with the government [of Correa]."

Nevertheless, important changes have been made to the normative framework of regimes of exception during the period, particularly with regard to the military jurisdiction over citizens. Indeed, as of 2008 it was ruled unlawful, an important step forward for the legitimacy of regimes of exception in Ecuador. Moreover, the explicit acknowledgement of principles of international law and the notification to the UN and the OAS are important developments in the "state of exception" established in the Constitution of 2008. While many of these changes are due to public debate and the activity of human rights organizations, the degree to which repressive regimes of exception were politicized or revised is by no means comparable to the case of Bolivia.

Next, the analysis carried out in this chapter provides evidence to support the negative opinions on administrative type decrees within the Ecuadorian press, in the framework of discussions on democratic governability. In terms of *legitimacy*, while there is no suspension of human rights there is a clear lack of accountability over public contracting procedures and financing, as well as a concentration of power in the executive branch.[64] Also, the fact that there is no clear remit for administrative type declarations of regimes of exception in the Constitution or legal framework (only situations of natural disaster are referred to) makes their formal legitimacy very doubtful, with consistent references to "internal commotion" proving rather hollow and repetitive. Moreover, while the aim of these decrees is to increase *efficiency*, the results are rather mixed. On the one hand, the series of decrees affecting both the electricity sector lasted from 2004 (if not before) until (at least) 2010, which suggests that the supposedly temporary measures that were implemented were, ultimately, highly inefficient. On the other hand, what can only be described as an avalanche of administrative-type decrees at the beginning of the *Revolución Ciudadana* seemingly kick-started a process of administrative and institutional change in a very effective (albeit widely debated) way. In this last case a degree of "popular" legitimacy seems to come from those citizens supporting the strong-man approach to politics, in a clear populist tendency.

However, the most potentially troubling declarations from the point of democratic governability are those administrative decrees which deploy the military to implement the decision, something reflected in debates in the national press. Indeed, in terms of *legitimacy*, the intervention of the Armed Forces is concerning both for the protection of human rights as well as the democratic precept of civilian control over the military. Moreover, the lack of oversight over public contracting procedures and financing are a cause for concern in terms of accountability, as with the fast-track administrative declarations. On the other hand, while the aim of these decrees is to increase *efficiency*, the results again are dubious: a series of extensions in effect as of 20th January 2009 up until the end of the period studied here placed Petroecuador under a long-term state of emergency which facilitated its intervention by the Naval Force, a situation which, rather than reflecting the efficiency of the measure, speaks of governmental inefficiency at providing an adequate policy for the sector and a negation of the possibility of ordinary politics.

Finally, regimes of exception within the disaster paradigm have clearly not been *efficient* in all cases. Indeed, the fact that the road system and the provinces surrounding the Tungurahua volcano have been subject to reiterated or semipermanent declarations of regimes of exception would suggest that their efficiency has indeed been limited. In relation to their *legitimacy*, the fact that there has been little public debate points to a de-politicization of this use of regimes of exception in practice and therefore higher levels of legitimacy. Crucially, given that the declarations of states of emergency or exception to deal with natural disasters offer the possibility of direct purchases and contracting with no evident oversight mechanisms (as in the case of the administrative paradigm), there should be concerns over transparency. It is important to note that the formal developments made in that sense in Bolivia and Peru during the decade under study were not mirrored in Ecuador. Furthermore, in those occasions when rights are suspended or military force is used the same concerns regarding repressive type regimes of exception could apply to those declarations made within the disaster paradigm.

In conclusion, the locus of concern regarding regimes of exception in third-wave Ecuador has generally moved from the human rights matrix to the transparency or accountability one, in the framework of declarations of regimes of exception within the administrative and the disaster paradigms. Consequently, providing more powerful and independent oversight procedures for the use of public resources and contracting procedures would be a way to democratize these mechanisms even further. Furthermore, the fact that there is no specific constitutional or legal framework for regimes of exception within the administrative paradigm means that they constitute a broad interpretation of regimes of exception (often with the justification of an "internal commotion") and could consequently be considered less legitimate than declarations of disaster-type emergencies or exceptions. Indeed, the reiterated or semipermanent application of these mechanisms makes this issue all the more pressing. Moreover, the continuing use of the military in the framework of regimes of exception to implement administrative decisions is particularly concerning from the perspective of the separation of powers and the protection of human rights.

Despite these concerns it is important to highlight the considerable developments at the formal level that have come about as a result of the "state of exception" established in the Constitution of 2008. Indeed, a lack of formality in publishing the decrees had previously made them rather opaque mechanisms within Ecuadorian politics. The fact that—according to the constitutional regime of exception—all decrees must include complete information and be notified to the UN and the OAS is a considerable step forward in terms of the compatibility of regimes of exception in Ecuador. Likewise—although thus far it has not been particularly effective—the (re)introduction of the Constitutional Tribunal as an oversight mechanism for the declaration of regimes of exception must be considered very welcome news.

It became clear during a conversation with an expert on constitutional law that the degree to which these formal changes will be effective in the future depends on the good faith of government in power at any time. Indeed, the fact that the justification of "internal commotion" has permeated declarations of regimes of exception throughout Ecuadorian history and continues to be present at the constitutional level leaves the door open for abuses: "For instance, you say a grave internal commotion according to the principle of necessity. But who's necessity are we talking about? The State? Society? The government? In my opinion this is rather dangerous" (Personal interview with the author carried out in Quito, July 2010). Consequently, these formal developments will only prove as democratic as the government that uses them in practice.

NOTES

1. This finding was highlighted in a prepublication, see Wright 2014a.
2. These declarations are available at www.derechoecuador.com. The search was carried out online and according to the nomenclatures used in the relevant normative frameworks of regimes of exception, in this case "estado de emergencia" and "estado de excepción." As well as the declarations, other relevant information including extensions in time or into different territories was also collected.
3. For instance the bulletins of "Conflictividad Socio-Política" published by the journal *Ecuador Debate,* (1980–2010) and the reports produced by the human rights NGO Inredh (2008).
4. Fieldwork was carried out by the author in Quito in June and July 2010. Those interviewed included a representative from a national human rights organization, an ex-leader of the CONAIE movement, a leader of Pachakutik, a general trade union leader, an ex-leader of a trade union of petrol sector workers, a legal scholar, a political economist, and a prominent political sociologist. The interviewees were selected according to the findings discovered throughout the study and in keeping to the snowball technique, according to the guidelines of Valles (2009). The identity of the interviewees is not revealed here in order to protect their opinions and comments and because what is of interest is their sociopolitical function and perspective. The interviews are on file with the author.
5. The electronic archives of two of the main national newspapers were consulted between 2000 and 2010: Hoy (www.hoy.com.ec) and El Universo (www.eluniverso.com). The first newspaper closed in 2014 due to financial difficulties.
6. Again, this is a very interesting development that will be returned to later.
7. Several articles from the newspaper Hoy quote different aspects of this report. "El Ecuador con 44 estados de emergencia vigentes," "Un país que sobrevive en la crisis del poder," "Una competencia por ver quién declara más movilizaciones," 10th February 2001. www.hoy.com.ec/Suplemen/blan122/negro1.htm_
8. Personal interview with the author in Quito, July 2010.
9. Personal interview carried out with the author in Quito, July 2010.
10. Articles from the newspaper Hoy quote a report carried out by the NGO Inredh on exceptional measures between 1924 and 1997. "El Ecuador con 44 estados de emergencia vigentes," "Un país que sobrevive en la crisis del poder," "Una competencia por ver quién declara más movilizaciones," Blanco y Negro, Hoy, 10th February 2001. www.hoy.com.ec/Suplemen/blan122/negro1.htm_
11. Sánchez Parga (1998) refers to this phenomenon.

12. It is worth noting that other emergency powers were used during this period but the number refers to states of emergency specifically.

13. Freedom of opinion (Article 23.9); inviolability of the home (Article 23.12); inviolability of correspondence (Article 23.13); freedom of movement (Article 23.14); freedom of association (Article 23.19).

14. Declarations of regimes of exception are understood as those decrees in which the President—referring to the relevant articles of the Constitution of 1998 or 2008 declares a "state of emergency" or "state of exception." During this time, 2 "states of siege" were declared, 52 cases of "emergency" and 11 cases of "disaster."

15. The decrees in question are DE435 of 2000, DE1806 of 2001, DE1811 of 2001, DE369 of 2002, De784 of 2003, DE1424 of 2004, DE2713 of 2005, DE430 of 2005, DE165 of 2005, and DE1130-A of 2006.

16. Personal interview carried out in Quito, June 2010.

17. "¡Atropello a la constitución!," article published on the 16th April 2005 in el Universo; Letters to the editor "Orellana y su grito de reivindicación" published on 30th July 2010 in el Universo; Letters to the editor "El inolvidable jueves 30" 5th October 2010 in El Universo; Opinion column "Detener la violencia" published on 6th February 2001 in El Universo; Buzón de lectores "Sobre el estado de emergencia" published on 6th April 2006.

18. On this episode see Freidenberg (2008)and Cárdenas Reyes (2003).

19. On this episode see Barrera (2001).

20. On this issue see Acosta (2005).

21. This is the nomenclature of the new regime of exception established in the Constitution of 2008 which is described in some detail later on in this chapter.

22. On this episode see Ortiz-T (2011).

23. The inclusion of both citizen and human security is an interesting move away from the previous, national security paradigm.

24. "Sin sustento legal" opinion piece published on 10th October 2010 in Universo; Hernán Pérez Loose "Excepción sin excepción" published on 5th October 2010 in El Universo; Pedro X Valverde Rivera "Indefinida e ininterrumpida" published on 8th October 2010, in el Universo; "Concluye este día el estado de excepción en Quito" opinion column published on 9th December 2010 in Hoy; "Innecesaria ampliación de estado de excepción" opinion piece published on 15th October 2010 in Hoy; "Injustificable abuso al amparo de excepción" opinion piece published on 13 de October del 2010 in Hoy.

25. As well as these cases, another two declarations of states of emergency were declared to deal with strikes (DE2625 of 2002) and roadblocks (DE1269 of 2006). Given that they were minor, isolated events that did not constitute a real challenge for the government they are not discussed in detail here.

26. It is calculated that less than 4% of Ecuador's population lives in the Amazon region (Freidenberg and Alcántara Sáez 2001).

27. "¿Hasta cuándo los paros?," editorial column published on 9th May 2002 in el Universo.

28. Data from personal interview with the representative of a human rights NGO, carried out in Quito, July 2010.

29. "Detener la violencia" opinion piece published on 6th February 2001 in el Universo.

30. See the extensive report carried out by Aguirre (2008) and CEDHU (2007). A reduced analysis of this episode was included in a prior publication (Wright 2013b).

31. The debate even reached the Constituent Assembly, see Resolución del Pleno de la Asamblea Constituyente, 14th March 2008, available at www.constituyente.asambleanacional.gov.ec.

32. See for instance the Carta Abierta (no date) directed to the "Presidente de la República, Asamblea Nacional Constituyente y Partidos Políticos y Ciudadanía en general" (President of the Republic, National Constituent Assembly and Political Parties and Citizens in general) and signed by the Comisión Ecuménica de Derechos Humanos (CEDHU), el Servicio Paz y Justicia de Ecuador (SERPAJ) and la Fundación Regional de Asesoría en Derechos Humanos (INREDH). Available at www.inredh.org.

33. Resolución del Pleno de la Asamblea Constituyente, 14th March 2008. Available at www.constituyente.asambleanacional.gov.ec. On this issue see also Becker, 2011.

34. Acción de Inconstitucionalidad Presentada por Luis Ángel Saavedra et al., caso 42–2007-TC.

35. It is also worth pointing out that the Inter-American Court of Human Rights case of Zambrano Vélez and others vs. Ecuador, in its sentence of 4th July 2007 (available at www.corteidh.or.cr) likewise warns about the use of military tribunals in the framework of the Security Law in Ecuador.

36. Sentence available at http://www.juridicas.unam.mx/publica/librev/rev/dialjur/cont/7/cnt/cnt11.pdf.

37. For several Ecuadorian analysts, the predominance of "principles" creates a degree of ambiguity in the new constitutional framework. Personal interview with constitutional law expert carried out in Quito, July 2010.

38. There was great public debate about this declaration of emergency with opinions both for and against the use of the military to deal with crime. The following articles were involved in the debate: "Seguridad y Polícia" opinion piece published on 2nd February 2000 in Hoy; "Derechos e impunidad" editorial column published on 7th October 2009 in el Universo; Letters to the Director "Estado de excepción y percepción de seguridad" opinion piece published on 20th December 2009, in Hoy; "Falta una política integral de seguridad" opinion piece published on 3rd January 2010 in Hoy.

39. This was confirmed by the representative of a national human rights NGO and a political economist in personal interviews carried out by the author in Quito in July and June, 2010.

40. Quito, June 2010.

41 DE1354 of 5th February 2004, DE2045-A of 31st August 2004, DE2427 of 30th December 2004, DE436 of 24th August 2005, DE 1202 of 3rd March 2006, DE1331 of 7th April 2006, and DE244 of 8th February 2010.

42. For example DE436 was extended by DE709 of 24th October 2005.

43. Apparently there is a direct historical precedent in the country, with a decree in 1997 in which the police force is declared in a "state of emergency" (DE416-A of 27 June 1997).

44. As Conaghan and de la Torre explain (2008, 271) one of the main objectives of Correa was a Constituent Assembly with full powers, something that he achieved after the elections of December 2007 (Freidenberg 2008, 94) via the popular mandate.

45. On Correa's first year in government see Conaghan and de la Torre (2008).

46. See for instance: "¿Emergencia indefenida?" editorial column published on 5th June 2008 in el Universo;; "Emergencia Social" opinion piece published on 4th February 2000, Hoy; Letters to the Editor "Emergencia y Prioridades" published on 11th June 2007, in Hoy; "Emergencia policial, sin resultados" opinion piece published on 23rd October 2008 in Hoy; "Abusivos decretos de emergencia," opinion piece published on 25th November 2008.

47. In this sentence it is worth remembering that one of the pillars of populism is the direct solution of problems. On the issue of neo-populism in Latin America see de la Torre 1997 and Gratius 2007.

48. These declarations are very similar to those presented in the section on fast-track administration, the main difference being the use of the armed forces to oversee the implementation of the administrative intervention.

49. These cases are very similar to DS27963 declared in Bolivia in 2005.

50. DE766 of 29th November 2007, DE1544 of 20th January 2009, DE1680 of 20th April 2009, DE1838-A of 22nd July 2009, DE101 of 19th October 2009, and DE228 of 19th January 2010

51. "Técnicos Petroleros" published on 28th August 2009 in el Universo; León Roldós Aguilera "La interpretación constitucional," published on 16th August 2009 in el Universo; "La verdad" published on 15th June 2009 in el Universo; Joffre Gampaña Mora "Nueva burla a la constitución" published on 12th February 2009 in el Universo; Hernán Pérez Loose "La trituradora" published on 23rd November 2010 in el Universo; Alfredo Pinoargote "Hipocresía y golpismo" published on 31st October 2010, in el Universo; "Petroecuador, emergencias, contratos y silencios," published on 14th July 2009 in Hoy.

52. Letters to the editor "Técnicos Petroleros" published on 28th August 2009 in el Universo; León Roldós Aguilera "La interpretación constitucional," published on 16th October 2009 in el Universo; Joffre Gampaña Mora "Nueva burla a la constitución" published on 12th February 2009 in el Universo; Alfredo Pinoargote "Hipocresía y golpismo" published on 31st October 2010, in el Universo; "Petroecuador, emergencias, contratos y silencios" opinion piece published on 14th July 2009 in Hoy; "Estados de excepción desvirtuados y sin resultado," opinion piece published on 20th April 2009 in Hoy.

53. "Estados de excepción desvirtuados y sin resultado" 20th April 2009 in Hoy.

54. Opinion of a constitutional legal expert expressed in a personal interview with the author carried out in Quito, July 2010.

55. Quito, June 2010.

56. DE800 (2000), DE1762 (2001), DE2333 (2004), DE952 (2005), DE1914 (2006), DE188 (2007), and DE1180 (2008).

57. DE421 of 2003, DE1260 of 2008, DE69 of 2009, DE365 of 2010, DE289 of 2010. DE1914 of 2006, and DE1693 of 2009.

58. For instance, it was not mentioned by the interviewees in Quito in June/July 2010.

59. Letters to the editor "Promesas al Agricultor" published on 18th January 2006 in el Universo; Letters to the Editori "¿Por qué se mueren las vaquitas?" published on 19th December 2009 in el Universo; Ricardo Tello Carrión "Otra vez la Josefina" published on 13th May 2010 in el Universo; and "Emergencia, un estilo de Rafael Correa" opinion piece published on 7th March 2007 in Hoy.

60. Data from personal interview with the representative of a human rights NGO, carried out in Quito in July 2010. See for instance the statements made by the Ecuadorian government to the Inter-American Court of Human Rights: Caso Zambrano Vélez y otros Vs. Ecuador, sentencia de 4 de julio del 2007, p. 8. Available at www.corteidh.or.cr. For the expert in constitutional law—personal interview carried out in Quito, in July 2010—there was actually little debate in the Assembly.

61. Quito, July 2010.

62. This is reflected in the lack of a register of certain decrees—called "ghost" decrees in this chapter—as well as the fact that typically several days (and sometimes weeks or month) pass between the declaration and its publication in the official register, meaning that oversight measures are made particularly difficult as they only come into effect once the decree has been officially published.

63. As of 2008, the Constitutional Tribunal has to declare the constitutionality of the declaration of the regime of exception. While this is an important oversight measure, in practice it has always found in favor of the executive, reflecting its lack of independence.

64. Again, between the declaration and the publication of the states of emergency or states of exception, considerable time passed, making the possibility of Congressional oversight very difficult. For instance, DE1546 was declared on the 12th of June and published on the 27th June.

Chapter 6

Lessons Learned

If I were asked to single out one lesson that I have learned about regimes of exception and emergency politics over the course of this study, it is the degree to which they are at odds with democratic institutions. In Peru I was told, "you cannot have a democratic government with islands of military dictatorship,"[1] in Bolivia that "the use of the state of siege should be very questionable, it is not necessarily a democratic mechanism,"[2] and in Ecuador that "it is the worst possible thing because you eliminate a democratic State and the rule of Law."[3] If I could point out a second lesson it would be that regimes of exception continue to be a very relevant fact of political life in the three countries under study, three decades after their transitions to democracy. They are not just a constitutional or legal possibility or "a nice topic for a historical study"[4] but rather institutions of great political and social transcendence, with very different applications in practice.

The main aim of this volume has been to offer a humble but rigorous contribution to our understanding of what emergency politics means in practice, with the secondary aim of evaluating how it relates to democracy. Specifically, I have concentrated on the use of regimes of exception in Peru, Bolivia, and Ecuador throughout the third wave of democracy and, particularly, during the first decade of the twenty-first century. While the focus of the study is thus reduced—and the lessons learned should be understood as of a limited scope—several important conclusions can be highlighted that could have important implications for our understandings and evaluations of emergency politics in other contexts. Consequently, this section offers an overview of the main lessons learned from the three empirical case studies and is divided into three sections which include: the key findings in relation to emergency politics in practice; next, the main observations on the relationship between regimes of exception and democratic governability; and finally a series of best practices.

FINDINGS IN RELATION TO EMERGENCY POLITICS IN PRACTICE

In Chapters 1 and 2, several important debates on emergency politics in general and in Latin American in particular were established. Consequently, in line with the tenets of grounded theory (Glaser and Strauss 1967) the following paragraphs reflect on the key findings with regard to: the incidence of emergency politics; the relationship between the norm and the exception; the nature of the exceptional threat; the link between extraordinary situations and measures (within the three and emergency paradigms); the role of Presidents as "declarers" of regimes of exception; and finally the importance of present and past institutions.

The first key finding is that emergency politics, as expressed through declarations of regimes of exception, has been a prevalent aspect of political life. Peru and Ecuador, in particular, show a similar incidence of regimes of exception—115 and 112 presidential declarations of regimes of exception between 2000 and 2010, respectively—and a general tendency for this incidence to increase over the decade. While Bolivia shows a lesser and, importantly, decreasing tendency toward the use of regimes of exception during this period, its total of 65 declarations of regimes of exception is still considerable. Consequently, given that regimes of exception are just one type of emergency politics, the results here point to a very broad use in the three countries in question. In fact, it may be worth asking how *exceptional* they actually are given that their use appears to be rather *routine*.

The next general, but equally important, finding relates to the various relationships that exist between the norm and the exception, beyond the clear divisions of Republican Exceptionalism (Lazar 2006). While in the majority of cases the application of the regime of exception was transitory, some important observations need to be made. As has already been highlighted, the elevated number of declarations of regimes of exception in the three countries essentially points to an everyday concept of emergency politics, which permeates and co-exists with ordinary politics, akin to the conceptualization of Honig (2009) and Wright (2012). On the other hand, certain cases reflect long-term or *de facto* exceptions, such as the use of repressive regimes of exception in Peru to deal with coca cultivation and terrorist activity or of administrative regimes of exception in Ecuador to deal with structural problems in the petrol and electricity sectors. This idea of a long-term exception is in line with concerns of authors such as Friedrich (1950) and Constant (1989).

The third variation on the relationship between the exception and the norm speaks of a learning process in that once an exceptional situation has occurred it is no longer unexpected and therefore can no longer be considered exceptional (Gross and Ní Aoláin 2006). No such learning process was discovered in the three case studies; rather there seemed to be a learning process in which a regime of exception became the classic reaction to a particular problem, something that will be highlighted below.

The study also offers an interesting perspective on the idea of the exceptional threat. As pointed out in Chapter 1, constitutional doctrine has traditionally conceptualized the exceptional threat as directly endangering the organized life of a community. Recently, however, a more nuanced or relative concept that refers to governmental incapacity to deal with certain events has been offered. Evidence from the three case studies here support the latter conceptualization in that few extraordinary situations found really constituted a direct threat to the life of the nation, except perhaps the cases of the earthquake in Pisco (Peru) or the eruptions of the volcano in Tungurahua (Ecuador). Consequently, the declarations of regimes of exception can be read as a manifestation of the lack of ordinary institutional capacity of these relatively young democracies. The (over)use of the vague concept of "internal commotion" in the case of Ecuador reflects this constructed element of emergencies, in line with securitization theory (Neal 2006).

Moving onto the specific uses of regimes of exception in practice, in Chapter 1 of this volume, the repressive paradigm was established as the classic type of emergency politics, in which coercion is applied (via the suspension of civil rights and/or the deployment of the military) in the face of political violence. In the three countries studied here, both the constitutional form and social representations of regimes of exception continue to correspond to this conceptualization. While multiple declarations of regimes of exception within this paradigm were found between 2000 and 2010, in numerical terms it does not constitute the dominant paradigm. Furthermore, in both Bolivia and Ecuador there has been a clear tendency for this use to decrease over the decade. Nevertheless, in Peru repressive emergency politics still holds fast and shows a tendency to increase over time. Three main uses were found for this type of declarations: to protect government from intense protest (in Bolivia and Ecuador); to deal with indigenous protest over the exploitation of natural resources (Ecuador and Peru); and to offer a permanent reply to coca cultivation and subversive groups (in the case of Peru).

Another type of emergency politics established from a political perspective in Chapter 1 of this volume was the disaster paradigm, in which extraordinary technical measures or humanitarian aid is applied to deal with natural catastrophes. While natural disasters are understood in all three countries as being a possible cause for the declaration of a regime of exception, little information is offered at the constitutional level on what measures can be taken in their name. Particularly in Bolivia and Peru, there have been interesting legal developments surrounding regimes of exception within the disaster paradigm, with Law 2140 offering a totally new paradigm of emergency politics within the risk management paradigm in the case of the former. In practice, the disaster paradigm shares similar features in all three countries: first, the identification of an adverse natural phenomenon (typically flooding, drought, epidemics, forest fires, and occasionally a real catastrophe such as an earthquake or volcanic eruption) that affects a community, infrastructure or economic activities; next, the establishment of extraordinary procedures for the adjudication of public contracts; and finally, the use of technical measures or humanitarian aid to deal with the situation. It is worth noting that in a handful of cases in Bolivia and Ecuador the military were called upon and/or human rights were suspended in order to ensure that the measures were successfully applied. In all three countries, the disaster paradigm is relevant, but particularly so in Bolivia, which as of 2000 has approached regimes of exception firmly from the idea of risk management.

The final paradigm of emergency politics established in Chapter 1 corresponds to an administrative logic in which exceptional administrative measures are applied to deal with administrative situations that are presented as an exceptional threat. Importantly, this corresponds to the second type of Roman dictatorship in which special measures were taken to get things done (Rossiter 2002) although there are no clear roots of this paradigm in Latin American constitutional history in general, including the three countries studied here. Likewise, while the regimes of exception established at the formal level do offer some administrative measures (including raising taxes, opening/closing ports, and changing the government's location, in the case of Ecuador), extraordinary administrative difficulties are not explicitly established as a potential exceptional threat. Nevertheless, in Ecuador, in particular, the administrative paradigm has also become synonymous with regimes of exception in recent years and shows an increasing incidence toward the end of the decade. Indeed, different sectors including the education system, prisons, the electricity sector, and the road system have all been subject to a fast-track intervention, which involves a complete administrative overhaul and/or exemptions from ordinary public contracting procedures, in line with secondary legislation. While this paradigm is effectively absent in Peru, in Bolivia there seem to have been a few tentative attempts at declaring administrative type regimes of exception to deal with unemployment, particularly in the mining sector.

Within this administrative paradigm, it is also worth noting a clear tendency in the case of Ecuador in which the military are called upon to implement or even administrate the measures that are declared. This is true of the government's approach to the management of strategic natural resources, particularly the petrol sector, and essentially is akin to rather violent interventionism and/or special privileges for the Armed Forces in the management of public companies.

An important question in relation to the use of regimes of exception in practice—and which brings their study firmly within the realms of political science—is whether this depends on the ideology of the President in power or indeed if he is in a minority government, in line with studies on Presidential crises in Latin America (Pérez-Liñán 2007) and the evaluation of a key informant in Bolivia.[5] In general terms, the evidence found in this study does not link the use of regimes of exception to certain Presidents, given that all of them have made use of these provisions throughout the period. Having said that, four more specific observations are worth making: first, that interim Presidents tended to shy away from declaring regimes of exception within the repressive paradigm; second, that there was a recurring situation in which, when a President was faced with a protest that directly threatened his government, he would declare a regime of exception; third, that repressive emergency politics in Peru is particularly linked with President García, perhaps reflecting a learning process from the fight against *Sendero Luminoso* in the 1980s; and fourth that administrative emergency politics in Ecuador is specifically linked to President Correa, reflecting his fast-track approach to political change and, potentially, populist approach toward politics in the framework of a minority government. In the last two cases it is possible to talk of a real Presidential style regarding the use of regimes of exception, although this is not true of all Presidents in the three countries in the period under study.

Another important question relates to the empirical and historical institutionalisms, given that regimes of exception should be understood as institutions of emergency politics. In terms of the relationship between the legal form and use in practice (empirical institutionalism), given the rather elliptic clauses at the constitutional level and the lack of laws to regulate regimes of exception (except in the case of Bolivia's Law 2140 in Bolivia), it seems that institutions do matter but discretion, informality, and innovation are equally important. In terms of the possibility of path dependency, this has been shown to be key to our understanding of the use of regimes of exception in the twenty-first century. Indeed, both constitutional forms and use in practice, particularly in relation to repressive regimes of exception, follow on from developments in the nineteenth and twentieth centuries. Consequently, Loveman's analysis (1993) still holds fast well into the twenty-first century. Nevertheless, there have been clear changes in Bolivia and Ecuador which can be explained by two critical junctures: the Guerra del Agua of 2000 in the former and the case of Dayuma in 2007 in the latter. There also appears to be a degree of path dependency in informal practices, given Presidential innovations in the use of regimes of exception to deal with certain problems that are then taken up and repeated by other Presidents. This has been seen to be the case for instance with regimes of exception to repair the road system in Bolivia and Ecuador, to deal with indigenous protest and coca cultivation in Peru, and to manage the electric and petrol sectors in Ecuador. In these cases the declaration of regimes of exception appears to be the automatic, knee-jerk reply to certain situations in line with previous use.

FINDINGS IN RELATION TO EMERGENCY POLITICS AND DEMOCRATIC GOVERNABILITY

Throughout this volume it has been argued that only once we know how emergency politics works in practice will it be possible to evaluate how it relates to democracy. In this sense, the framework of democratic governability offers a useful starting point for more inductive debates, given its two pillars of legitimacy and efficiency. In the paragraphs below I offer some observations garnered from the studies on Peru, Bolivia, and Ecuador, first from a formal point of view, next in general terms, and then according to the three different paradigms or types that have offered a conceptual lens for the empirical analysis carried out in the study: repressive, disaster, and administrative emergency politics.

First of all, in formal or normative terms it is important to establish that old debates on the suspension of rights rather than guarantees and military jurisdiction over citizens in the framework of regimes of exception have been largely overcome during the decade in question and these powers have been removed from constitutional and legal frameworks.[6] The fact that new regimes of exception have been established in both Bolivia (via Law 2140 and the Constitution of 2009) and Ecuador (with the Constitution of 2008), which are more in-keeping with international principles such as those established by Despouy (1999), should also be considered a positive development. Nevertheless, the fact that the constitutional clauses in all three countries remain very brief and are still focused on the repressive emergency politics paradigm mean that they do not entirely reflect political use and informal arrangements. Consequently, the declarations that are made in the name of regimes of exception often rely on secondary laws and/or Presidential innovation, meaning that their use in practice comes closer to the extralegal model rather than the constitutional accommodation one (in line with the scheme of Gross and Ní Aoláin 2006) and therefore should be evaluated differently.

Next, the sheer number of declarations of regimes of exception (almost 300 cases in three countries over an eleven-year period) is problematic given that it represents a high degree of abnormality within democratic regimes, protected by the idea of the black-box of the "exception" rather than mere governmental discretion. This could—and I argue should—be taken into consideration in measures of the quality of democracy as it represents a considerable reliance on measures that by their nature are meant to be exceptional. Furthermore, the fact that regimes of exception are repeatedly used in areas where State presence is low (such as the VRAE and Alto Huallaga Valley in Peru and Amazonian provinces in Ecuador) refer us back to old concerns expressed by Guillermo O'Donnell (1997). Indeed, the study carried out here casts a shadow of doubt over the capacity for institutions to resolve repeated conflicts and problems through mechanisms of ordinary politics, three decades into the third wave of democracy.

In terms of the use of regimes of exception according to the repressive paradigm, it is clear that in general terms they have been neither *legitimate* nor *efficient*. In terms of *legitimacy*, their continuing use to deal with episodes of social protest has been criticized in public debate given that it is seen to protect the government in power at the time rather than the State or the citizens as such. Furthermore, the role of the military in these situations is still problematic from the point of view of the separation of powers, although—as highlighted above—there have been some formal improvements regarding their role. In terms of the *efficiency* of regimes of exception declared within the repressive paradigm, it is clear that they have tended to radicalize protest and on occasions even precipitated certain Presidents' ousting, including Jamal Mahuad Witt and Lucio Gutiérrez in Ecuador and Gonzalo Sánchez de Lozada in Bolivia. Furthermore, the reiterated use of regimes of exception in a permanent state of emergency to deal with the cultivation of coca and subversive groups in Peru reflects the inefficiency of the measure, which is designed to be transitory. Two exceptions may be found to this general pattern of inefficiency: the "state of siege" declared in Pando (2008) and the "state of exception" declared in Quito (2010), given that the two episodes appear to have consolidated the power of President Morales and President Correa, respectively.

Next, with regard to the use of regimes of exception within the disaster paradigm, our evaluation from the perspective of democratic governability is mixed. In terms of *legitimacy*, it appears that natural phenomena are generally seen as a legitimate reason to declare a regime of exception, given their presence in constitutional forms and the fact that they are (perhaps erroneously) seen as a nonpolitical or man-made problem. Nevertheless, the fact that they facilitate the use of resources and the direct adjudication of contracts should be of concern from the perspective of transparency or accountability. Even more concerning are the handful of cases in which the military is deployed and/or human rights are suspended, given that the same concerns in relation to repressive regimes of exception are also valid in these cases. In relation to their *efficiency*, these types of declarations are essentially a call to arms in terms of offering technical measures and humanitarian aid and should be considered efficient to the extent that they deal with a specific problem over a short period of time. Nevertheless, the long-term or reiterated use of declarations of this type—as in the case of the Pisco earthquake, the Tungurahua volcano, or emergency works on Bolivia's and Ecuador's highway system—suggest that these transitory measures are rather a replacement for policy to deal with vulnerability, something picked up in public debate in national newspapers.

Finally, the administrative paradigm—which has emerged with great force in Ecuador and rather tentatively in Bolivia—is questionable from the perspective of democratic governability. First, in relation to *legitimacy*, given that there is no clear constitutional or legal basis for this use of regimes of exception—beyond the ambiguous idea of an "internal commotion" in the case of Ecuador—it is very difficult to approach it from a normative perspective. In any case, the idea of a fast-track or (as ultimately happened) long-term intervention in the management of a particular sector rather than a long-term policy approach is concerning for the prevalence of ordinary and therefore democratic politics. Likewise, the use of direct purchases or contracting is of considerable concern for transparency, with few real accountability mechanisms. In the considerable number of cases where the military is called upon to implement the administrative measures, we are undoubtedly in the face of a very problematic type of emergency politics for democracy, given the apparent lack of civil control over the military, even in what amounts to economic affairs. In terms of social or political legitimacy, public opinion appears to be divided in Ecuador and Bolivia, with some calls for the use of this type of powers to deal quickly and efficiently with difficulties in sectors and services and others criticizing what is seen to be a "perversion" of regimes of exception. In terms of their *efficiency*, the possible avoidance of conflict in Bolivia for instance would be seen as a positive result of the use of this type of mechanisms whereas the long-term application of regimes of exception in the case of Ecuador would point to their general inefficiency.

BEST PRACTICES

To end this volume on a more constructive note, it is worth pointing out some best practices in relation to regimes of exception that can be inferred as a result of the three case studies of Peru, Bolivia, and Ecuador in the third wave of democracy.

1. The first best practice is related to the importance of mechanisms of horizontal accountability, as exemplified by the debates in the Bolivian Congress during the state of siege in 2000. Beyond vague formal powers, both the legislative and judicial powers should be given real teeth to oversee the different uses of regimes of exception and their potential incompatibilities with democracy, not only the suspension of human rights and the role of the military, but also the use of financial resources, the direct adjudication of public contracts, and the evaluation of reiterated or semipermanent declarations of regimes of exception.
2. Another best practice is related to social accountability, which concerns a public politicization of the use of regimes of exception. The opinions of NGOs, politicians and the public undoubtedly helped to bring about positive change in Bolivia and Ecuador in relation to repressive regimes of exception. Likewise, the degree to which administrative decrees became politicized in Ecuador means that at least they were not carried out in a de-politicized vacuum. Given their widespread legitimacy, declarations made in the disaster paradigm have not been subject to public scrutiny but given the observations made in the section on democratic governability, it would be important for civil society to raise awareness of and evaluate their use.
3. At the formal level, another best practice is to change the constitutional or legal structure to reflect changes in informal practices. For instance, there appears to be a degree of fumbling around with administrative regimes of exception in Bolivia, given the lack of a clear legal background for these types of measures. As Friedrich (1950) warns us, often the legal form does not reflect changes in practice and so it is important to update regimes of exception at the formal level on a regular basis. The Bolivian Constitution of 2009 and the Ecuadorian Constitution of 2008 go some way to achieving this.
4. Finally, again at the formal level, it would be beneficial to establish different types of regimes of exception, clearly highlighting the specific situations and the specific measures to be used in their name. The three paradigms established here—repressive, disaster, and administrative—are one way of approaching regimes of exception and could be useful in this sense. One of the key problems with regimes of exception as they are established in formal frameworks is their brevity and elliptical nature, leaving a considerable amount of space for discretion, informal practices, and "imagined" extraordinary situations and powers.

As many key informants pointed out in personal interviews, these recommendations or best practices will only become relevant in contexts where the government has a real commitment to democracy and the Rule of Law.

To bring this volume to a close, it is important to reiterate that these conclusions are of a limited scope given that they are related to one particular type of emergency power (regimes of exception) in three, essentially similar, political contexts (Bolivia, Ecuador, and Peru). Nevertheless, the findings here confirm some of our existing knowledge and concerns over emergency politics and make new discoveries that should change the way in which they are thought of and evaluated. The study aims to have opened the door to a different and urgent research agenda on regimes of exception and emergency politics, beyond purely normative considerations and the specific context of the post 9/11 War on terror. Given that these mechanisms show no signs of disappearing from constitutional texts or indeed political life, the issue should be of great interest to Political Scientists in general and Latin Americanists in particular in the coming years.

NOTES

1. Personal interview with the head of a human rights NGO carried out in Lima Peru in April 2007.
2. Personal interview with a prominent historian held in Sucre in Bolivia in April 2007.
3. Personal interview with the head of a human rights NGO carried out in Quito Ecuador in July 2010.
4. As noted in Chapter 4, this comment was made by a former Bolivian President who did not have sufficient time for a full interview.
5. Personal interview with an adviser or the Constituent Assembly held in Sucre in Bolivia in April 2007.
6. Except in the case of Peru, where there seems to have been a set-back in terms of military jurisdiction since 2007, see Jaskoski (2012).

References

Ackerman, Bruce A. 2006. *Before The Next Attack*. New Haven: Yale University Press.

Ackerman, Bruce. 2004. 'The Emergency Constitution'. *The Yale Law Journal* 113(5): 1029–91. doi:10.2307/4135710.

Acosta, Alberto. 2005. 'Ecuador: Ecos de la Rebelión de los Forajidos'. *Nueva Sociedad* 198: 42–54. http://goo.gl/xpvXkh.

Agamben, Giorgio. 2005. *State of Exception*. Chicago: University of Chicago Press.

Aguilar Rivera, José Antonio. 1996. 'El Manto Liberal: Emergencias y Constituciones'. *Política y Gobierno* 3(2): 327–58. http://goo.gl/2fS3NC.

Aguirre, Milagros. 2008. *Dayuma, ¡Nunca Más!*. Quito: CICAME.

Albro, Robert. 2006. 'The Culture of Democracy and Bolivia's Indigenous Movements'. *Critique Of Anthropology* 26(4): 387–410. doi:10.1177/0308275x06070122.

Alcántara Sáez, Manuel. 1991. 'Sobre el Concepto de Países en Vías de Consolidación Democrática en América Latina'. *Revista de Estudios Políticos* 74: 113–30. http://goo.gl/Kq5Idq.

Alcántara Sáez, Manuel. 1999. *Sistemas Políticos de América Latina*. Madrid: Tecnos.

Alcántara Sáez, Manuel. 2003. '¿Calidad de la democracia o calidad de la política?'. In *Democracia, Desarrollo Humano y Ciudadanía: Reflexiones sobre la Calidad de la Democracia en América Latina*, compiled by Guillermo O'Donnell, Osvaldo Lazzetta, and Jorge Vargas Cullel, 289–93. Santa Fe: Homo Sapiens Ediciones.

Alcántara Sáez, Manuel. 2004. *Partidos Políticos en América Latina: Precisiones Conceptuales, Estado Actual y Retos Futuros*. Barcelona: Fundació CIDOB.

Alcántara Sáez, Manuel. 2006. 'La Agenda Política desde la Perspectiva de los Diputados: Los Problemas de la Vida Cotidiana'. In *Políticos y Política en América Latina*, edited by Manuel Alcántara Sáez, 117–38. Madrid: Siglo XXI.

Alcántara Sáez, Manuel. 2008. 'Luces y Sombras de la Calidad de la Democracia en América Latina' *Quórum. Revista de Pensamiento Iberoamericano* 22: 169–81. http://goo.gl/riXtbL.

Alemanno, Alberto. 2011. *Governing Disasters. The Challenges of Emergency Risk Regulation.* Cheltenham, UK: Edward Elgar.

Alenda, Stéphanie. 2003. 'Bolivia: La Erosión del Pacto Democrático'. *Revista Fuerzas Armadas y Sociedad* 18(1–2): 3–22. http://goo.gl/NjQ6XZ.

Altman, David, and Aníbal Pérez-Liñán. 2002. 'Assessing The Quality Of Democracy: Freedom, Competitiveness And Participation In Eighteen Latin American Countries'. *Democratization* 9(2): 85–100. doi:10.1080/714000256.

Amnesty USA. 2000. 'Bolivia: República de Bolivia'. Accessed June 11, 2007. http://www.amnestyusa.org.

Amnistía Internacional. 2000. 'Bolivia: el estado de sitio no puede condonar la violación de los derechos humanos'. Accessed October 31, 2011. http://www.amnesty.org.

Amnistía Internacional. 2009. 'Perú, Bagua seis meses después'. Accessed December 10, 2009. http://www.amnistiainternacional.org.

APRODEH. 2003. 'Pronunciamiento'. Accessed June 11, 2007. http://www.aprodeh.org.pe.

Arato, Andrew. 2006. 'Their Creative Thinking and Ours: Ackerman's Emergency Constitution After Hamdan'. *Constellations* 13(4): 546–72. doi:10.1111/j.1467-8675.2006.00409.x.

Arellano, Javier. 2008. 'Resurgimiento minero en Perú: ¿una visión moderna de una vieja maldición?'. *Colombia Internacional* 67: 60–83. http://goo.gl/uoPvpu.

Armitage, John. 2002. 'State of Emergency: An Introduction'. *Theory, Culture & Society* 19(4): 27–38. doi:10.1177/0263276402019004002.

Assies, Willem, and Ton Salman. 2003. *Crisis in Bolivia: The Elections of 2002 and their Aftermath.* London: Institute of Latin American Studies.

Assies, Willem. 2003. 'David versus Goliath in Cochabamba: Water Rights, Neoliberalism, and the Revival of Social Protest in Bolivia'. *Latin American Perspectives* 30(3): 14–36. doi:10.1177/0094582x03030003003.

Assies, Willem. 2006. "La 'Media Luna' sobre Bolivia: nación, región, etnia y clase social". *América Latina Hoy* 43: 87–105. http://goo.gl/7lKY3g.

Barreda, Mikel. 2006. 'De la Democracia Pactada al Proceso Constituyente: ¿Hacia un Nuevo Modelo de Gobernabilidad en Bolivia'. In *Bolivia: Fin de un ciclo y nuevas perspectivas políticas* (1993–2003), edited by Pilar Domingo, 65–92. Barcelona: Edicions Bellatera.

Barreda, Mikel. 2011. 'La Calidad de la Democracia: Un Análisis Comparado de América Latina'. *Política y Gobierno* 18(2): 265–95. http://goo.gl/Hht5fG.

Barrera, Augusto. 2001. 'Nada solo para los Indios. A Propósito del Último Levantamiento Indígena'. *Iconos. Revista de Ciencias Sociales* 10: 39–47. http://goo.gl/EIUMXb.

Bebbington, Anthony, and Denise Humphreys Bebbington. 2011. 'An Andean Avatar: Post-Neoliberal and Neoliberal Strategies for Securing the Unobtainable'. *New Political Economy* 16(1): 131–45. doi:10.1080/13563461003789803.

Ben-Asher, N. 2010. 'Legalism and Decisionism in Crisis'. *Ohio State Law Journal* 71(4), 699–760. http://goo.gl/64Ckqx.

Bercholc, Jorge. 2009. 'La Emergencia Permanente del Estado Democrático y el Control Parlamentario. El Parlamento Frente a la Crisis de la Representación Política, el Decisionismo y la Delegación Legislativa Permanente'. *Revista Aragonesa de Administración Pública* 35: 421–54. http://goo.gl/8teBJd.

Berger, Peter L., and Thomas Luckmann. 1986. *La construcción social de la realidad.* Buenos Aires: Amorrortu.

Berntzen, Einar, and Tor-Einar Holvik Skinlo. 2010. 'Peru and the Fujimori Presidential Breakdown in 2000: Continuismo Gone Bad'. In *Presidential Breakdowns In Latin America*, edited by Mariana Llanos y Leiv Marsteinstredet, 197–211. New York: Palgrave Macmillan.

Best, Jaqueline. 2007. 'Why the Economy is Often the Exception to Politics as Usual'. *Theory, Culture & Society* 24(4): 87–109. doi:10.1177/0263276407080098.

Bonilla, Heraclio. 1987. 'Peru and Bolivia'. In *Spanish America after Independence c.1820-c.1870,* edited by Leslie Bethell, 239–81. New York: University of Cambridge Press.

Bonometti, Petra, and Susana Ruiz Seisdedos. 2010. 'La Democracia en América Latina y la Constante Amenaza de la Desigualdad'. *Andamios* 7(13): 11–36. http://goo.gl/sTsE3e.

Brysk, Alison, and Gershon Shafir. 2007. *National Insecurity and Human Rights. Democracies Debate Counterterrorism.* Berkeley: University of California Press.

Buitrago, Miguel A. 2010. 'Civil Society, Social Protest, and Presidential Breakdowns in Bolivia'. In *Presidential Breakdowns In Latin America*, edited by Mariana Llanos y Leiv Marsteinstredet, 91–110. New York: Palgrave Macmillan.

Burt, Jo-Marie. 2007. *Political Violence and the Authoritarian State in Peru. Silencing Civil Society.* Nueva York: Palgrave Macmillan.

Cáceres Santa María, Baldomero, Cabieses Cubas, Hugo, Durand Guevara, Anahí, Soberón Garrido, Ricardo y Rumrrill García, Róger. 2007. *Hablan los Diablos: Amazonía, Coca y Narcotráfico en el Perú.* Lima: Programa Democracia y Transformación Global.

Carbonell, Miguel. 2008. 'Neoconstitucionalismo y derechos fundamentales en tiempos de emergencia'. *Estudios Constitucionales* 6(1): 249–63. http://goo.gl/Sptbh6 .

Carcelén Reluz, Carlos Guillermo. 2011. 'La Visión Ilustrada de los Desastres Naturales en Lima Durante el Siglo XVIII'. *Cuadernos de Geografía* 20(1): 55–64. http://goo.gl/HFsV10.

Cárdenas Reyes, Alejandra. 2003. 'La política económica de Lucio Gutiérrez y el Neopopulismo'. In *La región andina: entre los nuevos populismos y la movilización social*, edited by Consuelo Ahumada and Telma Angarita, 125–58. Bogotá: Observatorio Andino/Fundación Konrad Adenauer.

Cardoso, José Luis. 2006. 'El terremoto de Lisboa de 1755 y la política de regulación económica del Marqués de Pombal'. *Historia y política: Ideas, procesos y movimientos sociales* 16: 209–36. http://goo.gl/ElEIeo.

Carey, John M, and Matthew Soberg Shugart. 1998. *Executive Decree Authority.* Cambridge: Cambridge University Press.

Chappell, Ben. 2006. 'Rehearsals of the Sovereign: States of Exception and Threat Governmentality'. *Cultural Dynamics* 18(3): 313–34. doi:10.1177/0921374006071617.

Charvériat, Céline. 2000. 'Natural Disasters in Latin America and the Caribbean: An Overview of Risk'. *SSRN Journal* 434: 1–104. doi:10.2139/ssrn.1817233.

Cheibub Figueiredo, Argelina. 2010. 'The Collor Impeachment and Presidential Government in Brazil'. In *Presidential Breakdowns In Latin America*, edited by Mariana Llanos y Leiv Marsteinstredet, 111–28. New York: Palgrave Macmillan.

Cheibub, José Antonio, Elkins, Zachary and Ginsburg, Tom. 2011. 'Latin American Presidentialism in Comparative and Historical Perspective'. *Texas Law Review* 89(7): 1707–39. http://goo.gl/pK0E7v.

Clutterbuck, Richard. 2005. 'Peru: Cocaine, Terrorism, and Corruption'. *International Relations* 12(5): 77–92. doi: 10.1177/004711789501200506.

Cole, David. 2004. 'The Priority of Morality: The Emergency Constitution's Blind Spot'. *The Yale Law Journal* 113(8): 1753–1800. doi:10.2307/4135782.

Colomer Viadel, Antonio. 1990. *Introducción al Constitucionalismo Latinoamericano.* Madrid: Ediciones de Cultura Hispánica.

Comisión de la Verdad y Reconciliación. 2003. 'Cronología 1978–2000'. In *Comisión de la Verdad y Reconciliación: Informe Final, 28 de agosto del 2003.* Accessed June 11, 2007. http://www.cverdad.org.pe.

Conaghan, Catherine., and Carlos de la Torre. 2008. 'The Permanent Campaign Of Rafael Correa: Making Ecuador's Plebiscitary Presidency'. *The International Journal Of Press/Politics* 13(3): 267–84. doi:10.1177/1940161208319464.

Congreso de Bolivia. 2000. 'Octava Sesión Ordinaria de Congreso Nacional, Miércoles 12 de abril de 2000'. Accessed June 18, 2007. http://www.congreso.gov.bo/libros/leg_99_2000-VIII.htm.

Constant, Benjamin. 1989. *Escritos Políticos.* Madrid: Centro de Estudios Constitucionales.

Coordinadora Nacional de Derechos Humanos (Perú). 2004. 'Informe Anual 2003: Año de avances y retrocesos en la vigencia de los derechos humanos'. Accessed June 11, 2007. http://www.dhperu.org/

Cruz Villalón, Pedro. 1984. *Estados de excepción y suspensión de garantías.* Madrid: Tecnos.

Dahl, Robert. 1971. *Polyarchy: Participation and Opposition.* New Haven: Yale University Press.

Dávalos Muirragui, María Daniela. 2008. 'Estados de excepción: ¿Mal necesario o herramienta mal utilizada? Una mirada desde el constitucionalismo contemporáneo'. In *Neoconstitucionalismo y Sociedad*, edited by Ramiro Ávila Santamaría, 123–62. Quito: Flacso.

de la Torre, Carlos. 1997. 'Populism and Democracy: Political Discourses and Cultures in Contemporary Ecuador'. *Latin American Perspectives* 24(3): 12–24. doi:10.1177/0094582x9702400302.

de Wilde, Marc. 2010. 'Locke and the State of Exception: Towards a Modern Understanding of Emergency Government'. *European Constitutional Law Review* 6(02): 249–67. doi:10.1017/s1574019610200056.

Defensor del Pueblo (Bolivia). 2001. 'Informe al Congreso 2001'. Accessed June 11, 2007. http://www.defensor.gov.bo.

Defensoría del Pueblo (Perú). 2003. 'Restricción de Derechos en Democracia: Supervisando el Estado de Emergencia'. *Informe Defensorial* Nº 76. Lima: Defensoría del Pueblo.

Degregori, Carlos Iván, and Carlos Rivera Paz. 1993. *Perú 1980–1993: Fuerzas Armadas, Subversión y Democracia. Redefinición del Papel Militar en un Contexto de Violencia Subversiva y Colapso del Régimen Democrático*. Lima: Instituto de Estudios Peruanos.

Del Álamo Pons, Óscar. 2007. 'El Regreso de las Identidades Perdidas: Movimientos Indígenas en Países Centro-Andinos'. PhD diss., Universitat Pompeu Fabra.

Delfino, María de los Ángeles. 2000. El desarrollo de los estados de excepción en las Constituciones de América Latina. In *Constitución y constitucionalismo hoy. Cincuentenario del Derecho constitucional comparado de Manuel García Pelayo*, edited by Eduardo García de Enterría Martínez-Carande, 507–32. Caracas: Fundación Manuel García Pelayo.

DePlato, Justin P. 2014. *The Cavalier Presidency. Executive Power and Prerogative in Times of Crisis.* Lanham: Lexington Books.

Despouy, Leandro. 1999. *Los Derechos Humanos y los Estados de Excepción.* México: Universidad Nacional Autónoma de México.

Domingo, Pilar. 2006. *Bolivia. Fin de un ciclo y nuevas perspectivas políticas* (1993–2003). Barcelona: Edicions Bellaterra.

Dreyfus, Pablo G. 1999. 'When All the Evils Come Together: Cocaine, Corruption, and Shining Path in Peru's Upper Huallaga Valley, 1980 to 1995'. *Journal Of Contemporary Criminal Justice* 15(4): 370–396. doi:10.1177/1043986299015004004.

Durán Díaz, Edmundo. 1987. 'Los Derechos Humanos en los Estados de Excepción: Los Derechos Humanos y la Dignidad Humana'. In *Estados de emergencia en la región andina,* edited by Diego García Sayán. Lima: Comisión Andina de Juristas.

Eaton, K. 2007. 'Backlash In Bolivia: Regional Autonomy As A Reaction Against Indigenous Mobilization'. *Politics & Society* 35(1): 71–102. doi:10.1177/0032329 206297145.

Edelson, Chris. 2013. *Emergency Presidential Power: From the Drafting of the Constitution to the War on Terror.* Madison: University of Wisconsin Press.

Eguiguren Praeli, Francisco José. 1989. 'El estado de emergencia y su aplicación en la experiencia constitucional peruana 1980–1988'. In *La Constitución Diez Años Después*, edited by Enrique Bernales. Madrid: Friedrich Naumann Stifting.

Eguiguren Riofrío, María Beatriz and Jiménez Lozano, Arturo 2011. 'Análisis del conflicto socio-ambiental "Rosa de Oro" Cantón San Juan Bosco, Morona Santiago', *Revista Jurídica Cognitio Juris* 1(3): 45–58. http://goo.gl/2C8WtC.

Elster, Jon 1988. 'Introduction'. In *Constitutionalism and Democracy,*.edited by Jon Elster and Rune Slagstad, 1–17, Cambridge: Cambridge University Press and Norwegian University Press.

Espin Templado, Eduardo. 1994. Lecciones de Derecho Político. Madrid: Tirant lo Blanch.

Estellano, Washington, and Kathryn Nava-Ragazzi. 1994. 'From Populism to the Coca Economy in Bolivia'. *Latin American Perspectives* 21: 34–45. doi: 10.1177/ 0094582X9402100404.

Feldman, Leonard C. 2007. 'Terminal Exceptions: Law and Sovereignty at the Airport Threshold'. *Law, Culture And The Humanities* 3(2): 320–44. doi:10.1177/1743872107076386.

Ferejohn, J. and Pasquino, P. 2004. The Law of the Exception: A Typology of Emergency Powers. *International Journal of Constitutional Law* 2(2), 210–40. doi: 10.1093/icon/2.2.210.

Ferreira Rubio, Delia and Goretti Matteo. 1998. 'When the President Governs Alone: the Decretazo in Argentina 1989–1993'.In *Executive Decree Authority*, edited by John M. Carey and Matthew Soberg Shugart, 33–61. Nueva York: Cambridge University Press.

Figallo, Guillermo. 1987. 'Presentación'. In *Estados de Emergencia en la Región Andina*, edited by Diego García Sayán. Lima, Comisión Andina de Juristas.

Filmus, Daniel. 2003. 'Gobernabilidad Democrática: Conceptualización'. *Revista Aportes Andinos* 13: 1–4. http://goo.gl/8JE1TG.

Fitzpatrick, Joan. 1994. *Human Rights in Crisis: The International System for Protecting Rights During States of Emergency*. Philadelphia: University of Pennsylvania Press.

Fix-Zamudio, Hector. 2004. 'Los estados de excepción y la defensa de la constitución'. *Boletín Mexicano de Derecho Comparado* 37(111): 801–860. http://goo.gl/b2vsXH.

Fix–Zamudio, Héctor. 1999. 'Introducción' In *Los Derechos Humanos y los Estados de Excepción*, edited by Leandro Despouy. México, DF: Universidad Nacional Autónoma de México.

Flick, Uwe. 2014. An Introduction to Qualitative Research. London: Sage Publications.

Fontaine, Guillaume. 2003. *El precio del petróleo. Conflictos socio-ambientales y gobernabilidad en la Región Amazónica*. Quito: Flacso-Ecuador.

Frankenberg, Günter. 2014. *Political Technology and the Erosion of the Rule of Law: Normalizing the State of Exception*. Berlin: Edward Elgar Pub.

Freidenberg, Flavia and Manuel Alcántara Sáez. 2001. 'Cuestión Regional y Política en Ecuador'. *América Latina Hoy* 27: 123–52. http://goo.gl/8f0smE.

Freidenberg, Flavia. 2008. *El Sueño Frustrado de la Gobernabilidad: Instituciones, Actores y Política Informal en Ecuador*. Barcelona: CIDOB.

Friedrich, Carl J. 1950. *Constitutional Government And Democracy*. Boston: Ginn and Company.

Gamarra, Eduardo and Barrios Morón, Raúl. 1996. 'Seguridad ciudadana y seguridad nacional: relaciones entre policías y militares en Bolivia'. In *Justicia en la calle: ensayos sobre la policía en América Latina*, edited by Peter Waldman. Medellín, Fundación Konrad Adenauer Stiftung.

García Acosta, Virginia. 1997. Historia y Desastres en América Latina. Bogotá: La RED/CIESAS.

Garcia Sayan, Diego. 1989. *Habeas Corpus y Estados De Emergencia*. Lima: Comision Andina de Juristas.

García-Sayán, Diego. 1987a. *Estados de Emergencia en la Región Andina*. Lima: Comisión Andina de Juristas.

García-Sayán, Diego. 1987b. 'Perú: Estados de Excepción y Régimen Jurídico'. In *Estados de emergencia en la región andina*, edited by Diego García-Saýan, 95–125. Lima, Comisión Andina de Juristas.

García-Sayán, Diego. 1987c. 'Perú: estados de excepción y régimen jurídico'. *Síntesis* 3: 274–91.

Gargarella, Roberto. 2005. Los fundamentos legales de la desigualdad. El constitucionalismo en América (1776–1860). Madrid, Siglo XXI.

Glaser, Barney, and Anselm Strauss. 1967. *The Discovery of Grounded Theory. Strategies for Qualitative Research*. California, Thousand Oaks/Sage.

González Pérez, María Inmaculada y Mercedes García de la Torre Gómez. 2004. 'La Cooperación Educativa Internacional ante la Diversidad Cultural. Un Estudio Comparativo en la Región Andina'. *Revista Española de Educación Comparada* 10: 237–74. http://goo.gl/hBielp.

Gorman, Stephen. 1997. 'Antipolitics in Peru'. In *The Politics of Antipolitics. The Military in Latin America*, edited by Brian Loveman and Thomas Davies. Wilmington: Scholarly Resources Inc.

Graham, Carol. 1992. *Peru's APRA: Parties, Politics, and the Elusive Quest for Democracy*. Boulder: Lynne Rienner Publishers.

Gratius, Susanne. 2007. La Tercera Ola Populista de América Latina. Madrid: FRIDE.

Gross, Oren, and Fionnuala Ní Aoláin. 2006. *Law In Times of Crisis*. Cambridge: Cambridge University Press.

Hagopian, Frances, and Scott P. Mainwaring. 2005. *The Third Wave of Democratization in Latin America: Advances and Setbacks*. Nueva York: Cambridge University Press.

Hagopian, Frances. 2005. 'Conclusions: Government Performance, Political Representation and Public Perceptions of Contemporary Democracy in Latin America'. In *The Third Wave of Democratization in Latin America: Advances and Setbacks*, edited by Frances Hagopian and Scott P Mainwaring, 1–13. Nueva York, Cambridge University Press.

Hobbes, Thomas. 1996. The English Works of Thomas Hobbes of Malmesbury. Vol. 3, Leviathan or The Matter, Form and Power of a Commonwealth, Ecclesiastical and Civil. Aalen: Scientia.

Honig, Bonnie. 2009. *Emergency Politics: Paradox, Law, Democracy*. Princeton: Princeton University Press.

Humphreys Bebbington, Denise, and Anthony J. Bebbington. 2010. 'Extracción, Territorio e Inequidades: El Gas en el Chaco Boliviano'. *Ecuador Debate. Conflictos del Extractivismo,* 79, 83–104. http://goo.gl/Wy1Ss6.

Huntington, Samuel. 1991. *The Third Wave: Democratization in the Late Twentieth* Century. Norman: University of Oklahoma Press.

Huysmans, Jef. 2006. 'International Politics of Insecurity: Normativity, Inwardness and the Exception'. *Security Dialogue* 37(1), 11–29. doi: 10.1177/0967010606064134.

INREDH. 2008. 'Dayuma: La Represión que no Deseamos de un Régimen que se Proclama Ciudadano'. Accessed October 31, 2011. http://www.inredh.org.

Institut Internacional de Gobernabilitat de Catalunya. 2005. 'Perfiles Nacionales de Gobernabilidad: República de Perú'. Accessed June 11, 2007. http://www.iigov.org.

Issacharoff, Samuel, and Richard H. Pildes. 2004. 'Emergency Contexts without Emergency Powers: The United States' Constitutional Approach to Rights During Wartime'. *International Journal of Constitutional Law* 2(2): 296–333. doi:10.1093/icon/2.2.296.

Iturralde, Manuel. 2003. 'Guerra y Derecho en Colombia: El Decisionismo Político y los Estados de Excepción como Respuesta a la crisis de la Democracia'. *Revista de Estudios Sociales*, 15, 29–46. http://goo.gl/ZRXKSl.

Jaskoski, Maiah. 2012. 'Civilian Control of the Armed Forces in Democratic Latin America: Military Prerogatives, Contestation, and Mission Performance in Peru'. *Armed Forces & Society* 38(1): 70–91. doi:10.1177/0095327x11398449.

Karl, Terry Lynn. 1996. 'Dilemmas of Democratization in Latin America'. In *Democracy in Latin America. Patterns and Cycles,* edited by Roderic Ai Camp. 21–46. *Delaware: Jaguar Books on Latin America.*

Kekic, Laza. 2007. 'The Economist Intelligence Unit's Index of Democracy'. Accessed September 17, 2011. http://www.economist.com.

Klein, Naomi. 2007. *La doctrina del shock: el auge del capitalismo del desastre.* Barcelona: Paidós.

Kohl, Benjamin y Bresnahan, Rosalind. 2010. 'Introduction Bolivia Under Morales: National Agenda, Regional Challenges, and the Struggle for Hegemony'. *Latin American Perspectives* 37: 5–20. doi: 10.1177/0094582X10370172.

Kohl, Benjamin. 2010. 'Bolivia Under Morales: A Work In Progress'. *Latin American Perspectives* 37(3): 107–22. doi:10.1177/0094582x10366533.

Kohl, Benjamin., and Linda Farthing. 2009. '"Less Than Fully Satisfactory Development Outcomes": International Financial Institutions and Social Unrest in Bolivia'. *Latin American Perspectives* 36(3): 59–78. doi:10.1177/0094582x09334300.

Kruijt, Dirk and Kees Koonings. 2002. "Introducción: la violencia y el miedo en América Latina". In *Las Sociedades de Miedo*, edited by Dirk Kruijt and Kees Koonings. Salamanca, Ediciones Universidad de Salamanca.

Kruijt, Dirk. 2000. *Baile de Disfraces: Ensayos Sobre Viejos y Nuevos Actores en la Sociedad Militar y la Sociedad Civil de América Latina.* San José: FLACSO.

Laserna, Roberto and Villarroel, Miguel. 2008. Enero de 1970-Enero de 2008: 38 años de conflictos sociales en Bolivia. Cochabamba: CERES.

Lazar, N. C. 2006. 'Must Exceptionalism Prove the Rule? An Angle on Emergency Government in the History of Political Thought'. *Politics & Society* 34(2): 245–75. doi:10.1177/0032329205285406.

Leiras, Santiago C. 2010. *Estado de Excepción y Democracia en América Latina. Argentina, Brasil, Perú y Venezuela en Perspectiva Comparada.* Rosario: Homo Sapiens.

Leiras, Santiago. 2012. *Democracia y Estado de Excepción,* Argentina 1983–2008. Buenos Aires: Prometeo Libros.

Llanos, Mariana and Leiv Marsteintredet. 2010. 'Introduction'. In *Presidential Breakdowns in Latin America: Causes and Outcomes of Executive Instability in Developing Countries,* edited by Mariana Llanos and Leiv Marsteintredet, 1–13. New York: Palgrave Macmillan.

Lösing, Norbert. 1996. 'Realidad y Perspectivas de la Policía en América Latina'. In *Justicia en la calle. Ensayos sobre la policía en América Latina* , edited by Peter Waldmann, 381–404. Medellin: Biblioteca Jurídica Diké.

Loveman, Brian y Davies, Thomas M. 1997. The Politics of Antipolitics. The Military in Latin America. Wilmington: Scholarly Resources Inc.

Loveman, Brian. 1993. *The Constitution of Tyranny: Regimes of Exception in Spanish* America. Pittsburgh: University of Pittsburgh.

Loveman, Brian. 1997. 'Protected Democracies: Antipolitics and Political Transitions in Latin America, 1978–1994'. In *The politics of antipolitics. The Military in Latin America,* edited by Brian Loveman and Thomas Davies. Wilmington: Scholarly Resources Inc.

Machiavelli, Niccolo. 1987. *Discursos sobre la Primera Década de Tito Livio.* Madrid: Alianza.

Magide, Aquiles, and Wright, Claire. 2012. 'Los Derechos Civiles en México: Un Balance tras un Sexenio de 'Populismo Punitivo'. In ¿Adónde chingados va México? Un análisis político y socioeconómico de dos sexenios (2000–2012), edited by Salvador Martí i Puig, 253–66. Madrid: La Catarata

Mahoney, James. 2001. The Legacies of Liberalism: Path Dependence and Political Regimes in Central America. Baltimore, The Johns Hopkins University Press.

Mahoney, James. 2004. 'Comparative-Historical Methodology'. *Annual Review of Sociology* 30(1): 81–101. doi:10.1146/annurev.soc.30.012703.110507.

Manin, Bernard. 1995. *Principles of Representative Government.* Cambridge: Cambridge University Press.

Marcus-Delgado, Jane y Martin Tanaka. 2001. *Lecciones del Final del Fujimorismo: La Legitimidad Presidencial y la Acción Política.* Lima, IEP.

Martí i Puig, Salvador 2009. 'Los Múltiples Debates (y Realidades) de la Democracia en América Latina'. *Revista CIDOB d'Afers Internacionales* 85–86: 53–74. http://goo.gl/GkcTJR.

Martí i Puig, Salvador. 2014. 'Mexico a Decade on from Alternation: Understanding the Forms of Democracy and Citizenship that Exist Today'. In *Democracy in Mexico: Attitudes and Perceptions of Citizens at National and Local Level,* edited by Salvador Martí i Puig, Reynaldo Yunuen Ortega Ortiz, M. Fernanda Somuano Ventura, and Claire Wright, 245–58. London: ILAS.

Martínez, Rafael. 2006. 'La Consolidación Social de la Democracia como parte del Proceso de Democratización de las Fuerzas Armadas'. In *La Seguridad desde las Dos Orillas: Un Debate entre Europa y Latinoamérica,* edited by Rafael Martínez and Joseph S. Tulchin. Barcelona: Fundación CIDOB.

Mayorga, René Antonio. 2005. 'Bolivia's Democracy at the Crossroads'. In *The Third Wave of Democratisation in Latin America: Advances and Setbacks,* edited by Frances Hagopian and Scott P. Mainwaring. New York: CUP.

McEntire, David A., Christopher Fuller, Chad W. Johnston, and Richard Weber. 2002. 'A Comparison of Disaster Paradigms: The Search for a Holistic Policy Guide'. *Public Administration Review* 62(3): 267–281. doi:10.1111/1540–6210.00178.

Mejía Acosta, Andrés, and John Polga-Hecimovich, John. 2010. 'Parliamentary Solutions to Presidencial Crises in Ecuador'. In *Presidential Breakdowns in Latin America: Causes and Outcomes of Executive Instability in Developing Countries,* edited by Mariana Llanos and Leiv Marsteinstredet, 73–90. New York: Palgrave Macmillan.

Mesa, José; Teresa Gisbert and Carlos Mesa Gisbert. 2007. *Historia de Bolivia.* La Paz, *Editorial Gisbert y Cia.*

Molina, Gonzalo. 1987. 'El Estado de Sitio en Bolivia'. In *Estados de emergencia en la región andina,* edited by Diego García Sayán, 161–81. Lima: Comisión Andina de Juristas.

Morales, Juan Antonio. 1992. 'Cambios y Consejos Neoliberales en Bolivia'. *Nueva Sociedad* 121: 134–43. http://goo.gl/J2WQUJ.

Moreno Morales, Daniel E; Eduardo Córdova Eguívar, Vivian Schwarz Blum; Gonzalo Vargas Villazón; and Miguel Villarroel Nikitenko. 2010. *Cultura Política de la Democracia en Bolivia, 2010. Consolidación de la Democracia en las Américas en Tiempos Difíciles.* Cochabamba: Ciudadanía, Comunidad de Estudios Sociales y Acción Pública/LAPOP.

Neal, Andrew W. 2006. Foucault in Guantánamo: Towards an Archaeology of the Exception. *Security Dialogue* 37(1), 31–46. doi: 10.1177/0967010606064135.

Negretto, Gabriel L. 2003. 'Diseño Constitucional y Separación de Poderes en América Latina'. *Revista Mexicana de Sociología* 1: 41–76. http://goo.gl/YjyxNY.

Negretto, Gabriel L. y Aguilar Rivera, José Antonio. 2000. 'Liberalism and Emergency Powers in Latin America: Reflections on Carl Schmitt and the Theory of Constitutional Dictatorship'. *Cardozo Law Review* 21: 1797–2119. http://goo.gl/LVI7uQ.

Neocleous, M. 2006. 'The Problem with Normality: Taking Exception to "Permanent Emergency"'. *Alternatives: Global, Local, Political* 31(2): 191–213. doi:10.1177/030437540603100204.

Neuhouser, Kevin. 1996. 'Limits on Authoritarian Imposition of Policy: Failed Ecuadoran Military Populism in Comparative Perspective'. *Comparative Political Studies* 29(6): 635–659. doi:10.1177/0010414096029006002.

Nohlen, Dieter. 1991. 'Presidencialismo versus Parlamentarismo en América Latina'. *Revista de Estudios Políticos* 74: 43–54. http://goo.gl/FVrrwT.

Nolte, Detlef. 1995. 'Procesos Electorales y Partidos Politicos: Tendencias y Perspectivas en la Década de los Noventa'. *Perfiles Latinoamericanos* 3(5): 7–36. http://goo.gl/KxrpFH.

O'Donnell, G. 1997. *Contrapuntos: Ensayos Escogidos sobre Autoritarismo y Democratización.* Buenos Aires: Paidós.

O'Donnell, Guillermo. 2004. 'Accountability Horizontal: La Institucionalización Legal de la Desconfianza Política'. *Revista Española de Ciencia Política* 11: 11–31. http://goo.gl/2LpE4P.

Ochoa Gautier, Ana María. 2004. 'Sobre el Estado de Excepción como Cotidianidad: Cultura y Violencia en Colombia'. In *La Cultura en las Crisis Latinoamericanas,* edited by Alejandro Grimson, 17–42. Buenos Aires: Clacso.

Oriol Prats, Joan, and Iñigo Macías-Aymar. 2008. 'El Pacto Fiscal en los Andes: Desafección Tributaria en Bolivia, Ecuador y Perú'. *Documentos CIDOB América Latina* 27: 1–88. http://goo.gl/U3Bw1C.

Ortiz, Pablo. 2013. 'Capitalismo Extractivo, Minería y Derechos: ¿Pueden Cohabitar? (Coyuntura)'. *Íconos—Revista De Ciencias Sociales* 39: 11–23. doi:10.17141/iconos.39.2011.455.

Pachano, Simón. 2007. *La trama de Penélope. Procesos políticos e instituciones en el Ecuador.* Quito: FLACSO-Ágora Democrática-IDEA-NIMD.

Pachano, Simón. 2010. *Calidad de la Democracia e Instituciones Políticas en Bolivia, Ecuador y Perú.* Phd diss., Universidad de Salamanca.

Pajuelo, Ramón. 2006. *Participación Política Indígena en la Sierra Peruana: Una Aproximación desde las Dinámicas Nacionales y Locales*. Lima: IEP/Fundación Konrad Adenauer.

Paramio, Ludolfo. 2006. 'Nuevos Actores y Viejos Problemas'. In *Reformas Económicas y Consolidación Democrática,* edited by Manuel Alcántara, Ludolfo Paramio, Flavia Freidenberg, and José Déniz, 45–84. Madrid: Editorial Síntesis.

Paye, Jean-Claude. 2006. 'From the State of Emergency to the Permanent State of Exception'. *Telos* 136: 154–66. http://goo.gl/H815lg.

Pereira, Carlos, Timothy J. Power, and Lucio Rennó. 2005. 'Under what Conditions do Presidents Resort to Decree Power? Theory and Evidence from the Brazilian Case'. *The Journal of Politics* 67(1): 178–200. doi: 10.1111/j.1468–2508.2005.00313.x.

Pereira, Carlos, Timothy J. Power, and Lucio Rennó. 2008. 'Agenda Power, Executive Decree Authority, and the Mixed Results of Reform in the Brazilian Congress'. *Legislative Studies Quarterly* 33(1): 5–33. doi:10.3162/036298008783743309.

Pérez Mallaína Bueno, Pablo Emilio. 2000. 'La Fabricación de un Mito: El Terremoto de 1867 y la Ruina de los Cultivos de Trigo en Perú'. *Anuario de estudios americanos* 57: 69–88. http://goo.gl/3gBzBa.

Pérez Murillo, María Dolores. 2007. 'Imaginario Colectivo y Religiosidad Popular en los Andes Centrales'. *Minius, Revista do Departamento de Historia, Arte e Xeografía* 15: 203–17. http://goo.gl/3E5vCA.

Pérez-Liñán, Aníbal. 2007. *Presidential Impeachment and the New Political Instability in Latin America.* Nueva York, Cambridge University Press.

Peters, B. Guy. 1998. *Comparative Politics: Theory and Methods*. New York, New York University Press.

Peters, B. Guy. 2003. *El Nuevo Institucionalismo: La Teoría Institucional en Ciencia Política.* Madrid: Gedisa.

Pierson, Paul. 2000. 'Increasing Returns, Path Dependence, and the Study of Politics'. *The American Political Science Review* 94(2): 251–67. doi:10.2307/2586011.

Polga-Hecimovich, John. 2010. *Políticos, Militares y Ciudadanos: Un Análisis de las Caídas Presidenciales en Ecuador* (1997–2005). Quito: Corporación Editora Nacional-Abya Yala.

Power Manchego-Muñoz, Jorge. 1989. La Constitución Peruana de 1979 (los Estados de Excepción). Phd diss., Universidad de Valencia.

Quiroga, Hugo. 2005. La Argentina en emergencia permanente. Buenos Aires, Edhasa

Ralph, Jason. (2013) *America's War on Terror: The State of the 9/11 Exception from Bush to Obama.* Oxford: Oxford University Press.

Ramraj, Victor. V., and Arun, K. Thiruvengadam, Eds. 2010. *Emergency Powers in Asia: Exploring the Limits of Legality*. Cambridge: Cambridge University Press.

Ríos Álvarez, Lautaro. 2009. 'Defensa judicial de los derechos humanos en los estados de excepción.' *Estudios Constitucionales* 7(1): 249–63. http://goo.gl/P0GUPw.

Rodas, Hugo. 2005. 'Postideología y Rebeliones Sociales en Bolivia (1985–2003)'. In *Bolivia: Fin de un ciclo y nuevas perspectivas políticas* (1993–2003), edited by Pilar Domingo, 197–228. Barcelona: Edicions Bellatera.

Roe, Paul. 2008. 'Actor, Audience(S) And Emergency Measures: Securitization And The UK's Decision To Invade Iraq'. *Security Dialogue* 39(6): 615–35. doi: 10.1177/0967010608098212.

Rojas Aravena, F., and Claudio Fuentes Saavedra. 2004. *Gobernabilidad en América Latina: Informe Regional 2004.* Santiago de Chile: Flacso.

Romero Ballivián, Salvador. 2006. 'Análisis de la Elección Presidencial de 2005 en Bolivia'. *América Latina Hoy* 43: 31–61. http://goo.gl/1TWknx.

Rosatti, Horacio. 2004. 'Un Círculo Vicioso: Impacto de las Emergencias Continuadas en el Diseño Institucional de Argentina. Emergencia y División de Poderes'. *Revista Latinoamericana de Derecho* 1(1): 449–71. http://goo.gl/g8oXKu.

Rossiter, Clinton. 2002. *Constitutional Dictatorship: Crisis Government in the Modern Democracies.* Piscataway New Jersey: Transaction Publishers.

Rouquié, Alain, and Suffern, Stepehen. 1997. 'Los Militares en la Política Latinoamericana desde 1930'. In *Historia de América Latina. XII: Política y Sociedad desde 1930,* coordinated by Leslie Bethell, 281–341. Barcelona: Crítica, Grijalbo Mondadori.

Rousseau, Jean-Jaques. 1990. *El Contrato Social.* Madrid: Editorial Espasa-Calpe.

Rozenwurcel, Guillermo, and Claudia Vázquez. 2009. *Argentina ante la Crisis: Respuestas de Política Económica Subordinadas al Conflicto Político. Documento De Trabajo Nº 8 de IDeAS.* Buenos Aires: Universidad de San Martín.

Rubio Correa, Marcial. 1989. Fuerzas Armadas y Constitución en el Perú: 1979–1988. In *La Constitución Diez Años Después,* edited by Enrique Bernales Ballesteros, 223–59. Lima: Fundación Friedrich Naumann.

Safford, Frank. 1987. 'Politics, Ideology and Society'. In *Spanish America after Independence c. 1820-c.1870,* edited by Leslie Bethell, 62–73. Nueva York, Cambridge University Press

Salman, Ton. 2007. Bolivia and the Paradoxes of Democratic Consolidation'. *Latin American Perspectives* 34(6): 111–30. doi: 10.1177/0094582X07308264.

Sánchez Parga, José. 1998. *La Pugna de Poderes: Análisis Crítico del Sistema Político Ecuatoriano.* Quito: Abya Yala.

Schedler, Andreas. 2001. 'Measuring Democratic Consolidation'. *Studies In Comparative International Development* 36(1): 66–92. doi:10.1007/bf02687585.

Schmitt, Carl. 1985. *La Dictadura.* Madrid: Alianza Universidad.

Schmitt, Carl. 2009. *Teologia Política.* Madrid: Editorial Trotta.

Scott, James. 2003. Los Dominados y el Arte de la Resistencia. Txalaparta: Tafalla.

Serrafero, Mario. 2005. *Exceptocracia ¿Confín de la democracia?* Buenos Aires, Lumiere.

Servindi. 2009. 'Comisión Especial para Investigar y Analizar los Sucesos de Bagua. Informe Final'. Accessed June 11, 2007. http://www.servindi.org.

Skocpol, Theda y Paul Pierson. 2002. 'Historical Institutionalism in Contemporary Political Science'. In *Political Science: State of the Discipline*, edited by Ira Katznelson and Helen V. Milner, 693–721. Nueva York: W. W. Norton.

Smith, Keith. 2013. *Environmental Hazards: Assessing Risk and Reducing Disaster.* New York: Routledge.

Spronk, Susan., and Jeffery R. Webber. 2007. 'Struggles Against Accumulation by Dispossession in Bolivia: The Political Economy of Natural Resource Contention'. *Latin American Perspectives* 34(2): 31–47. doi:10.1177/0094582x06298748.

Steinmo, Sven, Kathleen Thelen, and Frank Longstreth, Eds. 1992. *Structuring Politics: Historical Institutionalism in Comparative Analysis*. Cambridge. Cambridge University Press.

Svensson-McCarthy, Anna-Lena. 1998. *The International Law of Human Rights and States of Exception with Special Reference to the Travaux Preparatoires and the Case-law of the International Monitoring Organs*. The Hague: Martinus Nijhoff Publishers.

Tamayo Herrera, José. 1998. 'El indigenismo en el Perú, Bolivia y Ecuador'. In *Filosofía de la Cultura,* edited by David Sobrevilla, 179–96. Madrid, CSIC.

Tanaka, Martín. 2005. 'Perú 1980–2000: Chronicle of a Death Foretold? Determinism, Political Decisions and Open Outcomes'. In *The Third Wave of Democratization in Latin America: Advances and Setbacks*, edited by Frances Hagopian and Scott P. Mainwaring, 261–88. New York: Cambridge University Press.

Tribe, Laurence H., and Patrick O. Gudridge. 2004. 'The Anti-Emergency Constitution'. *The Yale Law Journal* 113(8): 1801. doi:10.2307/4135783.

Tummala, Krishna K. 1996. 'The Indian Union and Emergency Powers'. *International Political Science Review* 17(4), 373–84. http://goo.gl/6vwLMs.

Valadés, Diego. 1974. La Dictadura Constitucional en América Latina. México, D.F.: Instituto de Investigaciones Jurídicas/ Universidad Nacional Autónoma de México

Valles, Miguel S. 2002. *Entrevistas Cualitativas*. Madrid: Centro de Investigaciones Sociológicas.

Vazquez Carrizosa, Alfredo. 1979. *El Poder Presidencial en Colombia: la Crisis Permanente del Derecho Constitucional.* Bogotá: Enrique Dobry Editor.

Vázquez Carrizosa, Alfredo. 1992. 'La Democracia Participativa y los Estados de Excepción'. *Revista Foro* 17: 16–23.

Villanueva, Víctor. 1997. 'The Military in Peruvian Politics'. In *The politics of antipolitics. The Military in Latin America*, edited by Brian Loveman and Thomas Davies, 92–101. Wilmington: Scholarly Resources Inc.

Vladeck, Stephen I. 2004. 'Emergency Power And The Militia Acts'. *The Yale Law Journal* 114(1): 149. doi:10.2307/4135718.

Wall, T. 2011. 'Engaging Empire At Home And In The Field: The Politics Of Home-Front Ethnography In States Of Emergency'. *Cultural Dynamics* 23(2): 127–41. doi:10.1177/0921374011411394.

Williams, Gareth. 2011. *The Mexican Exception: Sovereignty, Police, and Democracy.* New York: Palgrave McMillan.

Wright, Claire. 2012. 'Going Beyond the Roman Dictator: A Comprehensive Approach to Emergency Rule, with Evidence from Latin America'. *Democratization* 19(4): 713–734. doi:10.1080/13510347.2011.619779.

Wright, Claire. 2013a. Perú: el estado de emergencia como mecanismo de represión de la protesta indígena en el contexto de conflictos sobre recursos naturales. In *Entre el desarrollo y el buen vivir. Recursos naturales y conflictos en los territories indígenas*, edited by Salvador Martí i Puig, Claire Wright, José Aylwin and Nancy Yáñez, 265–92, Madrid: Ediciones la Catarata.

Wright, Claire. 2013b. States of emergency, courts, and global norms in Latin America. In *The politics of the globalization of law. Getting from rights to justice*, edited by Alison Brysk, 144–59. New York: Routledge.

Wright, Claire 2014a. *Executives and Emergencies. Presidential Decress of Exception in Bolivia, Ecuador and Peru.* Documento de Trabajo. Alcalá: Universidad de Alcalá.

Wright, Claire. 2014b. 'Indigenous Mobilisation and the Law of Consultation in Peru. A Boomerang Pattern?' *International Indigenous Policy Journal* 5(4): 1–16. doi: 10.18584/iipj.2014.5.4.4

Wright, Claire. 2014c. 'Poderes de emergencia y regímenes de excepción en América Latina. Una perspectiva política'. *Revista Mexicana de Análisis Político y Administración Pública* 3(1), 205–230.

Wright, Claire, and Salvador Martí i Puig. 2012. 'Conflicts over Natural Resources and Activation of Indigenous Identity in Cusco, Peru'. *Latin American And Caribbean Ethnic Studies* 7(3): 249–74. doi:10.1080/17442222.2012.723905.

Wright, Claire, and Ana Soliz Landivar. 2013a. *From Military Instruments of Dictatorship to Political Instruments of Democracy.* Working Paper. Hamburg: GIGA German Institute of Global and Area Studies.

Wright, Claire and Ana Soliz Landivar, 2013b. *De instrumentos militares de la dictadura a instrumentos políticos de la democracia. Regímenes de excepción en Bolivia* 2000–2010. *Política* 51(1): 31–59.

Wright, Claire, and Alejandro Hinojosa. 2015. NVivo 10. In *Métodos y Técnicas Cualitativas y Cuantitativas Aplicables a la Investigación en Ciencias Sociales*, edited by Gerardo Tamez and Karla Sáenz López, 460–76. México, DF: Tirant lo Blanch.

Zovatto, Daniel. 1990. *Los Estados de Excepción y los Derechos Humanos en América Latina.* Caracas/San José: Instituto Interamericano de Derechos Humanos/Editorial Jurídica Venezolana.

Zúñiga García-Falces, Nieves. 2005. Bolivia, Ecuador y Perú: Emergencia Social e Inestabilidad. In *Cartografías Del Poder*, edited by Manuela Mesa and Mabel González Bustelo, 277–93. Barcelona: Icaria.

Index

administrative powers:
administrative intervention, 102, 109–14, 138–44, 150, 160–61, 164;
public contracting, exoneration from, 72–79, 91, 106–14, 121, 138–51, 160–65;
raising taxes, 44–46, 75, 90, 123–27, 137–38, 160;
transfer of funds, 17–19, 113, 116, 124, 127, 137, 144.
See also emergency politics, paradigms of

Bolivia, places in:
El Alto, 110, 113, 116;
La Paz, 88, 93, 96–99, 110;
Pando, 97, 102–3, 110–12, 149, 163
Bolivia, regimes of exception in, 85–119;
constitutional form, 85–104, 109–14;
use, 94–119.
See also emergency politics, paradigms of

conflict:
armed, 15, 33, 47, 62, 82, 137;
el *Baguazo,* 65–68;
Guerra del Agua, 95–100;
Guerra del Gas, 100–101, 110, 113, 134;
la rebelión de los forajidos, 133–34;
over natural resources, 66–68, 101, 113, 128, 134–43, 149, 159–62;
political turmoil, 33–34, 53–54, 142;
protest, 36–37, 55–57, 62–71, 77–78, 85, 90–92, 95–113, 128–36, 142–49, 159–63;
Sendero Luminoso, 37–38, 58–64, 69–72, 77–78, 161.
See also emergency politics, paradigms of

democratic governability, 22, 51, 63, 78–80, 112–14, 122, 139–41, 149–50, 162–65;
efficiency, 52, 63, 78–79, 86, 94, 112–16, 122, 141–42, 150, 162,164;
legitimacy, 9, 18, 52, 59, 63, 66, 78–79, 86–88, 112–13, 121–22, 149–50, 162–65
disasters:
drought, 72–73, 77, 107–8, 144, 160;
earthquake, 72–79, 144–46, 159–60, 164;
epidemic, 44, 47, 72, 76, 107–8, 123, 144, 147, 160;

flooding, 72–74, 77, 108, 126, 144, 160;
volcano, 77, 146, 150, 159, 164. *See also* emergency politics, paradigms of

Ecuador, places in:
Quito, 133;
Sucumbíos and Orellana, 135–36, 145;
Tungurahua, 145–47, 150, 159, 164
Ecuador, regimes of exception in, 121–56;
constitutional form, 121–33, 139, 143–44, 149–51;
use, 130–52. *See also* emergency politics, paradigms of
emergency politics, concept of, 1–24;
Decemvirate, 1, 10;
Decisionism, 5–8, 13, 27, 32–33, 36, 88–89, 114, 124, 146;
Extra-legal model, 11–13, 20, 29, 34, 87, 91–92, 94, 162;
Iustitium, 1, 11;
Regimes of exception, 10, 27–35;
Republican Exceptionalism, 5, 6–8, 11–13, 18, 20, 27, 32–33, 36, 87, 89, 114, 158;
Roman dictatorship, 10, 25, 44, 138, 160;
Securitization theory, 14, 18–19, 92, 114, 159. *See also* emergency politics, paradigms of
emergency politics, paradigms of, 17–19;
administrative, 91, 94–95, 109–12, 127, 130, 139–41, 147–48, 151, 160, 164;
disaster, 18, 57, 63, 72–78, 91, 94, 108–9, 113, 144–51, 159–65;
repressive, 19, 22, 25, 32, 43, 48, 56–57, 63–72, 95–104, 131–38

human rights:
protection of, 19, 21, 39, 61, 65, 97–98, 104, 109, 112–14, 129, 137;
suspension of, 25, 28, 32, 40, 42, 58, 60, 62, 78, 106, 137, 146–52, 160–65;
violation of, 15, 26, 35–37, 78, 92, 97–98, 126, 129. *See also* emergency politics, paradigms of

military:
dictatorship, 26, 27, 34–37, 53–58, 87–91, 123–26;
justice, 16, 72, 133–38;
role in regimes of exception, 32–40, 59–67, 100–113, 133–38, 141–51, 157–66

Peru, places in:
Alto Huallaga Valley, 70–71, 75, 78–79, 163;
Arequipa, 65, 74;
Bagua, 65–68;
Lima, 59–60, 72, 75, 79;
Pisco, 76–78, 146, 159, 164;
VRAE, 70–71, 75, 77–79, 163
Peru, regimes of exception in, 51–83;
constitutional form, 53–63;
use, 63–80. *See also* emergency politics, paradigms of
political processes:
authoritarian regimes. *See* Military dictatorship;
Constituent Assembly, 57, 92–93, 103, 139–40, 147;
democracy, transition to, 27, 36–38, 56–57, 59, 92–93, 126, 130;
Independence, from colonial rule, 33–34, 52–54, 86–88, 122–25
Presidents:
Bánzer, Hugo, 91, 96–97, 98, 105;

Beláunde Terry, Fernando, 56;
Correa, Rafael, 121, 134–43, 147–49, 161, 163;
Fujimori, Alberto, 60–61, 64, 70;
García, Alan, 59, 64, 67, 124, 161;
Gutiérrez, Lucio, 132–34, 149, 163;
Mahuad Witt, Jamil, 132–33, 149, 163;
Mesa, Carlos, 100–101;
Morales, Evo, 95, 99–103, 108, 110, 114, 149, 163;
Noboa, Gustavo, 133;
Palacio, Alfredo, 135–36;
Paniagua, Valentín, 73;
Paz Estenssoro, Víctor, 89, 93;
Sánchez de Lozada, Gonzalo, 100, 163;
Toledo, Alejandro, 64–65

regimes of exception. *See* emergency politics, concept of

separation of powers:
Executive, role of, 10–20, 25, 28–48, 53–54, 90, 103–4, 108–14, 131, 143–50;
Judiciary, role of, 61, 71, 90, 98, 112, 126–30, 136–37, 148–51;
Legislative, role of, 21, 28–31, 43, 62, 80, 97–99, 104, 112, 126–37, 149;
oversight mechanisms, 66, 94, 108, 113–14, 143, 150–51, 163–65
state of emergency. *See* emergency politics, concept of

technical aid:
implementation of, 16–18, 26, 45, 72, 77–79, 100–109, 144–45, 159–60, 164;
plans and legislation, 44, 107.
See also emergency politics, paradigms of

United Nations:
monitoring of states of emergency, 16, 19, 38–41;
principles for states of emergency, 21, 137, 149, 162

About the Author

Claire Wright is a Political Scientist and Latin Americanist, concerned with two very important aspects of democratization throughout the region: emergency politics on the one hand and indigenous politics on the other. Her first degree was a Bachelor's in Modern Languages (French and Spanish) from Oxford University (Worcester College) and she completed a Master's Degree in Latin American Studies at the Universidad de Salamanca, in Spain. Following the successful completion of PhD in Contemporary Political Processes at the same university (her thesis won a university prize), she moved to Mexico where she is currently based as a full-time lecturer, at the Universidad Autónoma de Nuevo León. Claire has been a member of Mexico's National System of Researchers (SNI) since 2014 and is currently the head researcher on a project that studies processes of indigenous consultation in Latin America and which is financed by the National Science and Technology Council (CONACYT).

Claire's work has been published in important journals in her field, including *Democratization* and *Latin American and Caribbean Ethnic Studies*. She is the co-editor of the volume *Democracy in Mexico. Attitudes and Perception of Citizens at Local and National Level* edited by the Institute of Latin American Studies at the University of London. She has presented her work at conferences throughout Latin America, the US, Canada, and Europe and has been a visiting researcher at Flacso Ecuador, the German Institute of Global and Area Studies (GIGA), the Crick Centre for the Public Understanding of Politics at the University of Sheffield, and the Colegio Mexiquense.

www.ingramcontent.com/pod-product-compliance
Ingram Content Group UK Ltd.
Pitfield, Milton Keynes, MK11 3LW, UK
UKHW041629031026
15587UKWH00001B/168

9 781498 515276